Advances in Contemporary Educational Thought Series
Jonas F. Soltis, Editor

THE
CIVIC
IMPERATIVE

*Examining the Need for
Civic Education*

RICHARD PRATTE

Teachers College, Columbia University
New York and London

Published by Teachers College Press, 1234 Amsterdam Avenue, New York, NY 10027

Library of Congress Cataloging-in-Publication Data

Pratte, Richard.

  The civic imperative : examining the need for civic education / Richard Pratte.

    p. cm.—(Advances in contemporary educational thought series ; 3)
    Bibliography: p.
    Includes index.
    ISBN 0-8077-2922-1
    1. Civics—Study and teaching. I. Title. II. Series: Advances in contemporary educational thought ; 3.
  H62.P653 1988   88-15915
  320.4′07′1—dc19   CIP

ISBN 0-8077-2922-1

Manufactured in the United States of America

93 92 91 90 89 88   1 2 3 4 5 6

Contents

Foreword

Citizen. During the French Revolution, this appellation implicitly bestowed the ideals of liberty, equality, and fraternity on every individual addressed by it. Its use proclaimed that each citizen was a free person, entitled to be treated equally, and that each was joined to every other by a bond of kinship. In Ancient Rome, to be a citizen, *civis Romanus sum*, was to be entitled to the protection of Rome's laws and its civil customs no matter where one was in the world. Citizenship conveyed respect and rights that transcended political boundaries. In Athenian democracy, a citizen was a full member of the polis who shared its paideia, its obligations, and the benefits of living together in a mutually supportive attempt to create the civic conditions of living a Good Life.

Civic education, the conveying of the unique meaning, obligations, and virtues of citizenship, has been an essential aspect of education in every human society. Civic education carries the burden of ensuring that the younger generation will be able to join their elders in a meaningful form of unique group life that is permeated by a particular set of binding and guiding values. Today in America, there is a renewed concern about the school's role in the making of citizens. What are the most desirable characteristics of democratic citizenship and how might they best be transmitted? This book offers an answer to these questions.

In America, shrill voices have been raised in the aftermath of the 1960s liberated generation, the 1970s "me" generation, and the yuppie generation of the 1980s, bemoaning the ideal of individualism gone awry and the concomitant demise of a sense of community. Perceptive observers of the American scene have sought the root of these problems in our historical inheritance of two basic tenets of democratic life that are often in tension with one another. One extols the freedom and autonomy of the individual and the protection of individual rights. The other emphasizes group decision making, community participation, and social justice. One sees the advance of the individual as the aggregate advance of all. The other sees that

vii

any advance toward the good society requires a group effort where the stronger hold out a hand to the weak so that all may benefit.

In *The Civic Imperative*, Richard Pratte picks up these dialectical themes, examines them in depth, and argues for a new kind of civic education with an emphasis on community. He argues that the dominant form that civic instruction has taken in our schools has been aimed at providing civic literacy, a verbal familiarity with the structure of our political system and an understanding of our most valued political documents. Even though important, the narrowness of this conception of civic education should be apparent. To learn about democratic values and how government works is not yet to become an active citizen.

There has also been a less direct, more active attitude-developing form of civic education which is aimed at producing civic patriotism, the instilling of a sense of loyalty to our country and a willingness to serve and defend it. This brings about civic action, but it is often blind, uncritical, and chauvinistic.

Pratte opts for a third conception of civic education aimed at producing civic competence, the acquiring of the values, dispositions, and skills needed to act as a full-fledged member of a democratic community. In form, this is not a new conception, but in substance, as Pratte fills in his rendering of the meaning of civic competence, we are given a rich, well-argued image of what civic education in America needs to become before the close of the 20th century if we hope to redress the imbalances in our society and overcome our current civic malaise.

The problem with traditional approaches to civic education, Pratte argues, is that they aim too narrowly at making the good citizen and pay too little attention to developing the good person. His thesis is that in the long run, a good person—in the moral and virtuous sense—will make the good citizen. This means that our schools must teach moral and civic values consciously and in all subject areas and not just in civics or values clarification courses. The central values of the truly democratic citizen and good person for Pratte are respect for persons, belief in human dignity, concern for others, justice, fairness, tolerance, caring, and a commitment to reflective reason, respect for evidence, and honest critique. The good person lives an ethic of obligation and service to others. The virtuous citizen is one who views his or her own good as one with the good of others and has developed the social habit of acting for the benefit of others.

In his prescription for the needed form of civic education Pratte

draws on many contemporary theorists and on the legacy of John
Dewey to illuminate a concept of citizenship and democracy that
goes beyond the political and includes civic virtues and caring forms
of human association. He explores the idea of community service,
the distinction between private and public interests, and the separation of school from society and draws curricular implications from
all of these.

This is a work that offers a vision. It is a hopeful work. Pratte
is unafraid to tell us what we should do and what our society could
become if only we would take the need for civic education seriously
and give it our highest priority.

Jonas F. Soltis, Editor
Advances in Contemporary
Educational Thought Series

Prologue

> Our task of reconstruction does not require the creation of new and strange values. It is rather the finding of the way once more to known, but to some degree forgotten, ideals and values. If the means and details are in some instances new, the objectives are as permanent as human nature.
>
> *Franklin D. Roosevelt*
> *Message to Congress, June 8, 1934*

As we come to the end of the twentieth century, vast numbers of Americans find themselves increasingly puzzled and perplexed about the political climate here in the United States and abroad. Terrorism, political espionage, and irresponsible and immoral corporate acts affecting millions of people are matched by self-serving acts of local, state, and national public officials whose attitude toward the public seems to be "the public be damned!" And, reflecting and refracting all of this perplexity, educationists and journalists convey a general sense of civic and educational malaise to a distraught American public.

There are, however, signs of a fundamental change in the nation's political and social climate, a philosophical mood shift like those that seem to occur in America every generation or so. Political candidates and citizens are increasingly talking about compassion, more democratic approaches to deep-rooted social problems, and a new sense of community values. In this social pause, there are new images suggesting that the moral ecology of American life is altering. The change demands a new public agenda, a new sifting and discipline.

In the awareness that the problems of civic life today—homeless people on heating grates, a staggering national debt, the AIDS epidemic, teenage suicide, a weakened dollar abroad, nuclear disarmament, racism, and a neglected underclass—may in fact be a shattered mirror of a larger social picture, the present work began to take shape. This book is principally about how things should be in the civic culture, not about how things are, and since I do not think they are as they should be, some of it consists of criticism of the present civic culture. An important part of it, further, raises the question of how much formal education or schooling can help us to revitalize civic society. As I shall try to show, it can do a great deal, much more than it is presently doing. I hope to introduce a picture of civic life and a new set of social ideas that apply to it, which could also help us think both about what a reformulated civic culture might be like and the role civic education can play.

The main argument of this work can be stated simply: The nation's central political value has been and continues to be popular self-rule or democracy, but there is a gigantic gap between the ideal and reality. To realize the project of making incarnate the ideal of social justice in our lives and in our social institutions, a renewed democratic life of active, participatory citizenship is needed, and that in turn requires an enlightened discussion of civic purpose and civic education. In other words, we need to achieve a new, vital consensus, a civic/moral culture appropriate to our highest ideals and sentiments, embodying equality of opportunity and freedom for all, not only as a matter of social justice but as a question of America's long-term economic survival. I shall raise the question as to how many of the defects and problems that constitute today's "reality" properly belong to a departing economic order, an archaic conception of human life, and an older type of civic culture which are no longer adequate today. These defects do not readily attract notice, but they are in fact manifestations of an outmoded, inappropriate democratic social theory.

Thus, a subsidiary argument is that what is badly needed today is a revitalized civic culture that might command citizen loyalty and orient public decision and choice by reshaping society's purposes. The *civic imperative*, then, is to construct a new civic culture consonant with the objective conditions under which we live as well as with the highest of moral ideals. The first step is to create a new moral civic culture that is as appropriate for modern conditions as the old civic culture, at its best, was for its day and place. When that task is comprehended, the issue will define itself as validating and embodying the distinctive moral elements of American democracy, expressed not merely in the development of a shared culture, but through participation in the political sphere.

Academics, teachers, administrators, school board members, and, most of all, concerned citizens are my hoped-for audience. In America now, and indeed in many parts of the world, there is a great interest in civic education. I hope to address my arguments to those who want to examine the feasibility and admirableness of civic education and who want more or less urgently to frame it in a different form for a new generation.

Acknowledgments

I would like to thank many people who contributed, knowingly or unknowingly, to the discussions presented herein. Special acknowledgment is due to authors Alasdair MacIntyre (*After Virtue*, University of Notre Dame Press, 1981), William M. Sullivan (*Reconstructing Public Philosophy*, University of California Press, 1982), Robert Bellah and coauthors (*Habits of the Heart*, University of California Press, 1985), and Daniel Yankelovich (*New Rules*, Random House, 1981). I do not, however, wish to implicate them in any shortcomings of this work. Many thanks are due to my students at the Ohio State University and elsewhere, to audiences at papers given at various conferences, and to other colleagues and friends. Thanks go to my colleague Gerald M. Reagan, for the depth of his attention to my thoughts and aspirations. Thanks are also due to Charles M. Galloway and the College of Education, the Ohio State University, for releasing me from teaching duties during winter quarter 1986, thus enabling me to work full time on this project. Finally, I am grateful to John Dewey, whose many works inspired this effort and from whom I have learned, among many other things, to appreciate the importance of morality in community.

The Civic Imperative

Examining the Need for Civic Education

CHAPTER 1

The State of Civic Education Today

It will be argued throughout this work that, since citizenship is the highest political office in a democracy, civic education, engaged in systematically, must be a putative factor of first resort in shaping Americans for their role as participatory, virtuous citizens. Yet a problem exists: Americans are suspicious of civic education, perhaps fearing programs with overtones of partisanship, manipulation, and indoctrination leading to the politicizing of our dominant forms of social and economic organization (Cleary, 1971). In particular, there is a principle of American public education that has been long operative though rarely enunciated. This can be conveniently introduced by a brief passage by Green (1966):

> The principle is simply that nothing that people care very strongly about can be introduced into the public schools as a topic of study unless the strongly held opinions concerning it approach unanimity. In other words, if the topic is one about which people care very deeply, and if they are divided in their deeply held opinions, then to that extent, it cannot be introduced into public education. . . . It has its corollary. Anything can be introduced as a topic of study in the public schools provided it is a matter about which nobody cares a great deal or a matter which is widely believed to have no practical consequences. [p. 31]

Green calls the first the principle of concern and its corollary the principle of indifference. I, however, prefer to call Green's principle of concern the *principle of vigilance*, suggesting that the topics that come under its sway carry a concentration of significance, a density of vital concern. It is my hope that *vigilance* captures the pervasive sense of social and political controversy that surrounds the topic of civic education.

By the same token, MacIntyre (1984) cites the philosopher John Anderson, who urged that we "not ask of a social institution: What end or purpose does it serve? But rather, of what conflicts is it the scene?" (p. 163).

If we attend to these lines of thought, then we may understand why civic education is either neglected or taught in the least contro-

1

versial fashion: in order to instill a national loyalty or patriotism. According to Green (1966), we would expect increasing public contention and strife to assure that civic education would be the least controversial of school subject matters. By Anderson's account (MacIntyre, 1984), it is through an understanding of the conflict and the controversy that we can learn what the school's ends and purposes are.

Put in such general terms, it is a familiar story, still going strong, that current programs of civic education are uncontroversial. Civic education *per se* is uncontroversial precisely because the *control* over civic education is a matter about which the American public cares a great deal. Indeed, it is no exaggeration to say that today most Americans judge that they cannot afford to be indifferent to a matter as important as the control of civic education. In other words, the issues of civic education are divisive and tend to polarize the American public, not because there is no interest in civic education but because there is too much interest, resulting in a much publicized and debated conflict and vigilance.

Further, much of the conflict concerning civic education is fueled by the fact that students commonly are taught that in a democracy all power resides in the people; and that in a free-enterprise system all authority rests with the sovereign consumer, operating through the impersonal mechanism of the marketplace. Thus is hidden the public power of the organization—of corporations and lobbyists, the Pentagon, and so forth. In addition, similarly concealed by today's uncontroversial civic education is the power of corporations to set or influence prices and costs, to influence and control politicians, and to manipulate consumer response. All this is in conflict with what students learn in school, and when it comes to be recognized, if at all, it evokes indignation. Such power concealed by public schooling (and social conditioning) and then revealed seems deeply illegitimate and hence fuels the principle of vigilance.

Yet—and somewhat paradoxically—one of the most widely cherished beliefs in the conventional understanding of the American public is that the schools should forge a strong link between civic obligation and responsibility. Conventional wisdom enshrines the belief that the learning of civic virtue is paramount in any society; nothing whatever is accomplished without it. It is, however, a subject to be approached with a skeptical mind. In other words, although civic education can be socially malign, it is also socially essential. This fact alerts us to the task of examining the current state of civic education and rendering a judgment regarding its ends and purposes, in order to come to a decision of what a feasible civic flourishing would look like in the present.

THE CIVIC EDUCATION CONTROVERSY

It is important to see clearly that no nation-state in history has had the luxury of turning out new citizens who did not possess a modicum of civic competence. The historical force of this point is advanced by Butts (1980). He contends that the original purpose of universal education was the political education of the citizenry, a crucial factor in the success of the United States. Foshay and Burton (1976) give credibility to this point, stating, "Citizenship, we have said traditionally, is the main aim of schooling in the United States" (p. 4). Butts (1980), however, argues more emphatically that "education for citizenship is the *primary* purpose of universal education" (p. 6).

Although citizenship education has been an important function of public education, the goals and specifics of civic education are not entirely agreed upon. For some, civic education is the teaching of civic knowledge and skills—a civic literacy. Students learn the rights and duties of citizenship as a mere academic matter and keep politics and morality at arm's length. This approach, albeit uncontroversial, is in the minds of many a truncated view of civic education.

For others, the function of civic education is shaped by the fact that the public school is expected, as part of its responsibility or purpose, systematically to produce citizens possessed of a national loyalty, a sense of obligation to country, and a strong desire to serve it honorably, prepared, when necessary, to die in its defense. Most Americans, it would seem, are comfortable in thinking about civic education in these terms.

Of course, there are other views about the purpose of civic education. Numerous contemporary political and educational thinkers differ among themselves as to what constitutes a proper civic education. Butts (1980) states the uncontroversial view: "[The] goal of civic education for American schools is to deal with all students in such a way to motivate them and enable them to play their parts as informed, responsible, committed, and effective members of a modern democratic political system" (p. 123). Butts (1982) allows that, while this goal can be achieved in a number of different ways, all civic education curricula should include "basic aspects of political values, political knowledge, and the skills of political participation needed for making deliberate choices among real alternatives" (p. 392).

Butts's (1980) account of how civic education should operate in schools within a democratic society gives a central place to ten requisite political values. Five of these tend to support the goals and tendencies of a pluralistic society (*pluribus*): freedom, diversity, privacy, due process, and international human rights. Five others support the bonding goals and tendencies of a united society (*unum*): justice, equality, authority, participation, and personal obligation for the public good. The ten values are organized into a curriculum set which Butts calls "A Decalogue of Democratic Civic Values."

It is difficult to take umbrage with Butts's (1980) proposal; however, in passing, we may note two obvious deficiencies, if it is to be regarded as a viable proposal for determining a proper civic education curriculum. First, Butts does not explain how a democratic citizen will be shaped and be nurtured by the decalogue. Its strength is that there are indeed many different forms of life and good lives across the world, and it sounds a convincing moral precept that we ignore this at our peril. The weakness comes in at the point at which we recognize there is no agreement possible on the decalogue itself. The deep obstacle that this disagreement sets up, even among well-meaning educators intent upon educating children decently, is that the decalogue short-circuits what is most important and needed today: a wide-ranging, public discussion of (1) what a feasible and moral human flourishing could look like in the future and (2) which virtues and values really are basic to living well, and which are changeable. Butts also ignores, in large measure, the wider context of democratic theory and its bundle of assumptions about the nature of the good citizen and the good society; the value of individualism; and the intimate connections among economics, power, and morality, as well as what impels and organizes these.

The problems that lurk in these oversights can be conveniently taken up by confining our attention to the following. Assuming the advent of the decalogue in public schooling, how will students' beliefs be formed and changed? Will their behavior conform to general principles of good citizenship? Will justificatory reasons for political actions be considered and acted upon? Butts (1980) does not, of course, guarantee that democratic citizens will be produced by the decalogue; he is too wise for that. He does argue, however, that these values do specify, in a general way, what in any plausible view will be meant by a civic education in a modern democratic state. But only an optimistic thinker would accept Butts's "plausible view" as a clincher. If his proposal is to have compelling force, it requires something else, something more than the decalogue. Any viable civic education proposal must consider, *inter alia*, both the nature of meaningful self-development in relation to a larger whole (the society), as well as the nature of the relationship between the individual and society, between individual power and collective power.

By its own logic, the decalogue relies on something else, not fully explicated by Butts (1980); namely, a tacit assumption of an underlying moral consensus on such things as the nature of self-development and what it would mean to give individuals their due as citizens. It would be instructive to inquire of Butts as to what justifies this presupposition. Moreover, why would the decalogue be so congenial to promoting a new civic culture when it is patently more congenial to aspects of our current economic and social life, especially in moral terms? Butts's decalogue is refracted through the precepts and concepts of traditional democratic theory, which, it will be argued, can do nothing much about the state of the civic culture beyond loose moral exhortation to raise civic conscience to the level of a noblesse oblige volunteerism.

The grandiosity of Butts's (1980) decalogue, whatever its practical shortcomings, should not blind us to the fact that it is offered in response to a civic malaise. Whether or not his proposal is adequate, its rationale is clear. He has raised the clarion call for a reconstructed civic education; he has staked out the arena of civic education and its value components; and he has taken account of the brute fact of social heterogeneity and the need for a unifying force in American society. Finally, in particular, he fervently believes in the need for reinstating the notion of a public good. Admittedly this consideration introduces a much-debated and controversial topic, which we will examine in detail in this work. Briefly, however, the notion of public good requires a conception of the good life based on our willingness to admit that our identities are social in character and thus require a sense of moral decency and community. In short, individual self-development and public contribution are not antithetical. The rub, of course, is that many Americans are committed to individualism and to an individualistic logic, asserted in terms of autonomy, self-reliance, getting ahead, and keeping ahead of others, regardless of the cost in human suffering; and they therefore deny the value of the public good.

I think we can see from the foregoing that a clear, overall goal or purpose of civic education is sadly lacking today. This is a point that is implicit in this work. What is wanting is a careful consideration of a reconstructed civic education in order to bring about a revitalized civic culture appropriate to the transformation of American life.

THE NEW CHALLENGE

In reaction to this situation, voices are being raised. Parents, educators, businesspeople, and politicians throughout the land are forming grassroots coalitions to advocate the importance of education for the teaching of a common core of subjects—writing, science, mathematics, the liberal arts, and even computer literacy. Other concerned groups emphasize mastery learning, the raising of test scores, or simply the development of effective schools. Still others, with a deep concern for civic education, opt for character formation, calling for the development of student moral values such as civility, self-discipline, diligence, honesty, loyalty, decency, tolerance, and respect for the law (Wynne & Walbert, 1985).

These movements are bringing a new vitality and respect to public education, especially after many reports that have chronicled a dismal record for public education in terms of declining basic skills, foundering will, and a diminished ability to compete with a hi-tech rival like Japan ("The Bold Quest for Quality," 1983).

What many of the concerned groups recognize is that the tide of mediocrity in public schooling has begun to ebb. Although there are still many problem areas—for instance, a very high percentage of black youth who are functionally illiterate—educational quality or excellence has once again become part of the working agenda of hundreds of school districts across the country. It was reported that, over the three-year period of 1980 to 1983, 53% of the 16,000 school districts nationwide increased the number of credits required in such core subjects as English, science, and math; and 39% more upgraded their standards by 1985. During this same period, 69% of school systems launched efforts to increase daily attendance. No fewer than 20 states passed tougher certification laws, with the goal of making sure that a teacher has mastered basic skills before ever entering the classroom ("The Bold Quest for Quality," 1983).

It bears consideration that Ernest L. Boyer (1983), president of the Carnegie Foundation and former U.S. Commissioner of Education under Jimmy Carter, reported that public education had not failed. He argued that the first-rate American high schools, which educated 10% to 15% of all American students, are among the best in the world: "We do not suggest that schools can be society's cure for every social ill. A report card on public education is a report card on the nation. Schools can rise on higher than the communities that support them" (p. 6).

If Boyer is right, then any evaluation of the public schools would have to take into account community interest and support, especially in the teaching of civic education. In this respect, there is at present a sense of vigilance, if for no other reason than that the meaning of the term *citizenship* has become less and less clear. Yet in the first half of this century, there was little doubt that civic education was meant to strengthen patriotic attachment. A sense of patriotism and national loyalty was a frequently mentioned characteristic of responsible citizenship (Merriam, 1931). In other words, there was considerable agreement that the nation-society offers protection to the individual and as a result the individual owes loyalty to the society. Allegiance and protection are, in this respect, reciprocal obligations: allegiance or loyalty for protection, and protection for allegiance.

The Korean War helped bolster the traditional consensus that civic education was to strengthen patriotism. But in the late 1960s and early 1970s, there was a collapse of this consensus, a weakening of the principle of indifference about what was worth teaching and what was worth learning. The Vietnam War and its aftermath helped produce the principle of vigilance by mounting a challenge to civic education's reciprocal patriotic function, from which it has not yet recovered.

The challenge centered on the notion that the extent of civic allegiance incurred by the individual is not unlimited. Its scope depends on the individual, the nature of the nation-society of which that person is a member, the value that person places on the society, and that person's considered judgment about the goals and purposes of society. If the society advances ends and purposes the individual considers immoral or improper, patriotism and national loyalty are tested and challenged.

It also is clear that in a democracy the obligations of citizenship are extensive. Indeed, citizenship must include allegiance and obligation—a social cohesion—if the nation-society is to survive and continue to advance the interests of its members. One senses correctly, I believe, that national allegiance or loyalty is an obligation, but it is by no means an absolute requirement. There can be other obligations to which the citizen must be responsive. What comes to mind are certain "fundamental values" such as human dignity, mu-

tual respect, fairness, and benevolence; in other words, there needs
to be an ethic of obligation involving concern, caring, and tolerance
for others. In short, recent events, including the many civic and human rights movements, the Vietnam War, and Watergate and its
aftermath, have illustrated that civic education construed as national loyalty is a too-limited vision, a stew of private and public
obligation not calculated to advance democratic values or the public
good.

Consider, for example, the question of civil disobedience. A
sincere civil disobedience of the law may be engaged in when national loyalty conflicts with the value of human dignity or mutual
respect. When citizens believe that other citizens or innocents are
being wronged by the nation-society, respect for the dignity of the
individual being wronged requires them to turn to civil disobedience in order to try to bring about a change in the situation. Wise
citizens grasp that this type of tension or conflict over obligations is
essential to a democracy. A thinking loyalty, rather than an un-
thinking loyalty, is fundamental to producing a just democratic society.

The conviction that good citizenship involves a thinking loyalty
raises questions today regarding such issues as private interests
versus public interests; loyalty versus the right to define, at least to
some degree, the conditions of social justice; and finally, pride and
identification with one's country versus the right to criticize and re-
serve judgment about the values and limits of patriotism itself.

The main value being considered in the current discussion about
the ends and purposes of schools is that no longer can civic education mean an uncritical attachment to one's country, as a territorial
view of citizenship based on national pride too often leads to nar-
row-minded xenophobia. We must avoid at all costs a civic education that fails to question persistently the central and political
traditions of the nation-society, on the one hand, and on the other
hand promotes an overly zealous and critical attitude toward the organization and operation of modern governmental institutions, so
that civic distrust and negativism result.

It is imperative that we address this fundamental problem:
Given the extensive interdependence of the world-society, given that
immigration into the United States will continue to produce immense social heterogeneity and value conflict, and given that current school-reform movements are largely tied to economic goals and
purposes, can the American public school and the political community come together in fashioning, identifying, and agreeing upon

a viable civic education required for the performance of democratic civic competence? This is the gut issue, and how we answer it will go a long way in shaping the American national character as a dynamic entity capable of providing for the continued functioning of a modern democratic policy governing a large-scale, corporate, industrial, technological society.

THE CIVIC EDUCATION CURRICULUM:
ASSUMPTIONS AND RECOMMENDATIONS

The foregoing considerations have partly focused on the issues and problems attendant to civic life today, plumping for a renewed democratic life of active, participatory citizenship fueled by a virtuous moral/civic culture. But the concern of most discussions of civic life in a democracy is not the issue of an *individual* citizen who is not virtuous, but rather the *overall* lack of citizen virtue. We do not merely want to say that this citizen or that citizen is not virtuous; we want to say that schooling has not produced virtuous citizens *on the whole*. On what basis, however, is such a judgment to be made? How do we measure the lack of overall citizen virtue? Is it that political apathy is due fundamentally to a confusion arising from a lack of understanding of any vital connection between politics and daily affairs? Is it that citizens do not have stable objects of allegiance around which social purpose and loyalty may be formed?

The problems that lurk in the questions are not conveniently dealt with. The answer proposed here is that it all depends on what sorts of judgment about civic education we wish to make. If we wish to define civic education as the instilling of national loyalty or patriotism, in recent years the public school has not done well in this regard (Boyer, 1983). If we wish to define civic education as civic understanding of rights and obligations as well as civic skills, then the school has also not received good grades (Boyer, 1983). If we define civic education as developing virtuous citizens who view their good as individuals as being one with the good of the human community, then in this case the school also fails. But there is nothing inconsistent or paradoxical about this. It merely reflects the fact that civic education has been badly neglected in the public schools, and hence its effort has been, at best, mixed, very indirect, and tangential.

In order to further our understanding of the meaning of civic education for the contemporary scene, I shall address the role of the public school as an instrument for teaching civic education. In the grossest sense, experience shows, the exclusive function of the public schools is service to the social order. But the perfect measure of this function depends on whether or not the community delegates control over curriculum content to the school. The functionaries of school—teachers, administrators, and the like—are forced to listen, combine, and guess what the tendencies of the community are, what it desires to have students taught, and whither it wishes to be led. While public school personnel are much under the sway of the community's suggestions, they are not entirely so. Thus, a highly complex interaction is at work here, although it may at times appear that a purely active element—the community—is leading a purely passive element—the school.

Perhaps the most characteristic example of this view may be seen in the recent spate of suggestions that have been made regarding public education. Numerous national reports have advocated major changes in terms of paring down of schooling's traditional functions and purposes to the teaching of a common core of subjects, emphasizing "mastery learning," "effective schools," and so on. Consequently, some states have recently added decision-making or thinking skills to the traditional basics of reading, writing, and math. Certainly, a thoughtful response to the many national reports requires a much greater consideration on the part of school boards, administrators, and teachers than has been evidenced recently. That is, the changes made thus far reflect the uncontroversial course; the principle of vigilance is at work. But civic education is central to reform, to the proper functioning of a democracy, and it is absolutely essential that it be considered.

What are the issues of the project? My experience tells me that inquiries into questions with difficult solutions soon become confused if they are not examined in terms of basic assumptions. We must gain further insight, therefore, into the assumptions surrounding the issue of revitalized civic education.

Assumption 1: Individual Virtue Creates Community Well-Being

It is assumed that the role of the school in the social order is guided by several principles. The first and central principle is that one improves society by improving citizens and not vice versa. For one thing, the term *society* is an abstraction; society cannot be made virtuous, only individuals can. Moreover, it is foolish to assume that the institutions of society can be constructed so as to promote social justice and fairness without a proper consideration of the activities of the people who run them.

These points give significance to the question of how the school may advance overall citizen virtue as well as teach the skills of building a virtuous civic culture. The answer I propose is that it all depends upon our understanding and acceptance of the moral principle that a person's virtue as a human being is inextricably tied to the good of the human community. This virtue or morality is what concerns us here. Human interaction—that is, action involving two or more humans—is moral when it is based on shared virtues, practices, and values characterized by justice and fairness and informed by the principles of human dignity and mutual respect. It thus appears that a meaningful public dialogue centering around such values as social justice, fairness, and decency cannot take place unless the principles of human dignity and mutual respect are acknowledged and practiced. The moral maxim that one should never use another person as a mere means to an end is actually the formula for every human association. Where the perceived value or significance of a person is so degraded that it no longer has an effect on the relationship with another, there is little ground for speaking of social justice, fairness, and decency.

Assumption 2: Civic Education Is Influenced by the Total School Environment

A second assumption involves the peculiar aspect of schooling commonly referred to as the "hidden curriculum." If curriculum is viewed as all the experiences, both planned and unplanned, that learners have under the auspices of the school, then a civic education curriculum must attend to the operations of the school's "hidden curriculum." This includes teacher values and expectations, student clique and peer groupings, and school policies and practices. It must also attend to the values, learning styles, attitudes, and perceptions that all students bring to school. A civic education curriculum, in its broadest sense, will be influenced by the total school environment.

Thus, the possibility of a principled pedagogic practice and a revitalized civic education is fraught with difficulty and must be carefully considered. For instance, scholars of the "hidden curriculum" and of teaching/learning warn that students respond not so much to the style of individual teachers and the content of the curriculum as to the structure of the school and the dominant teaching paradigm (Harris, 1982; Willis, 1981). The latter, we are informed, stresses an educational exchange that is not always judged as fair by students (and by some teachers as well) (Willis, 1981). The structures of the school, moreover, would seem to be much more difficult to change than pedagogic practice or particular content.

Thus, even if teachers wish to teach a civic education for civic virtue, many find themselves in schools whose traditional purpose has been to mold new generations to a civic responsibility narrowly defined in terms of national loyalty and patriotism. Typically, teachers adapt to such situations. The most characteristic result is a feeling of disillusionment and a negative attitude toward teaching and schooling, commonly leading to the acceptance by the teacher of the idea of relative ineffectiveness ("You can't fight City Hall"). Teachers who make this adaptation come to see themselves as little more than cogs in the "system" and virtually helpless to do anything about civic education. They learn primarily to serve, especially if they want to retain their jobs. They tend to hold few realistic hopes of ever changing the system; survival, for them and their students, becomes the name of the game. Because of their characteristic devotion to their students, however, some perform significant humanizing work in the school by mitigating some of its harsh effects for their students and doing all in their power to make the schooling years as warm and humane as possible.

Another common adaptation of teachers is to acquiesce to the system by teaching civic education as subject matter, a unit or course of study, in order to instill political obligation and responsibility. This resolution of the difficulty is easy because this type of citizenship education is fashionable and uncontroversial in that it coincides with a popular view of what counts as a "sound" or good program of civic education. The critics of American schooling can look through the school program and find a place set aside for instruction in political obligation and responsibility. They therefore cannot say that the schools are doing nothing, or next to nothing, for civic understanding. Teachers also find comfort in these findings, holding not only that they do indeed "teach civics," but they teach it as subject matter through a rigorous and probing study of political rights and duties. This situation often leads, in circular fashion, to a defense of schooling in general as being the major means of instilling political obligation and responsibility, based solely on the fact that individual instances of narrowly defined success have been achieved.

This brings up a final point. It should be obvious that both teacher adaptations have very serious consequences as far as civic virtue is concerned. The first accepts the authoritarian and anticivic virtues of schooling and at best tries to mitigate the situation and make it a little more humane. This situation effectively means denying to students a program of civic virtue that is basic to strengthening the democratic purposes and practices of civic culture. The invidiousness and difficulty of this situation must be grasped by teachers, students, and parents, for teachers and students are caught in a very frustrating and compromising condition. Furthermore, the second adaptation succeeds mainly in building a set of civic understandings and practices for life within the school, while ignoring life outside the school. This resolution treats civic education as if the school were an institution set apart from society, and this is most unfortunate. Each adaptation in its separate way positively assists the socialization of new generations into the existing range of political forms, ideals, and values.

Recommendations

What needs to be done, however, is something quite different. Realistically, we need to ask whether educators could possibly do anything fundamentally different from what they are already doing, namely, either ignoring civic education or limiting it to the narrow sense of training students for citizenship in terms of teaching them obligations and responsibilities. This is a profound and difficult problem. Educators must be sensitive to the fact that any attempt to settle the problem runs the risk of lapsing into either a kind of uncritical authoritarianism or a loose and slippery educational quicksand. This means that discussions of the purpose of civic education must take place with the due consideration of a complex and controversial political reality, namely, the principle of vigilance. Teachers and parents must eschew political self-seeking, expediency, and mere preferences for a principled discussion leading to curricular reform. The difficult task in the period ahead will be to avoid a narrowly conceived, bitterly contested, zero-sum approach to this issue and to seek instead a new model that incorporates the vital center or critical mass on which a democracy depends. (More will be said about this issue in chapters 3 and 4.)

The assumption underlying this proposal is that educators and the community can achieve basic agreement on a viable curriculum that promotes civic virtue while recognizing a fundamental uncertainty about the correct solution to the task. All participants must understand that society is above all a community whose solidarity is maintained by a widely shared, continuing consensus capable of providing a shared and active moral life.

The distinguishing aspect of the present civic education crisis, sketched in the portrait of the principle of vigilance, is precisely the breakdown of the crucial link between the citizen and the community. That ruptured symbiosis threatens the intimate relationship of schooling to the development of civic virtue. The problem is exacerbated by the failure of educators to understand the issues involved, especially the need for an ordering of the ecology of human relationships based on a moral life lived in the commons.

The assumption, then, is that school must be a vital civic institution to a much greater extent than obtains at present. To put this somewhat differently, it is foolhardy for educators to be preoccupied with teaching a civic education that exhorts students to develop a strong sense of loyalty to the nation-society (patriotism) or that regards the learning of political obligation and responsibilities as sufficient for civic competence. Such an approach results in little or nothing being said about how political and social justice as well as a sense of moral decency are to be achieved. In effect, the school is engaged in a Sisyphean task of forming civic competence that bears little or no connection to how the world is today, especially the new tensions between public and private life found in a heterogeneous, modern, bureaucratic, highly technological society such as ours.

Why has the school persisted in this fashion? There are two reasons, I contend. First, we have failed to conceive of school as a social institution, suppressing the fact that school has a social life and value within itself. When schooling is isolated from social life it becomes mechanical in its functions, and civic responsibilities and obligations become school values, not life values carried over into the public sphere. Even a cursory examination of the overall goals of civic education means taking cognizance of the failure of schools to infuse students with an intimate understanding of their culture's tradition, a spirit of social continuity.

The second reason, I believe, is the principle of vigilance, which may explain the previous reason. Educators must take note of the great distrust the community as a whole has of any attempt to sanction a particular program of civic education. What teachers must do is make their classrooms miniature public spheres where the discourse of democracy can be debated and where the issues that arise in such a context can be collectively and seriously evaluated. In short, teachers and students can investigate historically how the nation-society was formed, how institutions helped shape its interests and vice versa, the techniques of power and their political usefulness, and the economic advantages that derived from them for particular individuals and groups. Using this approach requires that teachers realize that the community has never had much use for civic education *per se;* it is interested in the *control* of civic education, not the phenomenon itself. Most adults apparently care very little about civic virtue, which economically has little importance, whereas they are concerned with the complex means by which civic education is controlled and pursued (Kirst, 1984).

Thus, in order for the principle of vigilance to be negated, educators must commit themselves to the practice of civic virtue in the classroom, incorporating methods of teaching that afford opportunities for teacher-student cooperation, trust, and sharing. This must be done with due recognition to the fact that *all* subject matter can be taught in a mode that promotes civic virtue and hence betters the civic culture. What is suggested is that enlightened teachers can, with a large degree of safety, bestow human dignity and mutual respect on students; attend to their needs; foster an ethic of obligation that includes concern, caring, and tolerance for others; and promote critical social thought by making students aware of authority structures in schooling and how economic structures influence their lives. In so doing, teachers are aiming toward the overall goal of practicing civic virtue and achieving moral unity and integrity, all within the acceptable bounds of schooling purpose.

What students continuously need is not so much isolated civic lessons upon the importance of obligations and responsibility, of honor, or of the beneficent results that follow from a particular act of national patriotism. Rather, they need the chance to create and practice civic virtue, so that it may be effectively expressed in political conduct. This may be accomplished by teachers who provide instruction in all subjects that elicits an active response in practicing and carrying out the ideals of democracy in terms of the welfare of the classroom and the community. It may be achieved when students learn civic decency as a form of disciplined or controlled doing rather than as passive absorption of what one is told. Finally, it may be gained through continued practice of civic virtues as habits of execution (Dewey, 1975).

This perspective was expressed well by Dewey (1900/1966):

> To do this means to make each one of our schools an embryonic community life, active with types of occupations that reflect the life of the

larger society and permeated throughout with the spirit of art, history, and science. When the school introduces and trains each child of society into membership within such a little community, saturating him with the spirit of service, and providing him with the instruments of effective self-direction, we shall have the deepest and best guaranty of a larger society which is worthy, lovely, and harmonious. [p. 29]

To extend this point, civic virtue is best acquired in the course of learning different subject matter and through an ethic of practice whereby *social habits of willing action beneficial to others are established.* These habits or reliable means of social action are the desirable traits necessary for an enlightened civic competence. Put differently, the development of civic virtue is to be achieved through acceptance and practice of the ethical elements of the curriculum.

I wish to be as specific as possible about this last objective. To develop civic virtue through acceptance and practice of the ethical elements of the curriculum means that all subjects must be taught in such a way as to bring out and make central their moral significance in social, economic, and political life. Thus, in the teaching of mathematics, the ultimate significance of numbers is not abstract but social. They are part of the decision making that goes into buying a house, which is an activity that modifies and directs human relationships. In buying a house, it is useless simply to compute its cost, as we seek a house that is acceptable in a number of different respects, only one of which is its cost in dollars. Indeed, it might be argued that every decision to buy a house represents computations of a number of factors, resulting in a compromise of sorts. We could include in our decision to buy a house the moral courage to choose a racially mixed neighborhood, with the intention of helping to stabilize racial relations. Similarly, in the teaching of history, students will recognize the worth of a community, how past civic events contributed to or shaped it, and how civic virtue was exhibited when people stood up to be counted for something in political matters despite threats of danger from the mob or a tyrant.

The purpose of the school, therefore, is to insure that students acquire a civic virtue in such a way that they will better pursue their obligations and responsibilities as citizens, always active, engaged, and committed to seeking the public good. This purpose makes the civic element dominant and universal in all instruction, whatever the subject matter or topic. Were this statement not true, then the familiar belief that the ultimate purpose of all education is character formation would be sheer nonsense. As we are all aware, the primary focus of instruction must be, for the greater part of the time, upon cognitive and skill development activities. It is out of the realm of possibility to keep direct civic virtue considerations constantly uppermost. But it is not out of the question to have the goal of making the methods and strategies of learning, as well as the content of subject matter itself, such that they render civic character and behavior more socially enlightened, more consistently public and political in the best sense, and more morally focused and vigorous than they otherwise would be.

Only a little reflection is needed to see that civic virtue is not a matter of mere behavior; it is a matter of forming a civic disposition, a willingness to act, in behalf of the public good while being attentive to and considerate of the feelings, needs, and attitudes of others. Civic virtue, as thus described, has an internal landscape reflected in the obligation or duty to be fair to others, to show kindness and tact, and, above all, to render agreeable service to the community. This is what I understand and take to be the ineluctable purpose of civic education.

Obviously, the task of achieving the transition from what I have called the ethical elements of the curriculum to the development of civic virtue is not guaranteed. But it does provide us with insights that undoubtedly will enter into any proposed method of overcoming the gap between a formal study of civic education and developing civic virtue.

It seems to be the case that if we follow these suggestions there are definite conclusions to be drawn. First, we must reject the most hoary of all beliefs about civic education: that it can be taught as a separate subject matter unrelated to all other subjects in the curriculum. Second, we must discard the belief that didactic instruction, whether by preaching or by less explicit means, can instill civic virtue in those subjected to it. For instance, I find humorous the notion that instruction or courses can be given in elementary wisdom, intermediate wisdom, or advanced wisdom. But even today much of our explicit civic education—even if it is not sermonizing—suggests that it is a special subject encapsulated from others (Boyer, 1983). Third, the compelling argument, it seems, is that civic education is not separate from the social life of human beings wherever they associate; the school is a form of social life, not a preparation for life; and although the civic dimensions or aspects of students' experiences may be distinguished from what they learn and how they learn, they cannot be separated from it. Finally, educators should recognize the concerns of the community, especially parents, in the arena of civic education, but at the same time recognize that the community cannot provide the terms of civic education's content.

There is in civic education, in other words, an established or granted right to community control that may conflict with the claimed right to professional control by educators, and sometimes the two cannot be brought to terms with each other. In this case, educators, for reasons of which I spoke earlier, must exercise sound professional judgment about the teaching of civic education so that a type of virtuous citizen is formed that the principle of vigilance would otherwise render neutral. It is precisely in this effort, the struggle against parochialism and narrowness, or the recourse of professional knowledge and judgment against polymorphous community power, that the principle of vigilance is found to be vitiated and nullified.

THREE GOALS OF A CIVIC EDUCATION CURRICULUM

Up to this point, my remarks about civic education are unhappily abstract. More must be done to present a clear idea of achieving the transition from what has been called the ethical elements of the curriculum to the development of civic virtue or virtuous citizenship. Hence, I shall examine three goals of civic education that aim at insuring that civic education permeates the whole curriculum. In other words, it is not enough to offer a mere course or two in civic education, or to refer to civic education only incidentally, if at all. It must form a major item on the agenda of every course in every classroom.

Goal 1: The Development of Historical Perspective

Historical perspective involves a gaining of the knowledge of one's cultural traditions, including philosophy, law, language, government, economics, architecture, literature, and so on, by establishing a context of human life in a particular time and place. It includes, moreover, a knowledge not only of one's own cultural heritage—its central, political, and national traditions—but the contributions of diverse societies over time.

A cultural tradition, well taught, infuses students with an intimate understanding about a nation-state's contemporary situation, gives a world view, and provides different interpretations of current social and political events, as viewed through a historical perspective. This deepened perspective of traditional and contemporary values fosters a positive attitude with regard to the values of participatory democracy and heightens consciousness about the potential conflict between self-interest and a broader public good.

A historical perspective can show that institutions shape public opinion and it demonstrates how educational as well as other social institutions, including the mass media, can usually be transformed into instruments of power and propaganda for the dominant regime. Indeed, the concept of propaganda, or the manipulation of opinion, is an integral element of study in gaining a historical perspective. A clear example of this is the Soviet Union in 1917, where a small minority seized control of the machinery of state and used its powers to transform the educational system and mass media into a large instrument of propaganda.

As suggested earlier, every classroom offers opportunities for developing historical perspective. Students can prepare and display bulletin board materials that feature political issues or points of view on a variety of topics, or they can feature a who's who in local, state, national, and international news. Also, recognizing the birthdays of men and women who made significant contributions to world peace and social justice can bring these people to life, as students further probe the circumstances of their contributions. Focusing on events significant in the history of various nation-states is an effective way of informing students about the cultural heritages of others. Information about these events will provide individual students with special opportunities to identify with their own cultural heritage.

A political history calendar is a teaching device useful for immediate reference and display. It can be modified for junior and senior high school students, to highlight people who have made important contributions by promoting the ideals of justice, community, brotherhood/sisterhood, and freedom. Students can help create the calendar by doing research, planning the scope and sequence of presentation, and doing the artwork.

Chief among the insights, knowledge, and understanding gained from a historical perspective is the notion that democratic citizenship is a highly valued good and it can never be taken for granted. Citizens must govern themselves. Individual citizens must share in decision making to a greater or lesser degree. It bears repeating that any subject matter can build in each student a commitment to developing citizenship, to using democratic values as the means for justifying action, and to relating decisions to moral principles. Teachers must avoid the view that civic education is inextricably intertwined with political history, patriotism, and nationalism.

Perhaps the most positive contribution a teacher can make to the acquisition of historical perspective is to help students to see that present institutional arrangements are not just givens in the scheme of things; that in fact, other ways of distributing goods and services have existed and that change is possible.

Teachers can also create a classroom climate that encourages students to express their opinions and judgments about institutional arrangements, particularly the special forms of bureaucracy found in the modern corporation. By analyzing their opinions and judgments as well as those of others, by trying to see things from the point of view of others, and by warm and sympathetic concern for the welfare of others, democratic cooperation or "amicable agreement" can be achieved.

In addition, students can learn how to be constructively critical about sources of political information and, of course, to recognize the political dimensions of school as well as of city hall. Indeed, the historical perspective, as it fosters civic virtue and understanding on the one hand, or political chauvinism on the other hand, is one example of an issue/value pairing that can be studied as a way of helping students become more competent in dealing with contemporary economic, social, and political issues.

Teachers can find a wealth of material for teaching civic virtues in the reading and discussion of the basic documents that make up the American creed, throwing light on the political and moral dimensions of our democratic society. Here I refer to such documents as the Declaration of Independence, the Constitution of the United States, the Federalist Papers, *Democracy in America* (Tocqueville, 1840/1969), and Lincoln's Gettysburg Address. These documents, absolutely essential to an understanding of the principles of democracy, are unfortunately not carefully and thoughtfully read and discussed in most schools today.

This last point is important. A basic element in our present thinking is the thesis expressed by Lincoln that ours is a "government of the people, by the people, for the people." Another basic element is incorporated in Francis Scott Key's oft-sung phrase, "the land of the free." It is important for teachers and students to investigate the "slogan" aspects of these as well as how these beliefs contributed to the political stability of our present political system and the distributive system based on it. In other words, it is necessary to separate out the ideal and the reality.

In a similar vein, a historical perspective should make students aware of the darker side of past events: anti–Semitism, racism, forced ghettoization, ethnocentrism, authoritarianism, and political and cultural imperialism. Emphasis could be given to crises in societies that led to citizens supporting the erection of public tyrannies. Also, consideration could be given to how scientific and technological ideas filter through the institutional structures of corporations and governments, often being co-opted for narrow political purposes and antiegalitarian ends. What is to be avoided is blaming these problems on an amorphous entity called "society," without pointing precisely to the persons or groups responsible.

Finally, a historical perspective will show that the horrors of the past—for example, the Holocaust—expressed the denial of human dignity and mutual respect among citizens. The corrupting forces of the past, the horrors of history, are possible only within societies whose laws and institutions discourage their members from treating each other with dignity and mutual respect. Students will see that a moral culture scrupulously mindful of human dignity and mutual respect is a necessary condition for a web of civic trust, fellowship, and moral decency.

Goal 2: The Development of Social-Action Skills

Social-action skills suggest the ability to confer, discuss, debate, argue, plan, negotiate, compromise, and so forth. Underlying the use of these skills is the assumption that democracy is based on the consent of its citizens; that is, its authority or legitimacy derives from citizen consent. The polity is sufficiently differentiated so that individual citizens come together in a network of groups or associations, which both influences and competes for the loyalties of individuals, in order to maintain and create opportunities for political and social effectiveness.

Although the goals of social-action-skills development somewhat overlap the goals of developing historical perspective, actually teaching social-action skills means building a solid base of demonstrable communication skills in order to produce intelligent, cooperative, communicative, and responsible human beings whose interests encompass other citizens and the public good (Habermas, 1971, 1973)

It is hard to disagree with Greene (1984) who speaks of the need for educators to create classroom practices that can serve as pedagogical preconditions for educating students for participatory democracy:

> We need space . . . for expression, for freedom, . . . a public space . . .
> where living persons can come together in speech and action, each one
> free to articulate a distinctive perspective, all of them granted equal
> worth. It must be a space of dialogue, a space where a web of relation-
> ships can be woven, and where a common world can be brought into
> being and continually renewed. . . . There must be a teachable capac-
> ity to bring into being . . . a public composed of persons with many
> voices and many perspectives, out of whose multiple intelligences may
> still emerge a durable and worthwhile common world. If educators can
> renew their hopes and speak out once again, if they can empower more
> persons in the multiple domains of possibility, we shall not have to fear
> a lack of productivity, a lack of dignity or standing in the world. We
> will be in pursuit of the critical values; we will be creating our own
> purposes as we move. [p. 296]

What is abundantly clear is that citizens must possess a communicative ability for the purpose of exploring and developing the
conditions for a new public vision and civic life. The assumption is
that the development of social-action skills has the goal of helping
students come to an understanding, that is, reach a genuine consensus or agreement that culminates in shared knowledge, mutual
trust, and reciprocal accord with one another.

Hence, to develop social-action skills, teachers and students
must learn to take seriously their putative assertions, to recognize
that sometimes what are in fact tautologies are offered either as explanations of facts or as fresh factual findings from empirical research, and that facts are not values. This means, of course, that there
must be a rough epistemological equality among students which insures their freedom to enter into discourse, check disputed assertions, evaluate explanations, assess justifications, alter conceptions
of norms, reflect on the nature of an argument, modify a given conceptual framework, consider the nature of evidence and explanation, and discern propositions belonging in the *is* category from
those in the *ought* category.

What is suggested here is that every classroom can offer a rough
epistemological equality—really, an ideal free-speech situation—
where students enter freely into discourse, recognize the need for
inquiry in the pursuit of truth, and in the process are themselves free
of constraint or manipulation. It is important to note that there must
be such equality among students and a moral culture based on hu-

man dignity and mutual respect, if students are to have the freedom and initiative to participate in classroom discussion. This is, of course, an ideal, a recognizably hallowing practice, but a condition unavoidable in an education that develops social-action skills.

This connection between social-action skills and a moral climate can be made in a variety of classrooms where teachers build up a spirit of critical inquiry and reflective thinking skills, and encourage practice in their use. Teachers should remember that the most important way to gain social-action skills is to acquire practice in using them. This calls for providing experience culled from the real world, such as listening carefully to what people say in conversations, debates, or in news conferences. It requires looking with a sharp eye at what books, newspapers, magazines, political pamphlets, and polemical tracts report or advocate.

On a concrete level, students may keep running accounts of local, regional, or state issues they have selected from print or other media. An issue could pertain to a needed change and suggestions for making the change. This activity would chronicle the actual reporting of the issue and how, if at all, the issue was dealt with. Students can be asked whether or not they would take a stand on the issue and which means would lead to the best resolution of the issue. In this way they may come to understand how issues impact on and have major implications for their own lives. Once students have completed their individual assessments, comparisons can be made across the lines of neighborhood, gender, race, ethnicity, and so on.

Furthermore, students can develop social-action skills if they are given an opportunity to role-play a problem situation before they actually encounter it. Young children can use dolls, puppets, or masks; older students can be given role cards that define, at least in part, their roles in the situation. Ideas for role plays include the loss of the freedoms of speech, religion, and the press; the use of terrorism and murder for political purposes; the traditional problem of social order and discipline; the improper use of authority; and asserting one's will, even against community opposition.

It would follow from these considerations that we fail to treat students as social agents and choosers, as moral beings from which actions and choices emanate, when we treat them not as persons but as merely the bearers of title (student); or the players of a role (trouble-maker); or, worse still, as merely a way of securing a certain end (a means); or, worst of all, as merely an object (a thing). Although teachers and students, due to the institutional processes, of necessity cannot be equal parties in the school, they must be equally free to develop and nurture the social-action skills required for reaching amicable agreement about practical questions through rational discourse.

Goal 3: The Reduction of Ethnocentrism

To begin with, it is recognized that the previously discussed goals are not likely to be achieved if culturally conditioned prejudices and presuppositions about others are not dealt with in fundamental ways. That is to say that the effects of cultural conditioning are sometimes so pervasive that people whose experience has been limited to the norms of their own culture simply are neither in a position to develop a historical perspective nor likely to be able to exercise social-action skills when they cannot understand why a self-evident communication from them cannot be comprehended by others.

An important teaching goal is thus the reduction and elimination of ethnocentricism, or the point of view that one's own way of life is to be preferred to all others. This means taking into account the forces of cultural conditioning, especially how one is shaped by the language and norms of one's culture and how every person's perception of reality is shaped by cultural experience. Once teachers and students grasp how their own culture sets norms for modes of cognition, expression of attitudes and feelings, language, and so forth; and once they understand that this enculturation is not irreversible, they will not remain subject to cultural conditioning. Contrasts may be made with other cultures, with the hope of reducing and eliminating cultural prejudice and discrimination, replacing these with a broader understanding that, even among societies at the same level of technological development, we must expect differences in what is socially approved behavior.

Teachers in all subject-matter fields can help students develop skills in detecting cultural prejudice and bias in thought and action. English teachers, for example, can use selected pieces to discuss themes related to racism and ethnic discrimination, in order to enhance concern and caring for and tolerance of all cultural groups. This also increases students' ability to interpret customs and nonverbal behavior in differing cultural styles. Likewise, business teachers can include information on how cultures differ regarding notions of work, play, punctuality, leisure, and so on. Physical education teachers can help students understand that notions of fair play, rules, and other elements of games vary widely from society to society.

Surely mathematics and science can be presented with an eye to the contributions of other cultures to these fields, thus fostering acceptance of and respect for other cultures.

In effect, teachers should work to encourage students to view other cultural forms in their relative unity, rather than be alienated by the most obvious and external, possibly personally insulting elements. Teachers should act to expose, not mystify or strengthen, cultural processes in the classroom. It is difficult to exaggerate the contribution of this understanding to the elimination of cultural bias and discrimination.

The key to reaching this third goal is a flexible learning environment that allows for collective study, enriched learning centers, simulations and case studies, small- and large-group discussion, and peer and cross-age tutoring. Experimental learning is crucial here. For instance, students can be motivated to examine cultural messages, informal patterns, and cultural forms by being introduced to new material in a nonthreatening way that serves as a springboard to discussion, analysis, and follow-up practice. Above all, students can come to see how cultural groups rely on the ideology and imagery of ethnic identity that is intended to obscure as much as it is intended to reveal. Hence, to perceive the cultural realm—its scope and nature as well as its symbolic power—is to understand that the cultural level is in no sense free floating, but has a mediated relationship to the structural elements of society and underwrites their characteristic forms.

CONCLUSION

Our discussion in this chapter is of course a mere outline, a simplified setting out of the assumptions and goals of civic education. More detail is needed. The simple question for educators is whether or not we really believe that civic education is worth the effort. In other words, is there a justification or a moral defense of civic education? Much of the success of our democracy hangs on the answer. The degree to which we as citizens take civic responsibility seriously is more than a mere academic question. It impinges on our survival as a nation as well.

We have examined the status of civic education in the United States today. If not in total eclipse, at least the kind of civic education that has been equated with political chauvinism is clearly weakened. Civic virtue, too, has begun to change, as is discussed in the next chapter, from the concept of individualism and private interest to one of public involvement and public interest.

Let us step back and take a look at where this analysis leaves us. It is the central thesis of this book that a careful consideration of a restructured civic education is necessary in order to bring about a revitalized civic culture. What can be said about this?

The claims put forth in the foregoing discussions have been made in full awareness that on one level there is an inherent or essential contestability in them, namely, that these matters are essentially value issues. If social theory were a matter only of the arbitrary choice among preferences, a purely subjective activity, then it might be permissible to take a position and simply refer to it as "one more personal point of view." On another level, however, we recognize that value judgments are not merely matters of naked preference. I contend that the line of argument presented herein is a matter of considered judgment, of sound arguments and evidence on which to base a position. It is, therefore, not simply a matter of a gut feeling or attitude that decides the issue one way or another. This work ultimately must be judged by its arguments, data, and consistency over the whole range of democratic social theory and, of course, by its empirical validity and interrelation with all other aspects of our modern, complex nation-society.

Two Democratic Philosophical Traditions

In this chapter we shall see that a social theory serves to pattern how a governed and social life is to be executed. Two democratic social theory traditions, philosophical liberalism and philosophical civic republicanism, will be examined in order to explore the basis of the relationship between moral character and the civic community. We shall sharpen the basis for the distinction between the two traditions and, in the process, suggest that our current civic malaise, if left to its present course, holds great potential for tragedy. This understanding should suggest a reasoned foundation for the argument that philosophical civic republicanism has arrived at a propitious time to help reconstruct the civic culture and to inform a restructured civic education of service and obligation.

PHILOSOPHICAL LIBERALISM

Historical Development

The tradition of philosophical liberalism was conceived and nurtured as a revolt against established forms of government and the state. Its results, it seems, were actuated by a desire to reduce government's role to a minimum so as to limit the evil it could do (Sullivan, 1982).

Historically, the ideals of philosophical liberalism are rooted in the seventeenth-century thinking of Thomas Hobbes (1651/1958; Gauthier, 1969) and John Locke (1689/1946, 1690/1946; Macpherson, 1962, 1977). Together they fostered a set of beliefs and doctrines in which human beings are viewed as fundamentally self-rewarding, self-interested individuals; human associations and interdependence as necessary social evils; and the public sphere as an arena for the clashes of individual and group interest, which can be, more or less, if we work hard enough at it, civilly accommodated.

Since it is necessary to find justification for a movement of re-
sistance and revolt, Hobbes and Locke, and later Immanuel Kant,
appealed to some inalienable sacred authority that was resident, not
in the state, but in the struggling, protesting, resistant individual.
Thus was born "individualism," a social theory that bestowed native or "natural" rights upon singular persons, always in isolation
from any associations except those which they formed for their own
ends.

The adherents of philosophical liberalism saw the limitation of
the powers of the state as justified by the prior nonpolitical rights
inherent in the sacred individual. For any collectivity accepting this
theory, the primary criterion of success was a strongly individualistic society, sweeping away all notions of *the* public good as foreign to human nature and rights, save as *a* public good proceeded
from one's own voluntary choice and guaranteed one's own private
needs.

It is fashionable in ordinary speech to sum up the ideal of philosophical liberalism by the principle of individualistic logic, for it
honors individual capacity, protects individual rights and freedoms, ties "progress" to laissez-faire economics, and promotes the
politics of instrumental change while maintaining a long-term stability, usually defined as progress and prosperity, based on private
self-interest and joint interest politically felt.

The writings of Kant (1797/1981; Kemp, 1968; Korner, 1955) offered a much-needed counter to unrestricted individualism, by pro-
posing an elegant rational defense of the autonomy of the individual
governed or controlled by nonutilitarian rules. In effect, Kant
grounded the individual in a set of universal moral principles, rules,
and judgments supportive of the notion of human dignity and respect for persons as ends in themselves. His main purpose was to
establish the *a priori* principles of morality that apply, not merely in
the abstract to all rational beings *qua* rational beings, but to all human beings *qua* human beings. What Kant succeeded in doing, in
addition to advancing a conception of the individual as inherently
valuable or precious, was to legitimize, via thinly disguised Christian principles, the Hobbesian/Lockean view of the social sphere as
an arena of clashes between self-interested individuals.

MacIntyre (1984) addressed the relationship between moral
character and political community as seen from what he called "liberal individualism," or what I have called philosophical liberalism,
as follows: "For liberal individualism a community is simply an
arena in which individuals each pursue their own self-chosen con-

ception of the good life, and political institutions exist to provide that degree of order which makes such self-determined activity possible" (p. 195).

The loose premise of philosophical liberalism is, then, that nobody has a right to tell anybody else what to think or do, and that, since the central good of human life is individual freedom, which is exercised through what I have called the individualistic logic, the good life is best organized by allowing as large a space as possible in the public and private spheres for this self-determining activity. It is hoped that each individual will make choices compatible with the choices of others. Even if this does not happen, however, the paramount good is still the freedom of individuals to do what they desire, as long as that is their choice.

These observations about philosophical liberalism should express the point that it is deeply committed in its fundamental premises to an individualistic logic and to an ethic of individualism. Hobbes and Locke regarded individuals as self-interested egoists, driven essentially by their passions or desires. Social relationships, including civic ones, were important only insofar as they provided a context for an individual to advance his or her own self-interest. The Lockean social ideal, a moral ideal aimed at fostering social peace among self-interested individuals, appealed to the early founders of our nation-society, and today politics tends to be viewed as a procedural system of regulating clashes among private, self-interested individuals.

The critical problem of a social theory's justification is the standard of effectiveness and consensus, and there is little doubt that philosophical liberalism was ideally suited to the effective development of the United States as a sovereign nation-society over the past 150 years or so. Americans took to their bosom the premise that the unity of the social order was compatible with the proliferation of local and private associations through which citizens can combine to make their private, self-interest and joint interest politically felt. In this highly esteemed tradition, moreover, freedom or liberty was viewed as surrounding the individual, since freedom of association had to accord with the individual's understanding of self-interest.

The transformation of this social theory into social practice resulted in an eighteenth- and nineteenth-century American democratic polity that exalted both the supremacy of private self-interest and the role of multiple private associations functioning as means of political expression. There was, moreover, a strong denial of the meaning and values of a public good, since the common good was viewed as flowing from the individual's struggle against constriction, that is, from the attempt to secure the rights and freedoms of competitive individuals and not of humankind in general (Macpherson, 1977).

Now the question inexorably arises: Why did philosophical liberalism become the preeminent or foundational democratic social theory in the American consciousness and in practice? Why did we come to hallow the concepts of *rights, duties, obligation, freedom, liberty, individualism,* and *individualistic motivation,* which resulted in an instrumental, utilitarian political order? Why do we not think in terms of the ideals of other social theories in constructing our civic culture? For instance, how do we understand the meaning of one of the major public movements of today, the ecological critique? Those under the sway of philosophical liberalism react to the ecological critique in terms of the private individual's display of public power and the terrible specter each sees looming over private freedoms. The peace movement is viewed similarly, with the result that individuals yearn for a greater exercise of personal freedom and compete to gain the political power that decides the all-important matters of nuclear armament/disarmament, nuclear bomb testing, and the like. Why do we not think of the ecological critique as a plea for universal acceptance that resources must be equitably shared and conserved, and the peace movement as a statement about the interdependence of a species that is on the brink of annihilating itself?

As an explanation of this phenomenon, let us consider a brief account of a complex yet somewhat easily identified historical development. The U.S. economy went through two major alterations during the nineteenth century (Carnoy, 1974), each of which helped assure the dominance of philosophical liberalism. The first occurred in the 1820s and 1830s in the northeastern part of the country. The early textile mills of New England were the first examples of what was to be the factory system of industrial production in the United States. This was part of a new scientific-technological movement made possible by the invention and application of new mechanical appliances. A highly productive American market economy changed the nature of capitalist production and destroyed the preindustrial, agrarian social structures so basic to face-to-face participatory democracy or democratic localism.

The second alteration occurred by the end of the nineteenth century. The factory system had spread to the production of many goods, and production of some of these began to be concentrated in a few large corporations. These corporations developed monopoly capitalism, which created powerful new social conditions, notably, personal economic opportunities of unprecedented scale, large labor organizations, and anticapitalistic movements in the working class. Philosophical liberalism helped justify new political arrangements that supported, consciously or unconsciously, monopoly capitalism. Moreover, what is commonly called laissez-faire capitalism retained the Lockean notion that individuals are autonomous in such a way that they can be obligated only by their consent.

The basic principles of philosophical liberalism—individualistic logic, a distrust of governmental interference, and a desire to limit its operations—were peculiarly suited to being marshalled in support and justification of the new economic agencies of capitalist production and the distribution of commodities and services. The established doctrine of natural rights, for example, was employed to support the laissez-faire economic theory, based upon the belief in beneficent natural laws that brought about a harmony between personal profit and social benefit.

Throughout the nineteenth century and even today, philosophical liberalism has supported a circular flow operating between the individual and society. This circular flow is controlled by the medium of power exercised in the public sphere, an assemblage of inherently antagonistic and suspicious factions of civic elements competing for society's limited goods and services. Thus the political arena is where individuals, grappling with inherently conflicting self-interests and joint interests, agree to various kinds of compromises and are occasionally forced to restrain themselves in order to prevent fatal stand-offs or clashes.

Within this relationship is nested the view that individuals naturally seek the betterment of their own situations in life, and that for most this can be achieved only by hard work and effort. Moreover, each person is naturally the best judge of her own best interests and, if left free from the influence of artificially imposed restrictions, will express judgment in the choice of work and exchange of goods and services. Also, barring undue interference from the state, each person will contribute not only to her own happiness in proportion to the work and effort expended, but also to the overall prosperity of society. Social progress and prosperity, then, are the natural consequences of private, largely economic virtues. Finally, the chief functions of government are the protection of freedoms and property, the securing of the sanctity of contracts of private and commercial exchange, and the protection of citizens. In short, morally justified government action is restricted to enforcing certain conditions promotive of individual political freedom and a capitalist market economy. Indeed, the private, self-interested individual's view of the good life simply is the acknowledged good life of contemporary philosophical liberalism.

Thus, so long as the sanctity of the individual's private choosing space could be assured, and so long as the growth of the market economy could provide the prospect of individual material betterment, there would seem to be little reason to question the tenets of philosophical liberalism. Consequently, it has continued to have strong support into the present century.

The Poverty of Philosophical Liberalism

The foregoing historical account should not be construed as asserting that everyone believed that enhancing individualism and competitive individual economic advancement would promote the best democratic social order. The movements of populism and socialism aimed at bringing economic life within the orbit of self-governing, popular institutions (Canovan, 1981). Moreover, the so-called "progressives" of the late nineteenth century, those who sparked the political and social reform characterized as the "progressive movement," sought to manage social and economic developments, especially their social dislocations, by means of a restricted public administration, namely, city and state governments and regulatory agencies responsive to the will of the people (Hofstadter, 1955). Later, of course, the "New Deal" of Franklin D. Roosevelt continued this tradition, using public institutions, locally and federally, to check the abuses of laissez-faire economic consequences, in order directly and indirectly to care for and assist those unable to compete successfully in the marketplace.

Changes in the U.S. economy, especially those caused by the Great Depression, along with major alterations in the international situation following World War II and a growing understanding of ecological limitations and their consequences, have not only undermined our faith in social and economic policies, but have vitiated philosophical liberalism as a democratic social theory.

This can only mean that changes in the world situation, along with marked changes in the U.S. economy, have demonstrated that philosophical liberalism, although in its time an appropriate social theory, is quite unable to handle today's incalculable but vital human concerns. The operation of both governmental and nongovern-mental institutions is full of illustrations of this. For example, it has been assumed that total economic advance is simply individual ad-vance writ large. But this notion is faulty and pernicious because it sets up expectations that cannot be fulfilled, ever. Our faith in phil-osophical liberalism is breaking down because the problem is not just a matter of scaling down citizens' demands and expectations, which are extravagant in relation to actual effort by workers or the availability and use of technology. The problem goes deeper. The chief villain responsible for the current mismatch between social ex-pectations and economic resources is not an extravagant, unrealistic demand for society's goods and services that citizens unreasonably desire and want now, but cannot have now. The villain is found in the flawed philosophical liberalism tenet, the individualistic logic, confronted by radically altered world social conditions. Let us see what is at work here.

As suggested earlier, ever since Hobbes and Locke, philosoph-ical liberals have been suspicious and undermining of any attempt to define the social order in terms of the public good. Beginning with the American Federalists, especially Alexander Hamilton, the good social order has been defined in terms of mechanisms of control that could, on the one hand, reliably insure responsible political and so-cial stability while, on the other hand, generating over the long run a modicum of economic prosperity. In this social theory, there is no great mystery as to what is the common good; it is political and so-cial stability and economic prosperity. To insure the common good, there must be mechanisms operative at the level of the political and social system, as well as at the level of the economic system.

What was needed, in other words, was a reliable way of main-taining stability and prosperity. This was accomplished, at least in part, by harnessing private interests in the rough and hand-me-down calculus of utilitarianism. This meant that, in a nation-soci-ety, questions of public policy could be resolved by reducing all questions of political action to a calculation of the material benefits that would accrue to given proportions of the population. This is the utilitarian calculus, ratified by philosophical liberalism, as it is brought to bear in a free-market system. Individuals, through hard work and effort plus a bit of luck, would reap the benefits of the system and their rewards would "trickle down" to the bottom rungs of the economic and social ladder. In effect, the justification and le-gitimacy of the system was assured because it was the "greatest good for the greatest number."

A devastating challenge to the legitimacy of philosophical liberalism has come from Fred Hirsch (1976), a highly respected economist. His arguments are intricate, involved, and subtle. Their overall effect, however, is to deny that a natural symmetry exists between individual action and the aggregate effect of many individual actions in a modern economy. Hirsch makes a crucial distinction between *material* and *positional* goods. He informs us that the former include a wide range of goods and services whose output can be increased through improvements in productivity, without a concomitant deterioration in quality. Put in these terms, we can see that the material economy is the central concern of modern economics. Positional goods, on the other hand, refer to another wide range of goods (occupations, services, and other social relations) that are either scarce in an absolute or socially defined sense or are subject to crowding through extensive use. Vacationing at the seashore is a positional good, but it ceases to be so if the beach becomes polluted by a filthy ocean.

The critical point of Hirsch's (1976) analysis can be seen by looking at the relationship between employment and education as a special case (Green, 1971). It is generally understood that occupations in a modern corporate-industrial society are hierarchically organized to enable the identification of preferred occupations—jobs that provide high degrees of income, status, prestige, and control over one's psychological and physical space and time. Such occupations are preferred because their supply is limited and are therefore positional goods. Thus they are desirable relative to the majority of employment opportunities. Effective demand for such occupations increases as incomes rise, until, of course, they exceed available supply.

However, as the intensity of competition for preferred occupations rises, the price or cost of attaining these is driven up. This results in more resources being diverted to the pursuit of preferred occupations, with no corresponding increase in their supply. Or, if the supply is increased—as with, for example, bachelor's, master's, or doctoral degrees in education—then there is a negative effect on the quality of the environment that sustains the individual's pursuit of these positional goods.

This is now a familiar story. Individuals possessing relatively high educational qualifications are viewed as enjoying attractive professional and social opportunities (life chances). This situation produces a strong latent demand for access to such qualifications. Individuals themselves may be willing to pay the resulting higher fees for educational services; however, more often than not, the demand results in the state broadening access to postsecondary and university education and underwriting the cost of this extended schooling.

The problem Hirsch's (1976) analysis poses for philosophical liberalism is seen in the fact that the self-regulating aspects of the market economy do not, due to its internal logic, allow all or most individuals to advance their standing in the race for educational degrees. In other words, what is possible for the single individual to achieve is not possible for all individuals, and would not be possible even if they all possessed equal talent.

This unexpected result strikes at the heart of the matter. Philosophical liberalism presumes a symmetry between economic individual advancement and aggregate effects. This is not the case; hence, frustration results from an imposed hierarchy that confines socially scarce goods (really, positional goods) to those on the highest rungs of the distribution ladder. This clearly disappoints the expectations of those who believe in the individualistic logic that states that if anybody can, then everyone can. If the results of aggregate advance perforce must be inadequate or disappointing, then an essential condition of philosophical liberalism's definition of the common good—the "trickle-down" theory—is wrongheaded. The common good cannot be served, since the notion of collective benefit, based on the connection between self-interest and general interest, is truncated.

Hirsch's (1976) analysis indicates that there is a problem of great magnitude here; namely, translating individual economic improvement into overall improvement. One way of looking at the consequences of disappointing aggregate results is to see them as being caused either by inadequate economic hard work and effort or by excessive, irrational consumer demands. It is in this way that philosophical liberalism, as the dominant social theory, tries to make the best of a bad job. It encourages individuals either to intensify the competition to attain positional goods (look up, don't look down) or to be prepared to sacrifice and let such goods go to those whose hard work and effort have won them. Traditionally, philosophical liberalism has had a strong claim on the loyalty of citizens to their government, not only for holding the right attitude, but for developing a proper social conscience necessary for sacrifices to be undertaken.

But maledictions over the individual's excessive demand for goods and services, according to Hirsch (1976), cannot be sustained. In this respect, it is important to bear in mind that all goods are in some degree positional and are never simply material or natural. That is, the use of the phrase *material goods* can in fact be considered as superfluous, and it should be stripped of its purely economic definition. In practice, what constitutes an adequate income is only definable as whatever combination of economic resources an individual or family needs in order to participate in the life of the community. This points out that material goods are never merely economic; they are always nested in moral and psychological contexts.

Perhaps it may help to look at this point another way. Traditionally, under the spell of philosophical liberalism, we think of inflation as a technical, economic term. But is it? Hirsch's (1976) analysis informs us that inflation is at heart cultural, not economic. In this he is helped by economist Irving S. Friedman (1980):

> Existing methods of attacking inflation are simply wrong because they are based on a misunderstanding of the nature of modern inflation. The basic causes of modern inflation differ greatly from those of classic inflation. They are not confined to the economic field, . . . but are now deeply rooted in a society and in its political, social, and psychological structures. I call them societal causes. [p. 63]

Friedman contends that modern inflation is nested in a context that involves a tension between an expanding world population and the limits of world material resources. Inflation thus involves an economic phenomenon with psychocultural motivation. Indeed, it may imply a moral penalty imposed on the claim to a higher standard of living, which amounts to the current society's claim against its future. Instead of paying now, society decides to avoid the cost, at least for the present (Yankelovich, 1981).

On a related tack, philosophical liberalism, as the dominant social theory suffusing our consciousness and practice, helps deflect or make unassimilable the argument that our psychology of affluence cannot persist, that the resources of today can no longer support it. Hence, the ecological critique can be understood only insofar as the philosophical liberal's mind can absorb and decode it.

The immediate relevance of this compressed economic analysis is to show that during the past fifty years or so philosophic liberalism has been weakened as a viable democratic social theory. Since the 1930s, we have been divided over whether economic expansion or contraction best produces stability and prosperity. One group, the old liberals (today's conservatives), opposes the expansion of government simply as a means of combating the injustices and ravages of a competitive market economy. Another group, the new liberals, argues that the mechanisms of government provide the proper means for mitigating the harsh effects of the market. Both groups, however, approach unanimity on an underlying assumption: Society's fate can no longer be passively submitted to unguided, unrestricted economic mechanisms. Although they may engage in considerable debate over the notion of the proper means, usually couched in the familiar private-versus-public, voluntary-versus-compulsory dichotomies, both groups tend to offer solutions refracted through the precepts and ideals of philosophical liberalism.

As a democratic social theory, philosophical liberalism is challenged today because serious and haunting doubts have set in. It is obvious that it lacks an effective theory of human justice and fairness, one that would tell us how to deal with things gone horribly wrong in American society. The theory presents no meaningful guidance on how to situate the very idea of homeless people huddled around trashcan fires, the aged forced to take "hamburger jobs" in order to survive, executives taking huge bonuses while workers are laid off, and powerful government institutional functionaries using their power and influence to enhance their own interests at the expense of the American public. According to Yankelovich (1981), in one form or another, the judgment that the United States is lacking in a sense of human justice and fairness "has been made by the overwhelming majority of the American people—ranging from 70 to 80 percent" (p. 222).

The deep obstacle to loosening philosophical liberalism's hold over the American public is the argument that the United States, despite its problems, has an unquestionably superior quality of life over that of other countries. Ergo, philosophical liberalism is right and must be adhered to. It is a powerful argument, often applied. But is the claim true? In a study comparing the United States, Japan, Sweden, and West Germany, released in late 1986, the Economic Policy Institute reported that "on the basis of 17 measures of quality of life the U.S. performance was worst and Sweden's was best" ("Three Nations," 1986, p. 4). Significantly, the United States had the best performance on only three quality-of-life measures: home ownership, living space per person, and expenditure on medical care per person. It had the *worst* performance of the four nations in eleven categories, including infant mortality, male life expectancy, homicide rate, and unemployment. The central or dominating tendency of these findings, as would be expected, given philosophical liberalism, is that we do best on some materialistic measures, particularly those that speak to a private, individualistic ethic (housing and space), but we fare poorly on measures corresponding to moral values reflecting a concern for community and human decency (high infant mortality rate and unemployment).

Patently, philosophical liberalism carries less and less plausibility today. There are too many facts contradicting what it purports to offer. For one thing, it can never deliver what it promises to all people, and this insures bitter disappointment for a great many. What happens to those who do not "succeed"? Is there a place in such a system for the different values and virtues of minorities? What of the absence of fulfillment and the sheer misery that attend some economic successes; for instance, the hideous emptiness of rejecting one's ethnic group or social class?

These questions plead a strong case for a new American imagery, one based on other compelling views, such as those found in the World Watch Institute's *Report on Progress toward a Sustainable Society: State of the World 1985* (Brown & Wolf, 1985) and *The Uncertain Promise* (Goulet, 1977). These works make it increasingly clear that philosophical liberalism embodies a single, outdated, dysfunctional picture of the good life, one that must be abandoned.

The growing discrediting of philosophical liberalism is also reflected in the makeup of modern society. American society today is marked by an increasing percentage of service-sector income in its Gross National Product, not only in services such as the postal service, catering, and automotive repair, but also in social services such as marriage and birth-control counseling and the care of the young, the infirm, the disadvantaged, and the aged. The latter all fall under the general heading of social assistance or care. This stage of economic development is characterized by its unlimited potential, since service production has none of the limits imposed by material goods production—limits such as natural resources, capital, and land. There seems to be no end to the needs for which services can be rendered, and presumably no limit to the number of people who can participate in it, either as service producers or service consumers (professionals, semiprofessionals, and clients).

What is important is that the politics of a service society are unsure. The assumption of unlimited potential falls apart in the face of cuts in public budgets, which are becoming strained under the service load. Traditionally, philosophical liberalism supported politics rooted in a material-goods economy, which allowed debate as to whether the nation-society needed more wheat or more steel, more automobiles or more housing. But the new political service debate is different. We now debate whether we should have more doctors or more engineers, more teachers or more social workers, more law-yers or more law-enforcement officers. Politically, the question is whether we should trade health for a sound infrastructure; learning for family well-being; and justice for security and safety.

While philosophical liberalism established the language and rules of discourse that made it possible to set a public agenda by a clear-cut choice between wheat and steel, it is deficient in helping us decide between health and education. There is little in this social theory's framing of issues that impresses people whose faith in pa-triotism, national morale, and political morality has been shaken, those who want a new public agenda, one that veers toward a moral and decent civic compact. Today, it is felt, we need to find new in-tellectual resources, to deal not only with economic and political transformations, but with the normative transformations as well.

I suggest, in other words, that responsible and responsive po-litical action requires that we desert philosophical liberalism in fa-vor of its rival tradition, philosophical civic republicanism, a social theory incorporating the notion of public good. MacIntyre (1984) suggests just such a solution to our current dilemma, by arguing as follows: "Traditions do on occasion founder, that is, by their own standards of flourishing, and an encounter with a rival tradition may in this way provide good reasons either for attempting to reconsti-tute one's tradition in some radical way or for deserting it" (p. 277).

My point is that it would be foolish to claim that philosophical liberalism has never served America well; it did, for over 150 years. But it also negatively exploited differences, promoted social seg-mentation, and rewarded particularistic adaptation to a common culture. One of the central insights of our discussion is that today philosophical liberalism's formulations are defective, beyond recon-stitution, in several respects. First, as empirically evidenced, the consequences of laissez-faire economics are nasty and brutal for many disadvantaged Americans, such as the homeless, the aged, unorganized laborers, the black underclass, the disabled, and, in-creasingly, white-collar workers whose skills have become out-dated. Second, as normative social theory, it projects an ethic of independence and individualism no longer in keeping with the reality of global interdependence and mutual dependence. For ex-ample, it frames the ecological critique as a threat to personal free-dom. Third, as political ideology, it fosters a strongly individualistic form of competition which is destructive of a much-needed sense of civic compassion and decency.

THE NEW PUBLIC VISION:
PHILOSOPHICAL CIVIC REPUBLICANISM

As part of the answer to the problems discussed in the previous section, what is called for today is a new public vision, a new democratic social theory. The new public vision will include two ideals that will be explored throughout the remainder of this work. I speak of these as "ideals" because far too few Americans are attentive to or share a sense of what can be called *civic virtue* and the *public good*. *Civic virtue* (*arete*, or the good traits of moral and intellectual character) suggests the ideal of civic excellence—certain skills and character traits the possession and exercise of which tend to enable us to achieve a kind of integrity and unity of self. The possessor of civic virtue is guided by moral and intellectual considerations in an attempt to balance private interests with the *public good*. This is an ideal state whereby solidarity, friendship, trust, and tolerance are collective, communal relationships guided by moral principles and reasoning. The recognition of this role makes participation in public life something to be celebrated and valued, something that reflects credit upon the individual, rather than something to be ridiculed or grudgingly engaged in.

The common assumption at work here is that civic virtue has its proper exercise within the social context of the public sphere or political arena. To be a good person will be, at the very least, sufficient for being a good citizen. But what are the virtues that make a good person and, hence, a good citizen? It is clearly the case that different conceptions of virtue exist and, therefore, different conceptions of civic virtue exist. There is, of course, a crucial difference between the way in which ancient societies, say, Homeric Greece, viewed the relationship between moral character and political community and the way Christian medieval society viewed it. In every case, however, it is a fact that, outside a community of shared conventions, practices, and values, there can never be full human beings possessing a rich sense of personhood.

The central idea here is to conceive a view of human nature that accords human dignity and worth great value and is also in accord with the sociological view of civic involvement as a necessary part of the individual's self-development or fulfillment. The understanding is that to be a fully developed individual requires that individuality exist, but not outside of or prior to social relationships. To be an individual, in the most involved, mature sense, includes the capacity to achieve a responsible selfhood through secure objects of allegiance (social relationships), without which individuals are lost.

The most secure and enduring objects of allegiance are the notions of human dignity and mutual respect, along with the ideals of comity, solidarity, cooperative civic and community projects, and common devotion to the causes of compassion for others and social justice. Quite obviously, public and political concerns themselves depend upon the moral dimensions of social relationships, which in turn are ultimately grounded in the notions of human dignity and respect.

The human *telos*, for example, which is the good of a whole human life conceived as a unity (however it may be determined), cannot be achieved outside a community of shared conventions, practices, and values. It is the elaborate conventional, practical, and normative aspects of human life that condition our views of human good, and it is the polis, the political community, that nurtures these. But just what are the essential ingredients of human life conceived as a unity? I have argued that it is in association with others—in relationships characterized by human dignity, mutual respect, justice, fairness, benevolence, truthfulness, caring about others, and fellowship—that human nature most fully expresses itself.

Obviously, it must be conceded at the outset that the conception of human nature offered here is a normative one. This usage, however, is unavoidable, because civic virtue is a normative concept that cannot be understood apart from conceptions of the public good. Thus, although it is not my wish to link civic virtue and the public good to the practices of an ideal rather than to an actual state of affairs, in reality they do remain ideal in that they have been opposed by philosophical liberalism, the dominant social theory underpinning America's tradition of democracy. Let us consider this point.

If we look for a social theory tradition where civic virtue and the public good are not separated but inextricably bound together, certain benefits might accrue. This is not abstract talk about high theory in the upper atmosphere. There are in the American culture two examples of such a tradition, which exist as free-floating elements in the social/political system. The first is a large body of moral thought comprised of Jewish and Christian religious traditions; and the second is a civic republican tradition having its origin in the poleis of ancient Greece and later Rome, and further articulated in the humanism of the late medieval period and the civic humanism of early modern Europe (Pocock, 1975). The latter, of course, figured prominently in the formation of modern Western democracies.

In other words, while American social conditioning in the prin-

ciples of philosophical liberalism has been broad and deep, oppos-
ing or countering traditions have also been at work. Although the
older vision of the social order is still avowed in most quarters, it is
being challenged, and the new public vision, philosophical civic republicanism, has arrived with a modern relevance. It is called *civic*
republicanism, because it sees as both necessary and proper that the
public good be defined in terms of civic virtue, in terms of what individuals decide together, acting not as private persons but as citizens. It is called civic *republicanism* because it purports to use
democratic government in a positive and expansive role to achieve
a moral, public good (Sullivan, 1982).

It is important to clarify these assertations. As Arendt (1986)
noted,

> There exists another tradition and another vocabulary no less old and
> time-honored. When the Athenian city-state called its constitution an
> isonomy, or the Romans spoke of the *civitas* as their form of govern-
> ment, they had in mind a concept of power and law whose essence did
> not rely on the command-obedience relationship and which did not
> identify power and rule or law and command. It was to these examples
> that the men of the eighteenth-century revolutions turned when they
> ransacked the archives of antiquity and constituted a form of govern-
> ment, a republic, where the rule of law, resting on the power of the
> people, would put an end to the rule of man over man, which they
> thought was a "government fit for slaves." They too, unhappily, still
> talked about obedience—obedience to laws instead of men; but what
> they actually meant was support of the laws to which the citizenry had
> given its consent. [p. 62]

Arendt thus expresses how the founders of our nation-society relied
upon the philosophical civic republican tradition to play a creative
role in shaping the civic culture. This tradition was later manifested
in the eighteenth century as a project inherited from ancient Greece
and Rome, transmitted through the Middle Ages, especially in terms
of the Italian republics and their exaltation of civic virtue.

In this tradition, what is central is the notion of a rejection of
private interest in favor of a collective interest or public good. As
MacIntyre (1984) commented, "Republicanism therefore represents
an attempt at a partial restoration of what I have called the classical
tradition. . . . [It] inherited from the institutions of the medieval and
renaissance republic what amounted to a passion for equality" (p.
237).

What we should see in this claim is that equality points in two
directions. First, others should be given the same consideration as

oneself, at least in moral decisions; and second, others we think little of should be given the same consideration as others we think highly of or love. Equality, viewed as equality of consideration, runs counter to the tenets of philosophical liberalism, where in virtually every area of private life it is considered proper to favor one's own interests, the interests of those one loves, the interests of those who by dint of hard work and effort have gained for themselves a large measure of success or status, over the interests of strangers and those whose status suggests individual or cultural shortcomings.

Thus there exist today two quite different democratic social traditions. It is not unimportant to understand these, especially in the corner of human action and values called the school. Which tradition offers the best picture of society? How can this state of affairs even be talked about? The distinction needs developing. MacIntyre (1984) spoke of the relationship of two different moral traditions as follows:

> If two moral traditions are able to recognize each other as advancing rival contentions on issues of importance, then necessarily they must share some common features. And since some kind of relationship to practices, some particular conception of human goods, some characteristics which arise from the very nature of a tradition will be features of both, this is not unsurprising. [p. 276]

Philosophical civic republicanism, constituted by the Jewish Old Testament, Christian New Testament, and civic republican moral virtues, offers a viable challenge to the legitimacy of philosophical liberalism. While the latter tradition was a radical doctrine in its time, it is quite unable to handle the vital moral concerns of human beings today. Philosophical civic republicanism, on the other hand, offers the view that involvement in the political community or commons is essentially a form of moral activity. This tradition presupposes, in the first instance, that there is a one-to-one correspondence between the character of citizens and the human flourishing or welfare of the nation-society. It assumes, in the second instance, that anyone, not only those in a position of high status, should recognize that public actions must be guided by a self-interest promotive of civic virtue. In short, this tradition necessarily concentrates attention on the place of the citizen in relation to the public good. More than that, however, it forcefully articulates that what is needed today is a conception of citizenship calling for a civic education that nurtures a sense of human dignity, mutual respect, and an ethic of obligation to others; that is, a concerned, caring, tolerant attitude toward others. Such a civic education would cultivate civic compassion or civic decency, phrases used as a signal of recoil against the mean-spiritedness and indifference of philosophical liberalism.

Philosophical Civic Republicanism as a Tradition

The philosophical civic republican tradition, we have seen, has its roots in antiquity. It was, however, very much in the minds of the founders of this country, in their rejection of symbolic class divisions based on rank, and seen later in the North's opposition to slavery and society's rejection of the notion of real class divisions (although they do exist). Indeed, the failure of socialism and Marxism to take root in the United States may be explained, at least in part, by a small but actively supported sense of shared moral compact giving rise to equality of consideration of good fellowship, especially as manifested in rural communities and ethnic enclaves.

This manifestation of philosophical civic republicanism is further revealed in the face-to-face relationships of the early New England town meetings and in the *ad hoc* gatherings of frontier communities, where citizens ran their own affairs in a manner akin to Athenian democracy. It also erupted in the years before the Civil War in the Jacksonian movement, which asserted the rights of ordinary citizens against the ruling classes of the eastern seaboard. It was also seen in the antislavery movement, largely a Christian crusade, which increased the pressure on the proslavery factions and helped persuade people of the moral justification of a war against slavery.

Consider, also, a similar impulse exhibited in the late nineteenth-century agrarian-populism movement, which was a kind of rural radicalism with a particular socioeconomic base. This was a farmers' alliance, which claimed oppression by an unfair "system," a faith in the "people's government," and advocated using "socialistic" measures to put things right (Canovan, 1981, p. 52).

Finally, philosophical civic republicanism was also mirrored in the successful effort of the "progressives" to make American society more responsive to the people by promoting direct or participatory democracy through devices such as the referendum, direct election of senators, recall, the Australian ballot, and municipal reform. Most recently, the events of the civil rights movement, the campus opposition to the Vietnam war, and the religious Sanctuary movement are evidence of philosophical civic republicanism at work. In all of these stirrings of reform, there were evidenced parts of a tradition that assumes that citizens must take hold of the public sphere as a self-governing community as a necessary means of enhancing the moral quality of its members' lives. It is clear that these campaigns for greater participatory democracy and social justice were struggles against a view of society and politics where special interests tended to dominate, much to the detriment of the common or public good. It is possible, then, to distinguish an ongoing political counterforce rising here and there in American history, showing a clear alternative to the principles of philosophical liberalism.

This perspective helps us to see that, on the positive side, a major purpose of philosophical civic republicanism is to focus on direct democratic processes and participatory citizenship, as well as on nurturing a moral compact in politics. The bedrock issue has been and continues to be whether democratic morality will be taken seriously in the civic culture. In terms of its negative critique, philosophical civic republicanism regards its rival, philosophical liberalism, as assailing the eyes and ears with its individualistic norms and self-interests, which deny the shared moral concern or compact so necessary for promoting the well-being of the society.

An excellent argument for civic republicanism was made by the Frenchman Alexis de Tocqueville (1840/1969), who searched among the local and regional communities of Jacksonian America for the roots of the attitude toward association, participation, and mutual respect about which he wrote so glowingly. In the course of his broodings on the dangers of an increasingly egalitarian age, of the ancient phenomenon of popular tyranny, Tocqueville argued that the way to prevent the "evils" (excesses) of democratic society was to introduce fully democratic politics. He correctly pointed out that, in the United States, democracy had not so far given rise to tyrants, simply because ordinary citizens were in effective possession of political rights and they were used to acting politically to protect their interests.

Tocqueville's (1840/1969) assessment of republican life and its successes in America filled him with the conviction that the great task was to "educate democracy" if possible; that is, to put new life into its beliefs, to purify its mores, to control its actions, and gradually to substitute understanding of statecraft for inexperience and knowledge of its true interest for blind instincts.

Finally, Tocqueville saw clearly that democracy in America, which was really the implementation of the ideals of American civic republicanism, was intimately connected to the ability of local communities and associations, together with religious morality, to provide enduring objects of loyalty sufficient to sustain a moral civic culture. Of particular concern was his fear of the new spirit of economic enterprise, which he felt would turn citizens away from a vigorous civic life and spirit in the public sphere and toward the private sphere. Clearly, his worries in this regard have lost none of their relevance in the past 150 years.

The New Reality and the Morality of Reversal

One way of taking account of this is to say that a revitalized approach to democratic social theory suggested here is not really "new"; it has been evidenced in America's past, but it has largely been overshadowed by philosophical liberalism. Much of the vitality and energy of the "new" social theory derives from numerous familiar notions—trust, friendship, decency, benevolence, virtue, character, community, common good, moral consensus, human dignity, mutual respect, obligation or duty, concern, caring, and tolerance of others. These are in contrast to the notions of self-interest, individualism, individualistic logic, liberty, rights and entitlements, and contracts.

To put this in more rigorous terms, philosophical civic republicanism premises that questions about social power, freedom, rights and duties, liberty, distributive justice, and equality are not questions to be answered by the desires of self-interested individuals nor based on a calculation of the outcome in terms of the material benefits that will accrue to given proportions of the population. Rather, they are decisive moral considerations to be settled by collective sovereignty through moral public processes. Moreover, these matters, along with others, are the starting point for citizens' discussions of society's purposes, because they resonate with the need of humans for a life of public involvement, social justice, and willing service to others—the need, in other words, to be included in a democratic community whose operative principles are human dignity and mutual respect, and which amplifies an ethic of obligation to serve others.

From this perspective, philosophical civic republicanism values equality of consideration and participatory democracy. The latter term, however, sounds like a pleonasm. Since "democracy" is widely supposed to mean "government of, by, and for the people," how could a genuine democracy be other than participatory? This minor linguistic oddity, however, conceals an important point. The ideals and devices of participatory democracy arise precisely in political contexts where "democracy" in some sense is officially celebrated as a norm, but where dissidents judge that democratic practice does not live up to the promise of the norm. "Participatory democracy," then, is a label given by those who see and deplore the gap between the ideal and the reality of democracy and wish to make "government of, by, and for the people" a reality rather than a mere slogan.

Consequently, the history of philosophical civic republicanism in American life has two connected aspects, one practical and one theoretical. It is, on the one hand, the story of the vicissitudes of an ideal of participatory democracy and of the ways in which the stock of that ideal has risen and fallen in the United States. On the other hand, it documents the history of a minor tradition of moral aspirations and principles. Seen alongside philosophical liberalism, it has played only a tangential role in public affairs. Indeed, there has been scant use of the language, concepts, and arguments of philosophical civic republicanism in discussions concerning the shape of public policy. But it has served as an occasional and important human response or rejoinder to philosophical liberalism, by stressing the need for a moral compact among citizens, a moral foundation for politics. In this project it is assisted by a core of traditional morality, including such concepts as human dignity, mutual respect, community, equality of consideration, fairness, charity, service, concern, tolerance, and brotherhood/sisterhood, which has been used to tap a civic vision and generate a moral compact.

This conception of democracy has, it bears repeating, a central moral dimension. There is a strong case for saying that it applies the principles of *caritas*, the Christian love of one's neighbor, toward achieving and justifying an inclusive human community. The development of a moral community with a wide range of collaborative civic participation is neither inevitable nor easy to achieve. But if it is to happen, one condition, perhaps the supreme test, is that citizens acknowledge, in thought and deed, in our social behavior and in public policy decisions, that it is generally important to treat others with human dignity and mutual respect, that we ought to treat all people as if they were equally worthy of respect, and that in many contexts it is rude to slight someone else's values. Indeed, the litmus test of all democratic institutions is the contribution they make to the well-being of every member of society.

A major step, if not the starting point, in the attempt to restructure the civic culture in America must be the conception of democracy that issues from the understanding of virtues, preeminent among them the living of life as a shared concern, the exercising in our relationships with others an ethic of obligation, and compassion toward others. Put concretely, this means finding ways to overcome a highly individualistic, purely self-interested approach to everyday life. There are, of course, no instant recipes for achieving this goal, no patent medicines, no easy fixes. It is enough, for the present, to realize that American democracy must build upon the somewhat hidden but still living moral traditions of biblical religion and civic republicanism, wherever they may be found. As the older order recedes, we must consider this tradition at every point of application in our private and public behavior.

A major task, then, is to extend the moral principles of philosophical civic republicanism into the public sphere as well as into other dominant economic and social institutions of society. Effective strategies are needed for transforming the existing situation so as to recognize philosophical liberalism as the foe in the quest to sustain fully the institutions that democracy requires.

One strategy for binding Americans to one another, regardless of class, race, or religious differences, is by a commitment to an abiding object of loyalty, the civic culture. We need to realize that a democracy is only possible through a life that values human dignity, accords others mutual respect, helps citizens to know themselves in regard to the interdependent world in which they now live, responds actively to and shares an ethic of obligation to others, and promotes social justice for all.

A further strategy involves making operative the right of all democratic citizens to equal influence and consideration in matters that affect them collectively, and correspondingly in matters that affect them most closely. This condition would best be realized in a society in which as many opportunities as possible existed for democratic participation at all levels, including those that affect citizens most closely in their daily affairs. This calls for promoting genuinely associational civic activity, since it involves sharing responsibility for acts that create a quality of life different from the mere sum of material goods and individual satisfactions.

In calling for the implementation of these strategies, it is clear that participatory democracy and philosophical civic republicanism are bound together, because in a democracy citizens must be taught the value and skills of social action, of inquiry, discussion, and willing cooperation, as well as of the dangers of merely sitting in the dark, encouraging with occasional applause the prominent political players—their elected leaders. The issue is not simply more citizen access to a remote, uncaring government, along the lines, for instance, of progressivist programs for initiative, referendum, and re-call procedures, although these are important. Rather, what is needed is an improved quality of civic participation, one that reaches out to explore new moral purposes and goals.

What the foregoing signifies is a radical change in civic educa-tion, based on a need of citizens to learn a civic compassion and de-cency—to understand and care for others—while being tolerant and respectful of their values. This means, in part, helping students to see why citizens in a democracy are equal among themselves; why it is uncivil or rude to slight another's values; and that individual-istic logic incurs risks of encouraging snobbery, envy, and unfair-ness to others, and perhaps even of rationalizing their exploitation.

The assumption at work here is that democratic citizens must learn that humans are by nature social beings, that living together in harmony requires a shared concern, and that a shared civic life is possible only when members of the polity care for and are tolerant of one another. In short, a community supported by the principle of *caritas* must be formed. This requires a good sense of how to achieve this goal, for this is a difficult project. Good judgment suggests that civic education must be reckoned with. This claim is based on the fact that students spend considerable time in school and are ex-pected to experience a way of life or a set of experiences in school that put them in a good position to be civically competent. Civic education must be identified with the praxis of those who talk to-gether in order to act in common, for the public good. Students of different social classes and ethnic and religious backgrounds can come together in a civic education that shows them in practical con-crete fashion that, despite differences that exist between them, there are many bases for a shared concern, the fundamental one being re-spect for persons. Certain limits to this are recognized, of course, but if civic education is to be more than a romanticized notion, a gen-uinely accepted part of citizens' lives, then the necessity of making changes is no longer debatable.

The most telling argument for developing civic education is that there are some academic things all citizens need to know. These in-clude an understanding of democratic processes and institutions, the ability to use social skills that enable active participation in public debate, and a grasp of what a search for equality of consideration entails when based on moral obligations to others. In sum, students must learn what it takes to transform the individual into a good person and a good citizen.

There is a further point, closely connected to the foregoing.

Given that an educated citizenry is a desirable thing, we also need to be clear about the principle of majority rule. Oftentimes legally unrestricted majority rule is seen as *the* democratic solution to the problem of differences of opinion and judgment. However, the overruling of others by means of majority vote, while it may enhance rapid, clear-cut policy changes, can be very formidable in the suppression of the rights and wishes of minorities and very effective in the suffocation of dissent without any use of violence. It may also provoke resentment and hostility among the losers. Majority rule, uncaringly and uncompassionately employed, carries the danger not only of tyranny by the victors but of denigration of the dignity and worth of others. It implies mastery of others, or superordination; and it means the potential loss of the communal solidarity that comes when citizens join with others in "amicable agreement"—consensus among interested parties—in shaping the tasks and shared purposes of society.

This is not to say that majority rule is not a valued political practice; it can be, and sometimes expedience demands it. However, the democratic values of concern and caring for and tolerance of others demand that all interests be taken into account and compromises be reached that are acceptable to all parties. Political consensus is most likely to be achieved when those involved in the discussion and decision making exhibit a genuine appreciation of another's worth, sometimes operationalized as trying to understand more of what the other wants than the other has yet put into words.

In articulating this position, by helping students come to grips with its ramifications, educators must necessarily draw upon the language, concepts, and values associated with philosophical civic republicanism, since human dignity, mutual respect, kindness, compassion, and generosity are implicated. Students will come to see that these values tend to foster mutual feelings of good will among citizens, creating a sense of community yet maintaining an individual's sense of importance and worth. As applied to the affairs of school life, they help students to govern themselves, to pursue common purposes, to act on moral principle, and to participate fully in civic life as a good citizen. This will nurture a new concept of civic life, which for many Americans today is thought of as a morally indifferent arena or one not within the purview of morality.

Clearly civic education must play a vital role in helping students become reasonably civically competent and confident about the overall consequences of their actions. It must motivate them to act in ways that both uphold the existence of community and are highly beneficial for the members of that community. If educators can create a school community in which the major issues that affect different factions are decided by consensus among all parties and not by simple majority rule, students will be in a much better position to arrive at a reasonable and probably correct moral judgment about good citizenship than someone who merely mouths democratic slogans and generalizations. This is a civic education whose time has come, especially in a nation-society that is acutely aware of the intractability of many social problems, at least as they have been dealt with under the aegis of philosophical liberalism.

CONCLUSION

In this chapter we have examined and contrasted the dominant underpinnings of philosophical liberalism and philosophical civic republicanism. The former, it has been argued, presents enormous difficulties today, due to a too-exclusive commitment to self-interest, treating society as nothing more than an arena in which individuals seek to secure what is useful or agreeable to them. Traditionally, the values of philosophical liberalism have focused on a privatized self and encouraged citizens to scramble to obtain the goods and services of society first, before another individual or group seizes them.

Over the years, there has been increasing dissatisfaction with philosophical liberalism as a useful democratic social theory. Income redistribution and expert bureaucratic fine-tuning by state and federal governments have failed to meet the exigencies of runaway inflation, elected officials using public office to advance private interests, the depletion of our cheap energy supplies, public anxiety about nuclear warfare, and so forth.

As a response to this malaise, we have examined an alternative democratic social theory, philosophical civic republicanism, as a much-needed step toward bringing about a revitalized civic culture. Particularly, we have contrasted the moral dimensions of the two traditions, and I have argued that philosophical civic republicanism offers a better, or more just, basis for participatory democracy. So great a change, however, will have to overcome entrenched, traditional forms of rationality, action, and purpose, insofar as it will require a new ordering of values—"new rules," as it were.

These arguments have to get through to the general public in an assimilable form, and this is not an easy task. It is helpful to keep in mind an observation made by Dewey (1891/1972) that moral theory is "all one with moral insight, and moral insight is the recognition of the relationships at hand" (p. 94). This suggests that the basis for a revitalized civic culture is a moral compact, the foundation of which is found in moral relationships whose roots are in the principle that humans are possessed of inherent worth, human dignity, and all have an equal right to a moral civic existence. To ignore the moral dimension, or to leave it insufficiently fulfilled, is to neglect the very grounds on which a democratic society rests.

CHAPTER 3

The Moral Dimensions of Philosophical Civic Republicanism

In the last chapter we saw that social theory serves to pattern how a governed and social life is to be executed. Two democratic social theory traditions, philosophical liberalism and philosophical civic republicanism, were examined and contrasted in order to point out an obvious and critical deficiency in the former, namely, a deeply rooted self-interest translated into a highly individualistic logic and social view, as opposed to an individual-as-member social view. We explored, moreover, the basis of the relationship between the civic culture and civic education. I said that a good person will be a good citizen. To see how, something must be said about the moral foundations of philosophical civic republicanism, which are the ethics of obligation and commitment and of civic service. It will be argued in this chapter that the revitalization of the civic culture presupposes (1) philosophical civic republicanism; (2) a democratic minimum moral measure drawn from philosophical civic republicanism; (3) schooling that is a union of formal subject matter and an ethic of civic obligation; (4) the creation, in students, of the disposition of social habits of willing action beneficial to all by civic services; (5) self-development of good persons; (6) good citizens; and, finally, (7) a revitalized civic culture.

HUMAN DIGNITY AND SELF-DEVELOPMENT

The unique wonder of America, I believe, is not in its buildings, nor in its artifacts or its arts. Rather, I believe that its greatest value is found in its democracy. It would, of course, be dishonest and immoral to ignore the dreadful racial, ethnic, and gender scars of the United States, both past and present; and without a doubt the present state of affairs is less than ideal. The situation is the result of our failure to create a civic culture based upon a truly democratic moral foundation, and in this regard philosophical civic republican-

ism holds out the value of a common moral decency. It premises a
democracy dependent upon the moral culture of its citizens, an insight that gives cause, if not for optimism, then at least for a measure of courage and hope.

To create a moral basis for the civic culture, we must begin with
a recognition of a deep-seated inconsistency in American life: Traditionally, the American tendency has been to explain virtually all
actions, especially those in public life, as being a result of self-
interest. Americans have acted and talked that way even though they
frequently have acted with a deep concern and caring for the welfare of others, even to the detriment of their own particular self-
interest.

Clearly, the lives of citizens are regularly fractured by this pull
between private self-interest and common or group interest, producing occasions when one allegiance points in one direction, the
other in another direction. Oftentimes, the claims of the former
conflict with the latter in such a way that one may find oneself os-
cillating in an arbitrary way, rather than making rational, fair, decent choices. Commitment to sustaining a community of virtuous
citizens is too commonly incompatible with gaining success in the
economic arena. So there may be individual and group tensions between public claims to fair treatment and private claims of family and
friends.

If the lives of citizens are continuously fractured by choices in
which one allegiance entails the renunciation of another, it may seem
that the virtues internal to the effort of making and sustaining the
good citizen need to be ordered and evaluated in some way, if we
are to assess their potential for restructuring the civic culture. In
other words, any substantive application of civic virtues requires a
clear understanding of them.

The Principle of Human Dignity

I have previously suggested that the principle of human dignity
is so fundamental to a moral civic culture that any account that ignored it would be inadequate. It is time to support this claim and
specify the context of its application in civic matters.

The principle of inherent human dignity has been given at least
formal assent in the Virginia Declaration of Rights of 1776, in the
U.S. Declaration of Independence, by the French Declaration of the
Rights of Man in 1790, by the United Nations Universal Declaration
of Human Rights of 1948, and by the European Convention on Hu-

man Rights of 1953. It is, first and foremost, a philosophical rather than a practical concept, but citizens need to understand it in order to meet their obligations as members of a democracy. Most of us have come to understand it either through the Judeo-Christian tradition or through the ancient Greek and Roman ideals later incorporated into the fundamentally religious Renaissance ideal of Humanism, as in Giovanni Pico della Mirandola's oration *On the Dignity of Man* (1487/1965).

If the adjective *human* is taken seriously, the idea of human dignity must be the idea that there is a certain worth that, whether or not it is recognized, is inherent in all human beings, at all times and in all places. Thus, to assert the dignity or worth of persons is to make a highly significant claim about people, one that cannot be taken lightly. What is entailed by this claim? Chambers (1983) is helpful here, stating that

> we can say that *things* are things that may be used for the purposes of persons. Things take on instrumental or intrinsic value because of the experiences they provide for persons. Because persons do the valuing, things have no value outside the experiences of persons. . . . Persons, unlike the value provided by things, have value in themselves; they are of unconditional worth. To emphasize the difference, Kant says that things have *price*, persons have *worth*. [p. 120]

Chambers goes on to argue, following Kant, that "persons themselves must not be used *merely* as qualities and quantities in the pursuit of other persons' activities" (p. 120). In short, persons have intrinsic value or worth; they are "ends in themselves."

The working out of the principle of human dignity in the structure and conduct of American law, government, and economic and social life has been, to say the least, dismal. The most intolerable infringement on the principle of human dignity, however, is the denial of respect for persons. The imperative to respect persons is specified by Kant (1797/1981): "So act that you treat humanity in your own person and in the person of everyone else always at the same time as an end and never merely as a means" (p. 56). Kant's use of the term *merely* makes note of the fact that we can and do make use of other persons in some ways, but in so doing we must keep their personhood or self-development in mind. This suggests, in other words, that we cannot use other people as means only, but we can *use* them as means if, at the same time, we *treat* them as ends in themselves. In short, we can use others as means to our ends if, and only if, we do not block or limit their attainment of their own ends.

Obviously, certain obligations are associated with the principle of human dignity: impartiality, fair treatment, compassion, fellowship, integrity, loyalty, honorable conduct, and, above all, respect for persons or mutual respect. But why respect persons? I have said that we respect persons because, generally speaking, persons have dignity or worth. Put differently, if a person has worth, then we are required to embody in our relationships with that person what is called respect. But to see that point, we have to confront the question, Why respect persons? This question is frequently responded to with the retort that persons are moral entities entitled to respect because of their inherent dignity or worth.

This argument is deficient because it is circular. The question is this: What constitutes an adequate defense of human dignity? Let us consider a conceptual experiment proposed by Nozick (1981):

> If a human being was going to be valuable or precious, which characteristics would it have? Suppose a contest were being held to design a valuable or precious human being. A prize is to be given simply for succeeding; the winner does not have to justify the application of the terms "valuable" or "precious." [pp. 444–445]

He also suggests, on a more personal note, that you ask yourself, if you could give your child the characteristics of value or preciousness, which traits would you want your child to have?

According to Nozick (1981), there is little doubt that most people want their children to have dignity and respect, especially self-respect. Although it may not be clear why this is so, it is clear that a person possessed of dignity and respect has something dear or precious. Positively, we bask in the glow of their presence; negatively, we tend to envy them. This observation is not offered as an explanation of why this is so; rather, it is common experience that it is so. The possession of the characteristics of human dignity and respect positively radiate with value and preciousness.

The implication is that it is natural for us to want dignity, a sense of worth, and respect, especially self-respect. If it is natural for us to want these, it is in our interest to pursue them, and to grant them to others. In other words, if the adjective *human* is taken seriously, the idea of human dignity must be the idea that every human being is entitled to or owed a common measure of moral behavior. If somebody were to deny that she or he hankers after dignity and respect, we would consider the person in need of therapy, psychiatric help, or some such thing. The point is that people tend to prefer more, rather than less, dignity.

But, we ask, what is human dignity? Although there is room for disagreement, generally speaking human dignity consists of the status of individuals as ends in themselves, rather than as mere means toward some extraneous ends. The principle, of course, as we have seen, says something about respect for persons and, at the same time, indicates something about appropriate human treatment. These two considerations, it is evident, suggest that the principle of human dignity has great bearing on the moral significance of human beings. It is the main moral pull embodied in human rights movements, and it supports an ethical trinity of obligation—shared concern, caring, and tolerance for others—that appears to be a brake on tyranny, intolerance, totalitarianism, technology, and technicism. An ethic of obligation, in other words, rests firmly upon the moral principle that people value each other and treat each other with respect because they have a sense of one another's dignity or moral significance, as revealed in everyday contacts.

It follows that no action could be considered moral unless it stemmed from the principle of human dignity and respect for persons. Put differently, the principle of human dignity imposes on us an absolute moral obligation to meet the requirements of respect for persons. Its requirements can never justifiably be overridden by those of other moral principles, because it is itself the principle by which all such overriding must ultimately be justified. Human dignity, in other words, is the basis of such derivatives as rights and entitlements. Moreover, all moral transgressions against humans would be a violation of this principle. If none of the conventions of a social group involved according others dignity or worth, we would most reasonably regard that group as having no moral foundation at all. As Stanley (1978) argued, "The assertion of human dignity, then, is the constitutive act of moral consciousness. It is the entrance ticket to the community of formal moral discourse. To assert dignity is both to acknowledge the factuality of human creative agency and to accept responsibility for its use" (p. 70).

These considerations of human dignity are reinforced by the historical situation. When we ask ourselves why we should accord others dignity, it is illuminating to see what characteristics the deniers of human preciousness have pronounced. Although many examples of denial abound in ancient and modern history, we need look back no further than the Holocaust (which, incidentally, resulted in the formulation of the Universal Declaration of Human Rights adopted by the United Nations in 1948). It is no accident that the aims of the Holocaust were justified by the Nazis' claim that Aryan Germans had the right to life but Jews and other so-called "inferior races" did not. This terrible example highlights the implications of denying that certain human beings are persons of dignity or worth. It deprives them of all moral status, and, since they do not count as truly human beings, they can be "eugenically exterminated." According to Nazi morality, the principle of human dignity and respect for persons did not apply to "inferior races." Thoughtful people throughout the world readily acknowledge that the so-called "final solution" could not have been pursued at the expense of the lives of millions of innocents, had there not been a clear, conscious denial of the principle of human dignity in Nazi Germany.

The principle of human dignity, then, is important in social and political relationships because it gives moral sanction to respect for persons, a derivative notion. Moreover, human dignity is the main moral principle in the human rights and civil rights movements in the United States and internationally as well, especially since World War II (Cranston, 1964; Dworkin, 1977; Milne, 1986). It is important, therefore, to become aware of the moral authority of this principle and to be able to articulate it in terms of the duty one has to respect others, a fundamental aspect of the golden rule, a biblical injunction.

The heart of the issue can be summarized as follows: The principle of human dignity counters the philosophical liberal's notion of self-interest. The tenets of the latter, it will be recalled, withhold moral sanction from actions that contribute to anything beyond the individual's well-being, thus working perversely against civic actions having a community-of-interest grounding, a feeling good about oneself in terms of how what one is doing is affecting the realization of the others' ends as well as one's own end.

The significance of the principle of human dignity is that it offers a wholly different category of social relations for citizens. It gives, for example, an explicit sanction to the idea of social responsibility. Citizens have rights, but they have obligations as well. In addition to legal rights, there are moral human rights which obligate all human beings at all times and in all places. These moral rights are not merely correctives or brakes on government, but also form the basis of the moral relationships respectful human beings owe one another.

Let us be clear about this last point. Traditionally, philosophical liberalism plumped for "negative" rights, such as the citizen *not* being the recipient of certain kinds of acts. Such an approach obligates all others to refrain from making the citizen, the bearer of that right, the recipient of such acts. It also pushed certain "positive" rights, namely, the entitlement of a citizen to certain goods, opportunities, and services. The principle of human dignity, however, suggests that, since citizens have intrinsic value that is not reducible to their utility relative to the interests of others, then we are not to treat them merely as a means to bringing about the best consequences. We have a duty, in other words, to respect other persons. Anyone who has inherent value is due respect. Hence, the *duty-to-oneself* tenet of philosophical liberalism is supplanted by the *duty-to-respect-self-and-others* tenet of philosophical civic republicanism. This means not only respecting everyone's rights, but actively promoting modes of self-help to others, helping them to achieve their ends. In short, it means making the quality of social life better by helping and serving others.

Obviously, this latter tenet entails a strong sense of social obligation or responsibility, which, we see, exemplifies the principle of human dignity and mutual respect put into practice. Each citizen has an obligation to be predisposed to helping and serving others because to do so is to accord others dignity and respect.

It is perhaps difficult to disagree with this last point, at least in principle, but it is worth asking: What constitutes a moral democratic community? The question is of the greatest practical concern as well as of considerable theoretical importance. Our answer will affect practical civic decisions in all ways, particularly how we conceive of the purpose of civic education. This question also relates in an important way to the question raised in the last chapter, namely, How can we revitalize the civic culture? Both questions are answered, I believe, by the suggestion that a revitalized civic culture is dependent upon creating a moral democratic community whose members have dispositions characterized by social habits of willing action beneficial to others; who are, in other words, good persons and thus good citizens. This answer, however, does not give a working understanding of the questions. In order to operationalize this answer, it is imperative that we examine the conditions of human self-development.

Conditions of Self-Development

There is, first of all, the recognition that human self-development requires that citizens be part of an interconnected network of individuals, a *community*. What members of a community share are certain conventions. A community requires members to treat one another with respect in all their dealings, to refrain from unprovoked violence, from insulting and humiliating one another. If incivility were the rule, community would give way to a brutish Hobbesian "state of nature." A community also requires that members must accord others consideration, compassion, and tolerance. We all know how essential it is for someone to be a member of a concerned, caring, compassionate, and tolerant reference group, to be associated with people who share in a group's sense of well-being. No human collectivity can be carried on if its members are totally indifferent to one another's fortunes in participating in it. Indeed, to be denied such association is a powerful force in stunting a person's self-development. Further, the notion of a citizen is unintelligible apart from that of community, and both terms derive their sense from the idea that we achieve self-development, at least in part, as members of a collectivity, fragile and vulnerable as it may be.

A second condition of self-development is *identity*, which begins with the capacity to distinguish oneself from others. Merely distinguishing oneself is not enough, however; it must be coupled with "somebodyness"—a high self-esteem, having a good opinion of oneself—as well as with self-respect, treating oneself as having dignity and worth. Without a sense of identity, it is not possible to develop a sense of self or, for that matter, a personhood, self-esteem, or self-respect. A life lived without a sense of "somebodyness" would be strange indeed, for when we deny our identity, we not only threaten our self-esteem but severely challenge self-respect.

A third condition of self-development is *privacy*, the condition of being protected from unwanted access by others, either in a physical or psychological sense. Whenever one makes the claim to privacy, it is to control access to what one takes to be one's personal domain. Privacy plays a vital role in nurturing personhood. It is obvious, for instance, that those who run prisons and concentration camps realize that the key to destroying self-esteem and personal worth is to remove any semblance of privacy. Human beings, to develop properly, require personal control over some part of their environment, although how much special exclusivity is essential is contestable. But if we value human dignity and respect for others, we should respect the right to privacy and be morally observant, actually considerate, of others' personal spaces.

The fourth and final condition for self-development can be conveniently introduced with a brief passage by Lukes (1973):

> An individual's thought and action is his own, and not determined by agencies or causes outside his control. In particular, an individual is autonomous (at the social level) to the degree to which he subjects the pressures and norms with which he is confronted to conscious and critical evaluation, forms intentions and reaches practical decisions as the result of independent and rational reflection. [p. 52]

Lukes's statement defines *autonomy*, or self-direction, and it seems to me to strike at the heart of an essential condition of self-development. One must be an autonomous moral agent possessing an imaginative awareness of alternative forms of life; a cognitive perspective that permits engaging in conscious rational deliberation about them; and the ability to act with clear perception of the reasons for, consequences of, and justification of one's decision.

We should recognize that the condition of autonomy frequently involves an eschewing of the forces of custom, habit, and social expectation. It means seeing, for example, that different traditions of culture and civilization are different ways of being human. Rather than being under the sway of such forces, as a self-directed moral agent one expresses the ideas, beliefs, and values that one has ratified through critical, objective, and impartial judgment.

Thus, community, identity, privacy, and autonomy are the four common conditions of self-development. For the sake of brevity I shall henceforth refer to these simply as "common conditions." The adjective *common* is appropriate because the conditions are common to all human self-development, irrespective of the differences of culture or nation-states. Self-development, however, is never confined to these common conditions, although it always includes them. The common conditions, as suggested in the foregoing, generate particular moral virtues, which can be called "particular conditions." These are the conditions of self-development related to a particular way of life (Milne, 1986). The actual self-development of any individual will always consist of a union of common and particular conditions. Thus, as has been suggested, in a democracy, community will be linked with the particular moral virtues of civility and humaneness, identity with self-esteem and self-respect, privacy with respect and consideration, and autonomy with fairness and integrity.

It follows that the common conditions are necessary because they contribute to the whole upon which our self-development depends, but they must be joined by particular conditions, which flavor them and contribute the positive elements of how human beings will deal with one another in a particular society. Common conditions provide, in other words, the general framework of self-development, but particular conditions fill in that framework. In a democracy, for example, the latter require that citizens develop a sense of community for the sake of civility and humaneness; a sense of identity as a human being of worth not to be treated merely as a means, recognizing that others must be treated accordingly; a sense of privacy that asserts that one's space must never be arbitrarily interfered with; and the capacity for autonomy reflecting fairness, flexibility, and the ability to associate with others with courage and sincerity. In short, common conditions of self-development are adapted to meet the particular conditions of a democracy by their interpenetration with democratic or shared purposes.

Bok (1984) caught and expressed the dimensions of this intimate union in the following:

> Human beings . . . are not only unique but unfathomable. The experience of such uniqueness and depth underlies self-respect and what social theorists have called the sense of "the sacredness of the self." This sense also draws on group, family, and societal experiences of intimacy and sacredness, and may attach to individual as well as to collective identity. The growing stress in the last centuries on human dignity and on rights such as the right to privacy echoes it in secular and individualized language. [p. 21]

Bok went on to say,

> Without perceiving some sacredness in human identity, humans are out of touch with the depth they might feel in themselves and respond to in others. Given such a sense, however, certain intrusions are felt as violations—a few even as desecrations. It is in order to guard against such encroachments that we recoil from those who would tap our telephone, read our letters, bug our rooms: no matter how little we have to hide, no matter how benevolent their attentions, we take such intrusions to be demeaning. [p. 21]

To nurture this union of common and particular conditions, especially in education, is to give citizens the capacity for a minimum moral measure, a moral compact. The defense of this activity lies not in whether it is an achievable ideal, but rather in the understanding that these conditions provide the minimum measure of human self-development itself, irrespective of society or culture. This measure is applicable to all cultures and societies and does not deny that every human being is largely made what she or he is by particular cultural and social experiences. It presupposes social and cultural diversity but sets certain limits to its scope. The minimum moral measure proclaims, in other words, that common and particular conditions of self-development in any society must include the principle of human dignity and an ethic of obligations.

There is much support for this claim, not the least of which is the United Nations Universal Declaration of Human Rights of 1948, which states,

> Everyone is entitled to all the rights and freedoms set forth in this Declaration without distinction of any kind such as race, color, sex, language, religion, political or other opinion, national or social origin, property, birth or other status. [p. 2]

And,

> Now therefore the General Assembly proclaims this Universal Declaration of Human Rights as a common standard or achievement for all peoples and all nations as to the end that every individual and every organ of society, keeping this Declaration constantly in mind, shall strive by teaching and education to secure respect for these rights and freedoms, and by progressive measures national and international, to secure their effective recognition and observance. [p. 1]

This suggests the idea of common conditions that every human community should try to reach because doing so is in the best interests of its members, both as members and as private persons.

There is, of course, a vast difference between the status of a self-developed person in a democracy and the status of a self-developed person in a totalitarian regime. A democracy requires citizens whose common conditions are colored by democratic particular conditions or moral virtues. In virtue of their democratic membership, such citizens exhibit the character traits of objectivity, nonarbitrariness, impartiality, and the disposition to act with courage of conviction moderated by humaneness, decency, and tolerance. In so doing, they enjoy high self-esteem and self-respect. Moreover, the integration of these character traits is not only of central importance in personal self-development, it accords well with bonding citizens into a moral community, enabling all members, not just particular groups or classes, to live as well as possible. It is in harmony with the ideals of a democracy as a moral community, and it also sits well with the notion of democratic community members being moral agents, or good persons. Becoming a good person and, hence, a good democratic citizen, involves not only acquiring a well-balanced sense of the common conditions but cultivating the particular conditions—the character traits and dispositions—of a democratic way of life. This last point is vital. Without it, there would be no good democratic citizens—good persons who care about promoting the public good.

Since a totalitarian government gives no legal status to citizens with regard to what they can or cannot be subjected to, violations of human rights are commonplace. At best, the status of a self-developed citizen is insecure and human rights are at risk, since there is no obligation on the part of the government to protect human rights effectively. Moreover, citizens need not be committed to acting on the particular conditions of morality in their dealings with one another. Since they have no guaranteed rights and obligations as individual citizens, they have no correlative obligations to one another. Totalitarian regimes show a deep understanding of human vulnerability and the fragility of a human community. They are incompatible with making the most of human life, with an enlightened increasing of the rights and opportunities of human beings.

There is another way of coming to the same conclusion. If democratic citizens are to achieve a high degree of self-development, there are certain ways they must be treated and other ways which must be avoided. Much has been said about this, but it bears repeating that the link between common conditions and particular conditions must be grasped and schools should create environments in which children can practice and develop a democratic character.

In summary, I have attempted to show that the moral dimension of philosophical civic republicanism requires the principle of human dignity and offers a minimum moral measure for self-development in a democracy. The common conditions of self-development must be fused with the particular conditions of democracy via the ethical obligations of concern, care for others, tolerance, civility, humaneness, esteem, respect, compassion, benevolence, fairness, and integrity. The latter are to common conditions as food, shelter, and oxygen are to the human being. If these are not granted, then negative consequences follow, for this is precisely what the literature of psychology and medicine reveals.

THE ETHIC OF OBLIGATION: CONCERN,
CARING, AND TOLERANCE

A key element of this work is the contention that the values of philosophical civic republicanism are importantly different from the values of philosophical liberalism. A second element is that the latter tradition can only be understood as a remnant from the past and that, moreover, the problems that it has generated will remain with us until this is understood. What is needed today is not only philosophical acuteness but also a moral compact that will provide a nurturing context for the development of good persons. One way to develop our vision of civic education is to say more about the obligation to be concerned, caring, and tolerant citizens, all of which are character traits that are important particular conditions of democratic self-development. We are quite justified in asking what the substance of these conditions is, as they bear mightily on a reconceptualized civic education and on a revitalized civic culture.

To be more specific, the minimum moral measure obligates us to be concerned, caring, and tolerant persons. These virtues, however, should not be uncritically accepted, for they are fraught with considerable conceptual difficulties. A facile or glib assertion of their primacy as particular conditions bestows a soft-headed quality to much of the discussion surrounding them. The immediate task, then, is to understand them better, if we are to judge their role in bringing about good persons and hence good citizens. Once this is accomplished, we can judge their worth in revitalizing the civic culture.

Concern and Caring

Concern is an ambiguous term. In the civic context, one may be concerned *with* something (an organization or an activity); one may be concerned *about* something (an issue); or one may be concerned *by* something (an action, policy, or rule). The point of importance is that actions fully characteristic of concern for others, in all cases, cannot be explained without reference to a social context. Concern in this sense requires for its performance a social setting that involves complex conventions. The grammatical constructions also suggest a strong sense of knowing that one is concerned; the implicated individual knows he is concerned. No one, in other words, can be concerned in these senses without knowing it.

Thus the locution, "I am a concerned American citizen," suggests any one of the three uses of concern. Some citizens are concerned *with* the international arms race; others are concerned *about* violations of human rights; still others are concerned *by* the threats of international terrorists to world peace. In each of these instances, there is an attitude of interest, of being attentive, of being involved somehow, of noting and regarding, and of course, of vigilance.

Confronting the concept of concern directly, it seems that to be concerned is to have an interest, because a concerned person takes note and is aware of, and duly regards her relations with others. Concern, in other words, is something we can exhibit or show. But there is, of course, more, because to be concerned is to be of a certain disposition. For example, if I express an interest in my friend John's abuse of alcohol, I may say to him, "I am concerned about your drinking. It is out of control, and you need help." Here I am doing more than paying attention to and showing an interest in John; I am of a certain disposition. This shows in my uneasiness about his drinking, and I know it. At this point I am no longer a bystander, for I am involved in, occupied with, devoting myself to, and giving my time and effort in John's behalf, to help him recognize and deal with his drinking problem. My attention and interest are obvious, and my disposition is clear.

We should further note that the concept of concern is ambiguous in respect to (1) showing or taking a concern, such as my showing concern about John's drinking behavior and (2) having a concern, but not at the moment expressing it. In the first sense, concern is shown in the moment, and this is the episodic sense of concern. In the second sense, concern is not related to action but instead takes the form of a long-standing dispositional interest in some matters. Hence, there are the episodic and dispositional uses of the term *concern*.

What the analysis of concern reveals, as applied to civic education, is that we want students to be concerned democratic citizens. To achieve this end, we must teach them what is in their civic interest *qua* individuals and what is in their interest *qua* members. They must be given opportunities to show or take civic concern about something (episodic use) and to reconcile their concerns in practice so that they will have a unified civic concern (dispositional use), actually functioning as competent and willing democratic citizens. If civic virtue is understood as a progression from episodic to dispositional concern, then civic education will generally depend upon what is justified as being of concern and counted as important enough for taking action. I have suggested the principle of human dignity as one candidate in this regard. Others are the particular conditions of democratic self-development, namely, the moral virtues of fairness, civility, humaneness, esteem, compassion, integrity, and benevolence.

Caring, we should note, is also an ambiguous concept. It involves taking *care of*, which we do by being with, watching, looking after, attending to, taking action on, and taking up in our relationship with others. Babysitting is a clear case of taking care of someone, but it is a behavior that does not necessarily entail what might be called loving or holding dear. Caring also involves caring *for* someone, as in the locution, "I care for you," by liking, fancying, protecting, or enjoying her; by being empathic about, fond of, or sympathethic toward her; by taking to, coveting, loving, cherishing, being enamored of, and/or prizing her.

We are caring for someone when we show or have a concern, as seen in my concern about John's drinking behavior, and in so doing we demonstrate a certain frame of mind, namely, that we genuinely value our relationship. In this last respect, caring and concern are contrasted with ignoring, inattention, nonconnection, irrelevance, noninvolvement, and nonengagement. Where the two concepts overlap is that both, minimally, represent a strong sense of attention, interest, mindfulness, heeding, awareness, and vigilance. This linking or connection is illustrated in the behavior of parents who note, mind, heed, and so on the activities of their infants. If someone were to allege that such parents were not proper caretakers of their children, what would count against the allegation, at least in part, would be these same parental activities of caring and concern. Parents' love of their children is expressed in their evident intention to care *for* them, by taking pleasure in their presence, supporting their efforts, and affirming their sense of worth as persons. This point also may be seen in the example of Mother Teresa, who cares for the poor, homeless, and destitute of India. Her care for others goes beyond merely having an interest in other people—being with, looking after, feeding, and ministering to them. She truly cares for them by being concerned with, about, and by what they experience. Indeed, Mother Teresa's life activity is an unquestioned instantiation of an unending obligation to care for others, following the Christian principle of *caritas*.

In sharp contrast, we are guilty of *not caring for* when we fail to show or have concern about others, a condition we often hear descibed in the phrase, "He cares only for himself" (Noddings, 1984).

It is evident from the preceding that this interpretation of caring involves a basic ethical dimension. As we have seen, a clear example of such caring would be parental love. How, then, is this to be accounted for? I propose that caring for others is ethical behavior based for the most part upon the recognition that humans possess inherent value or dignity. Under this assumption, a caring disposition develops when one complies with the obligation or a sense of duty to treat others as persons of worth, as objects worthy of a caring commitment. It is as though caring persons are bound or intrinsically motivated to act ethically, as a matter of conscientiously performing their "duty" to others.

One clear consequence of caring is that everyone is apt to benefit. Its function, however, is to resolve the opposition between the interests of the individual *qua* individual and the interests of the individual *qua* member in such a way that it is beneficial to individuals *and* community.

This function spills over and attaches to the particular self somebody is and the particular ways people instantiate the myriad possibilities of being human. Within this conception, we care for all people by virtue of the general characteristic of being a person and having human worth, yet we also care for them for being themselves. The property of another person's being unique and its attendant spillover can satisfy the condition of caring for someone both in terms of an ethic of commitment, which is really an obligation to further that individual's ends, and in terms of the general property of being oneself.

Doubtless not all instances of caring for others are alike, even from the view of the person doing the caring. All people, even those we do not know, will be cared for simply because they are bearers of the general property of having human worth. But among those we know or know of, we may find some whom we are unable to care for as unique and particular persons. Thus, we make choices to care for some persons' particularity rather than others', even though we realize that it is possible for us to care in the same way for those others.

Since caring for another involves valuing, then it seems plausible that it is not a matter of all or nothing but of degree, and the degree of caring is proportional to the closeness one feels to another. Ordinarily, we care most deeply for those closest to us—our children, family, friends, clients, colleagues, fellow citizens, and so on.

We have established that caring for others is ethical behavior, but it is not owed to each and every thing—not, for example, to buildings or the Mesabi Range. There is, we have seen, something about people, some characteristic or property, by virtue of which we are obliged to care for them. The label we have used for this property is *human dignity*. For the want of a better word, let us call the obligation to care for others *service*. Thus, to care for another is to serve that someone, as a person possessed of the property of human dignity. Caring is thus service, a particular condition of self-development.

Ask anyone who willingly and unstintingly serves others what is ultimately satisfying about it and the answer will most commonly be framed in terms of wanting to help people. Press on and the answer is usually that the individual "loves" people, an emotional way of expressing *caritas*, or brotherly/sisterly love.

Ordinarily, service is not a policy issue and caring and loving are not political matters. Consider, however, how these terms have become almost ordinary in the language of social service in the United States today. When the first major program to provide governmentally insured medical service was proposed, it was not described as a system for expanding the citizens' access to the medical system. It was called *Medicare*. In the same vein, Albert Shanker, President of the American Federation of Teachers, noted in a 1987 address to the National Education Association that there are thousands of unemployed teachers. He further noted that there are large sectors of society in need of education or schooling. In order to meet the need for education, he called for a new government program to guarantee the lifelong educational rights of all Americans, to be called *Educare*. Similarly, if someone were to propose a system that would guarantee the rights of all citizens to legal services, what name might be considered for such a program? It would probably be *Judicare*.

As stated already, the requirement to be disposed to serve or care for all others is a duty, an ethical pull, of philosophical civic republicanism. Educators need to understand that, if we care only for those who have close particularistic ties of race, religion, national origin, and so forth, we restrict caring, such that we are not in a state of readiness, not predisposed to care for *all* others as a minimum moral measure. Particularism is parochial in the sense that it restricts the ethical bonding together of all community members, an important element of a democratic society.

This is not to say that the countenancing of particularism on the level of family is unjustified; it seems tenable, at least up to a point. Parents tend to give primary weight to caring for their own children over others, and this seems natural. On the level of political functioning in the civic culture, however, the moral weight of particularistic ties is highly suspect, for it misconstrues the role and function of citizens in a democracy. How, for example, can we exercise the broad and important civic responsibilities and duties of democratic citizenship if we make the lot of our fellow citizens who are not personally associated with us a matter of indifference, that is, if political decisions affecting others are made only in terms of caring passionately for those closest to us, say, family or friends? The problem is that particularistic caring for others does not coincide with standards of how to act under civic restraints. It is alien, in other words, to the minimum moral measure. What it suggests, moreover, is that we seriously entertain questions of fidelity, loyalty, and empathy in a subjective manner, as they apply to individuals *qua* individuals, but often without seeking impartial, objective, nonbiased moral approaches to individuals *qua* members of the human family.

To put it this way is to understate the crucial point: The ethics of service and social responsibility are intimately interconnected in the life of a democratic community. Being predisposed to care for all others is an ethical obligation, an ethical disposition of commitment and conscientiousness, which must be connected to political judgment in the impersonal, logical, objective sense, across a wide range of civic matters. That citizens can achieve such an understanding and honor this view through a revitalized civic education is an assumption implicit in philosophical civic republicanism. More will be said about this in chapter 4.

Tolerance

The concept of tolerance is not altogether clear, for there are many different uses of the word. Perhaps we can become clearer about the concept by considering what it means to say that an act of tolerance has occurred and what the evidence would be that it had.

Consider, for example, seventeenth-century England. After the restoration of Charles II in 1660, following the religious animosities of the Civil War and the Interregnum years, assuring the rights of religious minorities was a major problem. Limited progress in the direction of toleration of dissenters from the Church of England occurred on May 17, 1689, when Parliament passed the (Dissenters) Toleration Act. In this case, although the majority of Parliament genuinely disapproved of the dissenters' religious views, the members voted to oppose religious coercion of dissenters, thus exempting them from the penalties of certain laws.

What is brought out by this obvious case of religious tolerance is that there are two necessary conditions for calling someone's attitude and actions "tolerant": First, one party, *B*, must behave in a manner that another party, *A*, sincerely considers wrong, and *A* must be aware of this. Second, *A* must be capable of preventing or at least hindering *B* in this activity and must choose not to do so (Harrison, 1982).

Confronting this point directly, we see that we cannot describe as tolerant our response to an action that we sincerely approve of. Moreover, it seems that permissiveness is like tolerance in that permissive individuals allow other persons or groups to act without interference or the threat of interference. In this respect, permissiveness and tolerance toward others' actions are contrasted with restraining, interfering, censoring, regulating, dominating, dictating, commanding, ordering, overseeing, prohibiting, controlling, restricting, and confining those actions.

Where the two concepts differ, at least in part, is in permissiveness being a simply behavioral description, whereas tolerance involves both moral judgment and some sort of response. Tolerance always is contextually judgmental insofar as we consider consequences and then link these to a judgment about another's action that we sincerely disapprove of. Hence, it is always proper to ask of what we are tolerant and why. We are tolerant of another's action because of some reason or other, whereas we need no reason for being permissive of another's action.

Another point of difference has to do with caring. A significant aspect of being tolerant is caring for another human being, to a greater or lesser degree. Having the power to prevent or at least hinder another's action, which is a necessary condition of tolerance, and choosing not to exercise this option based on some moral ground or reason, suggest a disposition of caring and, of course, concern for someone.

The claim to an entailment between tolerance and caring deserves careful scrutiny. In part, I believe, the entailment is pragmatic: When we are tolerant of another's action we commit ourselves to accepting some hypotheses and not others about the conditions under which we ourselves act. Subject to this qualification, we ordinarily tend to favor "if-then" clauses in making our account. These specify quasipsychological conditions of ourselves as moral agents, such as weighing, judging, and deciding. I believe this is correct, since being tolerant implies a power relationship (preventing or hindering another's action) that is under the control of the person being tolerant. In this respect, tolerance must be the kind of thing that humans can and want to do because they wish to aid, benefit, help, or at least not hinder another they care for.

A positive test for isolating tolerance from permissiveness is to ask whether it is possible to treat tolerance as an approximate synonym for caring. For instance, when we speak of tolerance it is proper to consider its agents as attentive, interested, concerned, solicitous, taking pains, or seeing to it that their judgment in the matter has not been injudicious or unfair. This group of words evokes contexts in which some weighing of consequences of action takes place with deliberateness and mindfulness. Hence, it is a matter of real importance that it is always relevant to ask a moral agent, Now that you have made your decision, is the burden lifted? Clearly there may be a sense of discomfort, perhaps even pain, in making a tolerance decision, since it involves some action of which we sincerely disapprove. It is also obvious that what matters to the moral agent is to find some honest yet principled way to act in behalf of another. Given these points, the concept of tolerance is appropriately associated with the concept of caring for others.

On the other hand, permissiveness rarely is used as a synonym for caring. The impulse at work in permissiveness actually expresses a view of not caring or even a lack of concern. We may be permissive simply because we do not care enough or are not concerned enough in the matter to act otherwise. Indeed, when we speak of a "permissive" society, we convey a weakening of communal concern, interest, loyalty, and fidelity, and a loosening of social and ethical bonding. We could, if we wished, argue that such a society is an uncaring, unconcerned, loosely connected organization of self-interested individuals who are withdrawn into themselves and inattentive to the needs of others, who touch others but feel nothing, who are too occupied or privately engaged to be anything but permissive. By contrast, a "tolerant" society is neither unconcerned nor uncaring; on the contrary, egoism, self-interested pursuit, and privatism have only a small place in social relations.

What follows from this account is that permissiveness of all sorts, including sanctioning a class of actions that sincerely violates our sense of well-being, is not necessarily tolerance. We cannot rightly assume that mindless acquiescence to anything someone does is a fundamental expression of tolerance. What, for example, would we say about a group of young, able-bodied students who permitted other students to rape a female teacher in a public-school locker room? Would we call them tolerant, caring, or concerned regarding the sexual violation of the victim? I would hope not.

The conclusion is that tolerance and permissiveness are not synonyms; the former necessarily implies caring, concern, and the use of judgment, whereas the latter does not. What is not exhibited in a tolerance decision is indifference or noninvolvement; rather, it involves behavior that is responsive to the wishes of another. It may not be clear precisely where a line is to be drawn, but the mark of tolerance is the expression of these qualities such that the decision lies in the moral realm. To be tolerant, then, is to have moral character, to be virtuous. The exercise or practice of tolerance involves a respect for one's own values as well as those of others, mixed with a proper dose of concern and caring to produce a moral calculation or judgment.

It goes without saying that this need for respect weighs on both sides—on teachers and students—in education. Teachers must help students develop sound judgment, but first they must all view and weigh moral principles and values, stepping backward as it were, to look at different conceptions of the moral life. In the end, however, individual students must judge others by where they draw the lines, realizing that good citizens can disagree about the location of the lines while still holding that they must be located at some place other than the extremes. This understanding of tolerance makes intolerant persons easy to identify. Such people judge that those who draw the line on one side of their own are so lax as to be immoral, while those who draw it on the other side are fanatics.

THE ETHIC OF CIVIC SERVICE

The discussion of the ethical trinity of concern, caring, and tolerance in the preceding section attempted to clear the ground for a reconceptualization of our civic culture. To accept this logic is, indeed, to find oneself opposed to many of the tenets of philosophical liberalism.

It has been proposed that an ethic of obligation or conscientious commitment is fundamental to a revitalization of the civic culture. Such a commitment is really a set of virtues, including, among others, concern, caring, and tolerance. But as to what these virtues require for citizenship in a democracy there is extended disagreement. Their application in a society where the avowed aim is no longer the aggregating of self-interest but rather a realization of the public good presupposes a bond between citizens which constitutes a community. This is the bond of civic service.

The notion of civic service, however, means different things to different people. The type of service that I have in mind is a form of practice that embodies the ethical obligation to exhibit concern toward, willingly care for, and tolerate other citizens in shaping the life of a community. The ethic of civic service entails the practice of obligation and is due every member of the community. Moreover, it is essential to the constitution of any form of community, since it fulfills the vital social function of perpetuating community, whether in a household or a nation-society. This is how we, sometimes at least, think of service agencies and institutions such as hospitals and hospices; philanthropic organizations such as the Ford, Carnegie, and Rockefeller foundations; nonprofit schools; Boy Scouts and Girl Scouts; community civic groups; Greenpeace; refugee location agencies; and so on. Kindness, sympathy, empathy, and compassion characterize these organizations, and, generally speaking, our lives are enriched by them.

In this sense of civic service, then, there is a special kind of activity that nurtures civic virtues where they presently exist and develops them where they do not. Civic service is, obviously, a practical means for achieving the bond of loyalty, empathy, fidelity, and solidarity so fundamental to the well-being of a community. The centerpiece of civic service is an ethic for establishing *social habits of willing action beneficial to others*. It is civic duty done or labor performed for another, a contribution, a good turn, assistance, help, aid, support, or backing that we extend to others for the advancement of shared ends that will similarly benefit everyone. In short, civic service is the outward expression, through performance, of civic virtue. It aims at promoting the public good. General conformity to an ethic of civic service is reasonable to require of one another because it is enormously beneficial and these benefits are widely distributed.

It is worth asking, however, Is there a stronger conclusion, a stronger argument, for civic service? The case must be constructed by beginning with a consideration of the principles of philosophical civic republicanism. They premise a moral civic compact nested in an ethic of obligation. The moral compact is clear: One's duty is to civic service not merely because of the results of one's so doing, but because it is reasonably required by the community of which one is a member. In this way, the moral compact is hostile to a privatized, self-interested, self-seeking individual and society. There is in the moral compact an identity of shared interests and a marked stress on community solidarity. The bond of human community is willing civic service—help, aid, and support—which is given by citizens to one another and is, in an appropriate sense, equally to everyone's advantage. Civic service contributes to the public good.

Thus the strength of the above conclusion is warranted by the need to bring about harmony between the individual and society. Recognition of this need requires us to accept the ethic of civic service obligation in our relations with one another. In short, to be a good person will not in every view be identical to being a good citizen, but being a good person clarifies what is at issue in being a good citizen.

The nature of this link between an ethic of civic service and the public good, between being a good person and being a good citizen, is reinforced by empirical considerations. There is a long history in America of service as a way of expressing our obligation to fellow citizens. There is, for instance, the previously mentioned Christian principle of *caritas* and its notion of brotherly/sisterly love and service. This biblical tradition is replete with admonitions to sacrifice and love, to be charitable, and to follow the Golden Rule. Jewish communities, guided by biblical injunctions, have developed elaborate social service structures and agencies on a remarkable scale to serve sick people, stranded travelers, and widows and orphans. In addition, in civic republicanism there is a juridical language that stresses reciprocity and due process, and there is a long-standing labor movement that emphasizes belongingness, solidarity, and the virtue of friendship as bonds of community.

These historical examples, however, do not exhaust the range and variety of civic service. We render service to others when we pick up a discarded cigarette wrapper and place it in a trash container. A large enumeration of such civic services could be given, but it would only trivialize the point. Civic service goes on in its own way, never indifferent to human dignity, mutual respect, and the public good. Here we shall do our best to understand how it is learned and humanely exercised, how it becomes a "habit of the heart." I am deeply aware that an ethic of obligation cannot be left to chance. This means that educators cannot be indifferent to the fact that a disposition toward civic service will be formed only through effort and practice. If educators are sufficiently conscientious about this point, then students will grasp that civic service is a duty, and its performance is apt to benefit everyone.

What I wish to bring out is that civic service must be practiced, not merely discussed. I do not mean to suggest that civic service makes life smoother and more pleasant than it would be otherwise. Practice of the ethic of civic service is necessary in order to have communities, and thus is necessary for the sort of life we regard as worthwhile.

MacIntyre (1984) offers this clarification of the nature of any practice:

> A practice . . . is never just a set of technical skills, even when directed towards some unified purpose and even if the exercise of those skills can on occasion be valued or enjoyed for [its] own sake. What is distinctive in a practice is in part the way in which conceptions of the relevant goods and ends which the technical skills serve—and every practice does require the exercise of technical skills—are transformed and enriched by these extensions of human powers and by that regard for its own internal goods which are partially definitive of each particular practice or type of practice. [p. 193]

In addition,

> No practices can survive for any length of time unsustained by institutions. Indeed, so intimate is the relationship of practices to institutions . . . that institutions and practices characteristically form a single causal order in which the ideals and the creativity of the practice are always vulnerable to the acquisitiveness of the institution, in which the cooperative care for the common goods of the practice is always vulnerable to the competitiveness of the institution. [p. 194]

Although MacIntyre (1984) uses the term *institution* as sociologists do in speaking about organizations, the passages quoted make clear the nature of a practice by drawing two important contrasts. The first is that a practice is never merely a set of technical skills, and the second is that practices must not be confused with institutions.

Taking up the first point, no one has written, at least to my knowledge, that technical means are totally divorced from human needs and wants, cultural standards, political decisions, individual choices, and the like. No one has argued that technical skills and human motives have parted company in an absolute way. MacIntyre (1984) wisely recognizes this and insists that practice can advance only by maintaining a delicate relationship with institutions (organizations). Failure could eventually impose a one-sided, tyrannical pattern on either practice or institution. The weight of his message is clear. The crisis of steering practice in the institution order does not mean that no one is at the wheel and that the car literally drives itself. It does mean, however, that the relationship between car and driver, practice and institutions, is intimate; and that the essential function of an ethic of civic obligation is to provide the moral grounding for civic service practices which, left alone, could not resist the corrupting power of institutions.

MacIntyre's (1984) second point is appropriately aimed at the widespread influence of institutions, especially their corruptive power. We now realize that we live and breathe in the interstices left to us by our institutions, particularly our political institutions, and they grow more constricting all the time. But fault and blame are not at issue, institutions are not villains, they are, simply, institutions. MacIntyre's point, it seems to me, enables us to say that we need "new rules," moral or ethical, to buttress democratic practices better and thus resist the corrupting, undemocratic power of institutions.

Today, there is much controversy regarding the role of the executive branch of the federal government in what is called the Iran-Contra deal. Following the reasoning of MacIntyre (1984), it is evident that democratic practices are fostered by certain types of social institutions and endangered by others. If institutions do have corrupting power, the work of creating and nurturing democratic institutions has itself the characteristic of a practice. Thus the Senate and House investigations and the appointment of a special investigator regarding the arms deal to Iran and money payments to the Contras take the shape of congressional practice. Whether or not this practice exhibits moral integrity will depend on the way it can be and is exercised in sustaining the institutional forms—the constitutional division of power and its checks and balances—that are the social bearers of the practice.

It is important to grasp, moreover, that this account shows that democratic practices would be impossible if divorced from a viable social ethic. A democracy requires both an ethic of obligation and an ethic of civic service practiced so that citizens are bonded in an affective way. The two traditions that form the core of philosophical civic republicanism—Judeo-Christian religion and civic republicanism—have long recognized that civic institutions require the exercise of an ethic of civic service, for in this ethic resides democracy's real cohesion and consequently its strength. Where the ethic of civic service stops, the weak, disadvantaged, and helpless—those most in need of aid—fall into the pit of neglect and become "things" or "problems" to be dealt with by impersonal institutions.

If we are to revitalize our social institutions in order to avoid their corrupting influence and vices, we must practice concern, caring, and tolerance within them, to bolster human dignity and respect, especially self-respect. If we view such ethical civic service in light of an obligation or a duty to assist, help, and bolster one's fellow citizens, then our institutions will exhibit the practice of a new compassion, a phrase heard today which signals a rejection of the impersonal mean-spiritedness of institutions.

The push for civic service should not be viewed as a subordination of self-interest to the interests of others, but rather as a fusion of all interests into a single one, the public good. Thus we could say that political office holding—where the function of the office is that of contributing on behalf of the larger, impersonal whole, the engaged citizenry—is a civic practice of idealized personal unselfishness, of doing good for others that also makes one feel good, of fulfilling one's role of individual *qua* member. In short, when we practice civic service in accord with an obligation to help others, then that activity gains a hold over us and over our institutional forms and practices. It becomes a necessary characteristic of community.

In summary, the important questions (How should we treat differentiated strangers? How do we justifiably deal with individual interests when they conflict with community interests?) are answered by making an ethic of obligation, of civic service, central to the practices of the community and the school. Civic service practices are incredibly important for civic education because they are not only in every citizen's self-interest, but in every citizen's interest as a member of a community.

No doubt this may strike some as too strong a claim. What tempers the claim, however, is the fact that persons are not required to abandon self-interest entirely, which would be nonsense and foolhardy. As Milne (1986) explains it, "they must pursue self-interest in ways compatible with the community's interests." (pp. 41–42) Somehow—and this is the major problem of civic service and practice as well as of civic education—self-interest must be adapted to, coordinated, fused, or made one with the community's interest. To fail in this is to run the risk of having a community where individuals have the benefit of social life without meeting its share of burdens.

CONCLUSION

There is little doubt that there are some who prefer that social theory avoid the use of moral notions or who believe social theory does well enough without using any moral ideas. These views reflect, however, the erroneous idea that social theories are value free, devoid, say, of a theory of the good life. Clearly, in every case social theories employ moral notions.

Now at this point it is obvious that we can no longer afford to stand idly by and assume a business-as-usual posture while our nation-society and the world undergo a vast transformation. An ethic of obligation is sorely needed, as is an ethic of civic service. If an ethic of civil service as defined herein is practiced in a community, institutional forms, the social bearers of the practice, will be revitalized. Educators must recognize that civic service as a practice can and will revitalize the civic culture, depending on the way in which the minimum moral measure is exercised or applied. Patently, the integrity of civic service as practice requires the principle of human dignity and the particular conditions of mutual respect, concern, caring, and tolerance. Conversely, the corruption of institutions is always in part an effect of society's vices. This point applies with great force to the relationship most persons have to their institutions, but especially to schools. If we are not careful, our educational institutions can be highly destructive of the ethic of civic service and its practice. More will be said about this in subsequent chapters.

CHAPTER 4

Democracy, Citizenship, and Community Service

It was argued in the previous chapter that the starting point for a much-needed revitalization of the civic culture must be the philosophical civic republican view of a moral compact and, as a form of virtuous self-development, the practice of ethical civic service. Nested in this proposal, so far as it applies to civic education, is the notion that formal education must produce good persons through an ethic of civic service, not in some vaguely hoped-for, inhaled sense of civic obligation and responsibility.

In this chapter I wish to advance further the view that democracy implies a moral compact as an objective reality, not as a sloganized ideal. Central to the argument is that democratic citizenship involves a moral compact promotive of a civic consensus directed toward reaching the public good. Civic education for the public good implies an "other-regarding" community service program aimed at developing democratic civic values and virtues, the practices of obligation and commitment so fundamental to the moral compact.

SELF-DEVELOPMENT

In attempting to operationalize the notion of self-development discussed in the previous chapter, four common conditions—community, identity, privacy, and autonomy—were proffered in an attempt to show that individual fulfillment and public contribution are not antithetical. Rather, a concern for self and a concern for others are balanced in the pursuit of particular conditions, a pursuit that necessarily involves practices of ethical obligation.

I shall proceed on the view that the process of self-development in private affairs parallels that of democracy in collective affairs. Thus, democracy is simply self-development writ large. Otherwise stated, the democratic community is expected to achieve at the collective level what the self-developed person is expected to achieve at the individual level: a sense of moral decency.

It barely needs saying, then, that the ideal citizen of a true democratic community would be the self-developed, self-integrated individual, the possessor of a clear sense of identity and of a need for privacy, yet communitarian and autonomous in the sense that the good life is pursued within the community that defines it. The potential for conflict between these elements is great. It is admittedly difficult to identify the moment at which one moves from the individual *qua* individual to the individual *qua* member, from the self-developed, self-integrated person to the communitarian citizen. Perhaps we can say that the passage is made from self-interest to group interest when the citizen is predisposed to treat other citizens warmly, caringly, sympathetically, fairly, and justly. This predisposition, it has been argued, may serve to mark the move to a moral/civil society in formal ways.

In any case, it should be noted that self-development, based on the principle of human dignity and mutual respect, looks to achieve a sense of solidarity within community. There are matters that concern the interests of everyone, and in these cases the principle of the public good can be applied. It is contended that the self-developed agent is aware of this and chooses the public good by employing a moral sense (common and particular conditions) that is fair and undistorted by cultural stereotypes, a coercive indoctrination, and happenstance. In this view, then, civic education in a democracy is education for the self-development of a good person, whose attitudes rest on the principles of human dignity and mutual respect and who exhibits a sense of solidarity within the community.

According to the philosophical liberal's view, the notions of self-development and the public good are poles apart. Self-development is equated in a consistent way with individualism and asserted in terms of an unrestricted self-interest. Thus self-development is acting autonomously without restraint to secure what is useful or agreeable to oneself. Any conception of society as a community united in a shared vision, the public good, is negated on this account. The public good, if it exists at all, consists of the aggregate of self-interest.

In the philosophical civic republican view, however, the notions of self-development and the public good are compatible. Both are identified in a consistent way with a moral compact, an idea central to the social theory since other basic notions are defined in terms of it. Thus self-development follows the principles of the moral compact that we consent to as free and equal rational beings. We understand that the public good *in the long run* accords with shared attachments and interests; that is, we frame individual decisions autonomously but from a shared point of view. Our interest is for self *and* for others, balanced in the pursuit of enhancing the dignity of all. It reflects a concern for the welfare of one's neighbor, as well as caring for and tolerance of others.

Moreover, and not to be diminished by its obviousness, this social theory does not define a good citizen solely as a member of this or that community, but as a participant in a moral compact that is the common concern of the community. Obviously, such a citizen would wish to participate energetically in the process of creating and administering the rules under which he lives. The ability and willingness to act cooperatively would enable a citizen to do these things well. This point should not be lost on educators.

These points suggest that the democratic community is marked by wide discussion and participation among concerned, caring, and tolerant citizens who take an active role in the formulation, ratification, and implementation of social policies. But, of course, our judgments will not always coincide on all questions, and in fact many if not most social issues may still be insoluble. Wherever possible, it should be stressed, when citizens attempt to act as moral agents, framing judgments from a moral compact, they are more likely to reach an agreement that is satisfactory and enduring.

This view of the matter has important ramifications. Civic education is not simply a curriculum sequence intended to bring as an end result a citizen with the appropriate moral sentiments or civic virtues. As far as possible, civic education foreshadows in its content and teaching the common and particular conditions of self-development at which it aims and by reference to which citizens may one day recognize their responses as morally validated. Civic education, therefore, will acknowledge our mutual dependence and interdependence and prescribe a generosity of spirit in the pursuit of community and the public good.

DEMOCRACY

I have been using the term *democracy* as if it were perfectly unambiguous, which is not the case. Experience and scholarship inform that the term has many meanings, but the most common and most accepted employment is caught in the notion that citizens must govern themselves (Benne, 1987). The most striking difference between human life and all other kinds is that it is characterized by activities that are possible only in a community with elaborate conventions. The point I wish to stress is that of living a life informed by democratic conventions. Democracy is, in Abraham Lincoln's words, "government of, by, and for the people." A number of astute observers, many from foreign lands, have long understood the significance, durability, and strength of Lincoln's definition. To most, it conveys the notion of self-developed citizens who enjoy the right persistently to question and inquire of their government, without fear of the consequences of that inquiry. It also signifies a government to which these citizens accede voluntarily, and which they, as individuals, or through their elected agents, manage and control. What all the observers have not fully understood, however, is that the words embody an ideal, not the reality.

The consideration of this last point is involved in making the concept of democracy intelligible, if for no other reason than the recognition that this is as far as simplicity will take us. For instance, George Bernard Shaw (1929/1956) questioned Lincoln's formulation of democracy in the following way:

> Now for the three articles of the definition. Number One: Government of the people: that, evidently is necessary: a human community can no more exist without a government than a human being can exist without a coordinated control of its breathing and blood circulation. Number Two: Government for the people, is most important. But Number Three: Government by the people, is quite a different matter. . . . We repudiate Number Three on the ground that the people cannot govern. This is a physical impossibility. Every citizen cannot be a ruler any more than every boy can be an engine driver or a pirate king. . . . Government by the people is not and never can be a reality, it is only a cry by which demagogues humbug us into voting for them. If you think this—if you ask me "Why should not the people make their own laws?" I need only ask you "Why should not the people write their own plays?" They cannot. It is much easier to write a good play than to make a good law. And there are not a hundred men in the world who can write a play good enough to stand daily wear and tear as long as a law must. [pp. 116–117]

Although Shaw stacks the cards against the common citizen's ability to make good laws, he does present a view that challenges the formal sovereignty of the people acting individually in their civic function. From this perspective, democratic citizens are not fit to make the laws that govern them; their choice is only that of selecting representative elites who will make decisions or take action for them.

Within the portrait just advanced, however, something is amiss. The point of democracy is that those involved, those who will be most affected by the decision to be made or the action to be taken, must actually take part in the decision making, and they must assume the responsibility for the decision. Of course, the notion of democracy as participation and discussion by those involved in decision making is precisely what Lincoln intended: government of, by, and for the people.

This claim connects closely with what political power is and what it is for. Obviously, political power should be possessed by those who know how to use it, but it should be controlled by those who are the recipients of its effects. (Recall the point made in chapter 1: The community wants to *control* civic education; hence, the principle of vigilance.) The crucial qualification for exercising political power is not some special knowledge of how governance functions, but citizenship exercised by rational and humane choice of means and ends in the public sphere. There are and can be no better judges on public matters than citizens, because the proper exercise of power is nothing more than the direction of society in accordance with the civic or public spirit of its citizens.

This complex interplay suggests at least two points. First, civic education is not designed to make students into good citizens, but to make them into good persons. This means that students must be systematically inducted into the moral compact. If we try to picture a society in which no one had the slightest wish to act on the values of the moral compact, we would see an indifference—if not a disdain—for human beings that would make our own sense of worth impossible. Second, civic education must systematically induct students into political problems whose solutions require application of the ethic of civic service, a practice that we have defined as the willingness to connect private self-interest with the public good. This means that students must be taught to implement democratic practices—thoughtful deliberation; studying issues; becoming familiar with the pros and cons of a hotly debated topic; and honing the skills of debate, compromise, comity, and consensus building—in order to deliver fair, rational, and humane solutions and settlements to the questions of selecting the means and ends of civic life. Thus democracy entails meaningful citizen participation involving "other-regarding" virtues and the recognition of another's good faith and desire for justice, in order to establish the short- and long-term interests of the political community as well as to maximize the self-development of citizens. But unless there exists a common foundation, which in philosophical civic republicanism is a moral compact that nurtures friendliness, warmth, and respect between citizens, reasoning and debate would be pointless.

The Gap Between the Ideal and the Real

It is not my purpose to trace the origin and development of our idealized political democracy, what is sometimes called the "American Creed," as embodied in the great documents: the Declaration of Independence, the Constitution, the Gettysburg Address, our legal code, and significant Supreme Court decisions. Suffice it to say that the idealization of such norms as justice for all, the inherent dignity and worth of human beings, mutual respect, and equality before the law offers a strong concept of democracy that is really an ideal, an illusion outfitted with the power of common hopes and aspirations.

There are, of course, several sharp contrasts between our idealized democratic norms and the actualities of political processes and social institutions, and it may prevent misunderstanding if they are mentioned. First, the several ruptures between our idealized norms of democracy and reality are due to the everyday consequences of living in a human community and the activity of democratic party politics. Conceived of as a system, American society consists not in one collectivity, but in a ramified system of disparate collectivities. The circulation of power in this pluralistic cross-cutting consists of the process of persuading those in positions of authority to binding support of policies through cultivating the belief in the need for or purposes of such policies. This is accomplished either in the constituency itself, by the use of direct influence and voting, or via such indirect means as interest-group lobbying efforts.

Second, the perennial problem of achieving unity and solidarity within a highly diverse society cannot be solved without a minimum moral measure. This involves the grounding of the nation-society in a consensus, an acceptance on the part of members, regarding their belonging together, in the sense of sharing, over time, common values and interests. This minimum moral measure must be articulated within communities capable of effective collective action. A nation-society possesses unity and solidarity in relation to the proportion of its members who are committed to a minimum moral measure through which discrete individual interests can be integrated and conflicts resolved.

This brings up the final point. The dominant literature of philosophical liberalism comments regularly on the ways in which individuals seek support for their views of the economic and social order and of associated action. The coming together of those with similar interests, values, or purposes is integral to the winning of such support, to the pursuit of power. Individuals and groups seek support to advance their own special interests, to extend to others their personal and social values, and to win support for their perception of the public good.

These considerations point to the clash of democratic ideals with reality. Guided by the principles of philosophical liberalism, both business and governmental organizations exercise considerable power over citizens, so much so that the real world is one of large interacting organizations—corporations, unions, the state—whose existence has become the basic fact of modern life. In this respect, their pervasive effect is not considered wholly benign. Each year hundreds of thousands of intelligent high-school and college graduates looking for employment have second thoughts about the values and purposes of modern corporate and governmental organizations. There must be some misuse of power, some denial of the ideals of democracy, when those who are considered sophisticated do not believe what they read or hear in the public-interest advertising of the great corporations. For many thoughtful citizens today, government and business are widely regarded as the common enemy, since they are extensively concerned with the intrusive, limiting, and otherwise malign tendencies that limit the democratic ideal. Government, for example, seems to be less the instrument of limiting those who seek to abuse power, and more an abuser of power in its own right (Bachrach, 1967; Dahl, 1961; Domhoff, 1983; Mills, 1956).

It is against this background that I wish to examine the lack of fit between idealized democracy and the reality of concrete political processes and social institutions, and, of course, the question of the implications for civic education. This is not an easy task. Let us therefore turn to Dewey (1927), whose work is a most interesting and illuminating treatise on the subject.

Dewey (1927) argued that the public is becoming less and less involved in political processes having a direct bearing on its well-being:

> In spite of attained integration, or rather perhaps because of its nature, the public seems to be lost; it is certainly bewildered. The government, officials and their activities, are plainly with us. Legislatures make laws with luxurious abandon; subordinate officials engage in a losing

struggle to enforce some of them; judges . . . deal as best they can with the steadily mounting pile of disputes that come before them. But where is the public which these officials are supposed to represent? . . . Is the public much more than . . . a geographical expression? [pp.116–117]

The theme of a lost and bewildered public is basic to Dewey's account. This phenomenon has not abated today and has spawned numerous political offspring, ranging from the libertarian movement to a new kind of socialist vision and to the leftist thought of neo–Marxists. For instance, Nozick (1974) resonates to a Lockean interpretation of the spirit of the American republic by restating a laissez-faire view of the good society. Commoner (1979) opts for a "social governance" of the economy, with greater power placed in the hands of the public than presently exists; and Harrington (1980), on a similar tack, puts his faith in left-leaning politics supporting a "new consciousness." Jurgen Habermas (1969, 1971), a critical theorist and member of the Frankfurt School, explores a legitimation crisis possibility, implying a change in the identity of the social system itself. Today, he argues, advanced capitalism is characterized by the spread of oligopolistic structures fundamentally antithetical to participatory democracy. Thus, each author, in his own way, speaks to the problems and issues Dewey (1927) addressed.

Let us return to Dewey (1927), to look at some classic questions he asked: "What after all, is the public under present conditions? What are the reasons for its eclipse? What hinders it from finding and identifying itself? By what means shall its inchoate and amorphous state be organized into effective political action relevant to present social needs and opportunities?" (p. 124). Dewey's point is that the American public is no longer able to perform its political responsibilities because of rapidly changing economic and social conditions. Chief among these are an expanded role of government, the growth of large-scale economic organizations, and the breakdown of face-to-face relations in towns and cities. Today, we might say, the mass media are less and less involved in investigative reporting of substantive political content. We witness the emergence of trained specialists or "managers" of political affairs. We also observe the latest and perhaps most formidable form of domination: bureaucracy or the role of an intricate system of bureaus in which no one can be held responsible, and which could properly be called rule by nobody. It is this state of affairs, in which it is impossible to localize responsibility and to identify the cause, that is among the most potent factors in the eclipse of the public and accounts for its inchaote nature, as well as its tendency to become out of touch and control and, sometimes, to run amok.

Today, as in the 1920s only more so, the U.S. economy is characterized by (1) large-scale organizations that are actually multinational cartels; (2) increased state intervention to stabilize the economy; (3) an expanding role for research and technology; (4) an unwillingness to concede to citizens a rough epistemological equality, that is, to support the notion that their political judgments are as valid as all others; and (5) the preeminence of the role of instrumental reason or technical decision making in political life. These and other present-day realities have limited the democratic ideal by restricting citizens' participation in the public sphere.

Matthews (1984), an ex-Cabinet officer and presently President of the Charles F. Kettering Foundation, spoke to this issue as follows:

> There can be no vital political life, no viable institutions of government, no sense of mastery over our shared fate, no effective common endeavors of any kind without there being a foundation of public awareness and spirit. . . . Certainly if there were a public sphere, we would have more choices in solving our problems. Now we are limited to two options in making corrections. We can increase the responsibilities of the private (i.e., business) sector or we can improve the performance of government. But if the public sphere were once again real and available, we might not only have a third set of options, but we might also have options that would get us closer to the problem behind the problems. If the idea of the public were available to us, the question of who is attending to giving us the healthiest, the richest, and the best public life possible would become important. . . . Civic literacy, the capacity of people to think about the whole of things, of consequences and potential, becomes education of the most crucial kind. [pp. 123–124]

This statement bears forcefully on the fractured relationship between the democratic ideal and reality. Commonly, history shows, we have accepted this distorted relationship without very much difficulty. In terms of our traditional democratic social theory, philosophical liberalism, economic well-being served as the operational definition of stability and prosperity. Its successes encouraged Americans to live with less than justice for all. In this situation, society increasingly operated under direct political regulation and democracy became a very formalized system of bureaucratic social agencies and institutions. More and more aspects of life became politicized; the power that once operated directly over the decision-making process was now superseded by the more visible hand of the state. This development, in turn, stimulated ever greater demands on the state. Indeed, a provident federal government has acted by more than doubling the national debt to $2.2 trillion in 1987.

Today, however, we have come to realize that the active role of the state in adjudicating many disparate demands is fraught with danger. For one thing, it costs too much in terms of our relations with the rest of the world. Consider, for example, the demands of anti-Cuban groups in the United States and of those supporting dé-tente with Castro's Cuba. The problem is that we have not identi-fied what type of rules or protocols would serve to deal with this issue. What this problem brings out is that a society such as ours contains antithetical relations of power which try to permeate and constitute foreign and domestic policy. The state, as a major mech-anism of decision making, is weak at planning because it is too commonly reactive to the interest groups. If social and political le-gitimacy are to be maintained, then the state takes on a peculiarly negative character, oriented toward the avoidance of risks and the elimination of dangers to the political and economic system, not to-ward the realization of a clearly stated common interest or public good. This is why our political system seeks to react to pressure by making constant adjustments and scores of bargains, *quid pro quo*; and this is why it is consistently tied to identifying damages rather than righting wrongs.

Thus, regarding the Cuban question just posed, our political system pays attention to questions such as, Which group, the anti–Cuban or pro–Cuban, would most likely be adversarial and hostile if a decision went against it? Which group would most pre-dictably refrain, both politically and economically, from responding to the decision? In other words, which group would invest itself and which group would divest itself regarding the articulation of the de-cision? At the same time, this type of decision making, if it is to project the image of being fair and just, must conceal why it does what it does; thus it is in every aspect the antithesis of that seeking after the moral public good which is so basic to philosophical civic republicanism. Such decision making does not provide the context of moral meaningfulness that, in turn, can connect citizens' aspira-tions for themselves with the aspirations of their community, so that the public good can be achieved.

On a similar tack, the gap between the democratic ideal and reality is further exacerbated when social and political issues are believed to be technical problems whose solutions can be discovered only by experts conducting research and applying technology. Citizens, in the process, lose their participatory function, since they cannot be expected to understand the presumed complexity of today's problems. Hence, democratic participation is reduced to the mere making of plebiscitary, or ballot box, decisions about alternative sets of leaders who are believed truly to understand the role of research and technology in decision making. This describes our present situation, wherein the public sphere, which is ideally a political space providing a forum for the exercise of citizen functioning, has become primarily an arena for the choosing of political administrators or managers, who then employ technician-experts to guarantee the solution of social and political problems as technical problems.

The dimensions of this state of affairs can be appreciated by considering the fact that most social institutions employ much more refined varieties of technological *information* than ever before. Yet mastery of *knowledge* appears to be waning in the sense that ever less of what is known can be digested, taught, learned, or utilized by any given individual, group, or organization. A corollary of this development afflicts the public sphere, namely, the view that scientific knowledge itself constitutes a power that is greater than the bulk or weight of the citizenry, a power to which all in fact must bow, even though in a democracy citizens are supposedly to share in the decision-making process. The experts of science, and especially social science, are called upon to solve social issues arising out of medicine, social care, pedagogy, criminology, and so on.

The phrase *technological politics* aptly describes this approach, whereby the rule of technological circumstances supplants other ways of choosing and even acts upon and enforces decisions that are commonly considered political. As the technological solution spreads into the public sphere, it presents to the public the solution as a finished whole, yet the knowledge upon which the decision was made usually does not become part of shared social and political experience. On the contrary, the detailed information and theory appropriate to a particular technique, apparatus, or organization becomes the exclusive domain of specialists and experts in that field. Obviously, so the thinking goes, nonspecialist citizens cannot be expected to know anything about the subject. It would require too much time and effort for citizens to learn the inner workings of all the social and political arrangements that impinge on them.

Characteristic of this situation is the fact that experts stress the "problem of complexity" in public decisions, seeking to use surveys, systems theory and analysis, computer science, new methods of coding great masses of information, and so forth. They justify themselves by claiming to make decisions employing a trenchant weapon or two to simplify and resolve all contradictions, order incoherences, and rationalize the excesses and shortfalls of citizen demand by an "objective" accommodation of means to ends.

Winner (1978) described this one-dimensional thinking as follows:

> Those who now unconsciously employ such terms as "imput" and "feedback" to refer to human communication forget the origins of such words and the baggage in meaning and sensibility that they carry. Feedback, some will be surprised to discover, is not the same as a response. Over the past two decades the language and mentality of systems analysis have become an increasingly central part of political awareness in advanced industrial nations. A comparison of the modes of expression in public discussions of our time to those of the 1930s reveals the direction of the drift. In the earlier period political language included a substantial emphasis upon the moral concerns of a community suffering certain difficulties. Looking at issues of unemployment, hunger, old age, and human welfare, public spokesmen were apt to raise questions about the "responsibilities" or "obligations" of the society to persons in need. Today the tendency is to see such problems as those of the malfunctioning of a complex social mechanism requiring new "incentive structures" and other "policy tools" in order to bring the system back to proper order. [pp. 223–224]

It may be that Winner overstates his case regarding the concern of past public officials for the welfare of citizens, but he is quite right in asserting that the new vocabulary and its employment are rarely questioned, and citizens are judged to have little understanding of them. Hence, it is the specialist/expert rather than the citizen who rules.

Indeed, the more deeply we consider the gap between the democratic ideal and the reality of today, the more we see how the age-old problem of who governs and what governs is unreconciled. Under present circumstances citizens are thought to be ill-equipped to handle the exercise of power. In addition, even though there are enormous differences in the distribution of wealth and privilege within the United States today, these have caused few major con-

flicts, since most people have been, until recently, sufficiently sat-
isfied in their material needs to ignore both the erosion of their
political power and the inequalities of class.

Thus we have a situation in which social critics and reformers
make their case against a social system that makes a mockery of the
democratic ideal, at least for some, but they are largely ignored by
the American public itself. The public, it would seem, has little or
no quarrel with the social system, for it believes that the social system has little or nothing to do with the political system and vice
versa.

Compounding this problem is the recognition that, even if one
did have a mind to raise tough social and political questions, especially to raise the specter of an unjust system, one would run the
risk of being labeled a "radical," a "commie." It is, I think, a rather
sad reflection on the present state of affairs that a great negative
weight attaches to such action. It is important to take a look at what
happens at those times when citizens come together in a show of
solidarity, to challenge and oppose the command of the public sphere
by privatized interests. In such cases the challenges to these entrenched economic and political interests too often are viewed as
anti-authoritarian, anti-intellectual, anti-bureaucratic, technically
simplistic, and, above all, antidemocratic. The entrenched forces,
with a little skill, can manipulate the media to create the appearance
of a threatening public crisis surrounding the protest. This is not to
say that the entrenched forces always lie or deceive; they may, however, read and publicize the situation very selectively. From this
carefully packaged portrait, if it is well orchestrated, may come an
acceptance by the public of a truly dangerous social situation. Hence,
"political protest" too often is manipulated to suggest a radical, and
potentially subversive, experience, rather than a serious opposition
reflecting a granted right to exercise one's voice as a citizen.

Yet it is fair to say that there also are many good citizens who
appear to be disinclined to quarrel over the issue of the lack of fit
between the democratic ideal and the reality. In fact, they are quite
ready, even eager, to give power and authority to those who possess, through education and training, formalized knowledge and
techniques, even allowing consumer protection "experts" to speak
and act in their behalf.

At this time, then, the democratic ideal is seen to wobble. For
instance, citizens are consistently puzzled about how to judge the
competence of political candidates, because to judge anything presupposes criteria of evaluation and their application. The evaluation

of office seekers, the future servants of citizens, is extremely difficult, even if agreed-upon criteria were available, because candidates are "packaged" by mass-media manipulators and public opinion research. A "clean" political campaign, generated and informed by a close examination of economic, political, and social issues, presented and officially documented by candidates, is a democratic ideal, perhaps even a nostalgic, offbeat, fantastic, notion with little connection to reality. We may be on the verge of a rude awakening to the realization that not only does a gigantic gap exist between the democratic ideal and reality, but special knowledge, especially of media manipulation, can itself contribute to this schism. Moreover, special knowledge can be oppressive and antidemocratic, since it is shielded from citizen judgment and criticism. Hence, the democratic ideal of an enlightened citizenry, a necessary condition for participatory democracy, may be a myth today.

From the portrait of the schism between the democratic ideal and reality just sketched, a dominant view emerges. We glimpse the specter of philosophical liberalism, in the primacy of self-interest over interdependence and of privatism over the public good, and in the dominance of specialist-experts over citizens in deciding the acceptable and unacceptable in national and international politics. Under this social theory, citizen participation in the public sphere has been curtailed by privatized sensibilities, the dominance of advanced technologies, corporate wealth and power, and media manipulation. These constitute an unorganized but systematic web of collaborative connections which, if completely understood, might well be the epitome of antidemocratic, morally indecent, policy making.

Obviously, the full sense of democratic citizenship—and here I refer to *clear-minded citizens interpreting a common set of values by making policy choices which they impose upon one another in the pursuit of an integrated commitment to self and others*—is an ideal rather than a reality. It is the quest for this kind of citizenship that is generative of a commitment to philosophical civic republicanism. In the recognition that participatory democracy is asleep at the switch, that citizens are woefully bereft of mutual reciprocity in their relationships with one another, that the public sphere is controlled by factions using their awesome size and power to tailor political decisions to suit their own efficient workings, what matters is how one feels about democracy. The elephant can do his dance if you ask him to, but he sometimes crushes a beautiful maiden during the performance.

Let us briefly reconsider what has been said thus far. Today many citizens believe that they have no competence to judge and control their own societal means and ends through political processes. Politicians often seek office on behalf of their own pecuniary interests or on the behalf of affluent supporters. For evidence of this, one need only review the historical success of the railroads, oil companies, food and drug producers, public utilities, and Madison Avenue in controlling the political agencies that supposedly determine what they do and how. In short, our democracy appears to have become in reality, protective rather than participatory, unfriendly, inimical, and even hostile to widespread citizen reciprocity in civic relationships and to the ideal of concern for the public good.

According to Arendt (1963), Thomas Jefferson, the committed republican among the framers of the American constitution, already had

> at least a foreboding of how dangerous it might be to allow the people a share in public power without providing them at the same time with more public space than the ballot box and with more opportunity to make their voices heard in public than election day. What he perceived to be the mortal danger to the republic was that the Constitution had given all power to the citizens, without giving them the opportunity of *being* republicans and of *acting* as citizens. In other words, the danger was that all power had been given to the people in their private capacity, and that there was no space established for them in their capacity of being citizens. [p. 256]

Jefferson's prophetic concern does much to illuminate the reasons for the huge gap between the democratic ideal and reality, which characterizes the present malaise in American life. Most citizens are caught between the narrowness of their everyday affairs and a vast array of local, national, and international events which, at the very least, bedazzle, puzzle, frighten, and mystify them. Beyond a certain point, we simply do not wish to know or be concerned, much less care, about events surrounding us. Little thought is given by most to the idea of a moral society and its requirements, its symbols, and its effects. Consequently, the democratic ideal becomes as slippery as squid in a fish market.

Participatory Democracy and Citizenship

Fortunately, the one-dimensional portrait of democracy described in the foregoing is not guaranteed: Protective democracy is never fixed. There is no denying the fact that this appears to be an era of rapidly increasing relative ignorance among citizens; that is, if ignorance is measured by the amount of available knowledge that an individual "knower" does not comprehend, then the gap between knowledge and ignorance—relative ignorance—is growing. However, it is also a fact that there is increasing evidence that some citizens wish to bring participatory democracy into a more dominant position in the civic culture.

Consumers, for example, have become more militant and have at last begun to ask for their money's worth. What was a mere trickle at first has become a veritable Niagara of consumer insistence regarding the quality, health, and safety of the goods they purchase. Citizens regularly recall office holders for abusing their offices, and Watergate and its aftermath have created a more skeptical attitude toward elected officials and the mass media. A number of attempts to build human-centered and responsive institutions, places that would be more reasonable environments for social intercourse, are now accepted by those who found it simply impossible to continue with the old habits (Wirth, 1987). These settings include day-care centers; flex-time for employees; no-smoking work, entertainment, and restaurant areas; worker self-management in factories and bureaucracies; and self-sufficient communities in both urban and rural areas. Moreover, a new breed of scientists, engineers, lawyers, and white-collar activists now pursues human rights matters in education, housing, employment, the environment, and so forth. It is perhaps premature to judge the success of these moral/civic practices, but clearly there is a disillusionment with the old system. The success of this potential cultural transformation hinges on how skillfully the seekers of a new moral compact can, in the economic conditions of today, discard the harmful and obsolete practices of the past and nurture the moral practices of their undertakings. For a start, we need to capitalize on the small but precious human and animal rights movements, to build a new but powerful set of moral practices that will gradually infuse all of civic culture.

The lesson, I believe, is intuitively evident. A part of the foundation for establishing a vital participatory democracy is a moral compact grounded in the principle of human dignity and mutual respect as well as an ethic of obligation or service. Put differently, the tradition and practice of participatory democracy begin not with dividing the rulers from the ruled, but with establishing a rough epistemological equality among all citizens. This suggests that if democracy is to exist and thrive, the norm of elite rule runs counter to it. An epistemological equality denies the existence of any certain method for establishing an objective hierarchical relationship between conflicting human values and aspirations.

The concrete implication of this project, it seems to me, can be appreciated only in comparison with the ends and purposes that bureaucratic/technocratic politics tend to emphasize. In contrast to, say, the good of efficiency or feasibility, epistemological equality acknowledges a truth we all know: No one has the final word about the social relationships that constitute the public good and how the good society should be organized. This does not mean, however, that arguments and evaluations of different particular beliefs, practices, and concepts cannot be engaged in, that accounts of the rise and decline of different social theories cannot be considered, and that the nature of the moral community and moral judgment in general are such that they cannot be examined and judged. This point informs that neither science nor technology can have the final word in terms of yielding an objective specification of the good life for humans or of resolving, once and for all, our moral dilemmas.

Seen in this light, science and its language objectify one "reality" in order to examine it under the conditions of a recognized, restricted mode of inquiry; and technology is a tool properly used to better the human condition in terms of production and services, not as a final arbiter of human values. Allowing science and technology to rule is to put the cart before the horse. Hence, the conclusion is that a democratic civic culture would be inhabited by epistemological equals, at least in their roles as citizens, who do not shrink from the responsibility of political decision making and who demand greater credit for intelligence and moral judgment regarding these.

Mention of a "rough" epistemological equality demands two points of clarification. First, this does not mean that political decisions would never be informed by specialists or experts. Perhaps a navigational analogy would help here. The captain of a passenger liner would not consult the passengers and defer to their feelings and opinions regarding navigational matters. The captain might, conceivably, allow passengers to vote on whether they wished four rather than three meals a day, whether they might have a longer recreational period during the day, and so on. Likewise, the elected servants of citizens might let the experts determine, for instance, the level of spending on education, the location of nuclear plants, and so forth. The natural tendency, though, would surely be for the citizens to settle the important policy issues regarding education and nuclear energy. "Important" policy issues consist of what is perceived as important relative to a set of citizen or public interests. Obviously what is important relative to one set of interests may be unimportant or altogether irrelevant relative to another set of interests. Nevertheless, given any *one* particular set, what is important and relevant is a question of objective fact, although the problem of the resolution of *several* conflicting interests is not a matter of objective fact. Participatory democracy, then, would tolerate a fair degree of expert decision making, being careful to treat social analysis not as an exact science but as problematic in the sense that it involves value choices.

The second point is that the arena of political decision making in the civic culture, the public sphere, will have to be sufficiently flexible to insure that all citizens have rough epistemological equality. In this respect we are guided by the democratic ideal, since it offers the political vision of the people ruling those who govern them. All democratic political institutions are manifestations of power; they petrify and decay as soon as the living power of the people ceases to uphold them. The value the citizen has in this tradition is seen not merely in the emphasis given to the guarantee of legal and political rights—that each citizen's word is counted in the same way—but in the requirement that the civic culture be a moral order which nourishes the moral compact. Thus there is a relationship of mutual reciprocity between the moral order and its members, a reciprocity that constitutes the basis of moral civic life.

What type of moral order is proposed here? The idea is that the essence of power in a democracy is not the instrumentalization of any individual's will, but the formulation of a common interest directed toward reaching agreement, toward serving the public good. Power, in other words, means the consent of the governed that is mobilized for collective goals. This view presumes that government without exploitation or domination does no damage to one's dignity or self-respect; government without exploitation is not a denial of human dignity (Walzer, 1983). If we cannot all govern, even for a short time, we must be governed by those who have a fundamental moral understanding, who pursue justice justly and reinforce the agreed-upon collective goals, the public good. Hence, from this perspective, a rough epistemological equality entails agreement-oriented discussion and debate aimed at producing consensus. Democracy, in other words, is a political arrangement of those who take counsel together in order to act in common. It rests on the assumptions that (1) in the give and take of public discussion, insights to problems will assert themselves, and (2) all citizens must of course, be free to enter the public discussion as equals. Obviously, the give and take of public discussion can be manipulated, but it is less likely to be if we bestow epistemological equality on all citizens who are oriented toward reaching agreement and not primarily toward their respective individual successes.

From this perspective, a revitalization of civic culture along the lines of epistemological equality among citizens gives concrete meaning to the principle of participatory democracy. Gouinlock (1986), following Dewey, contended that

> the obvious plurality of moral values need not be an impediment to the increase of moral concord. Dewey, as we have seen, concludes that there is a plurality of basic moral criteria. At the same time he argues that they are antagonistic only infrequently; and he points out that conflicts between them are not usually oppositions of good and evil, but of positive but incommensurable values. . . . There can be no perfect agreement. Yet, even though we do not agree precisely about anything, we are no doubt capable of constituting a more or less effective moral community. Our differences are not great enough to convert pluralism into mayhem. There is a simple reason for this: The benefits of mutual tolerance, cooperation, and friendship vastly outweigh whatever benefits there might be in distrust, interferences, and antagonism. There are few persons, if any, who are absolutely intolerant of any moral values not identical to their own. Otherwise, we are all pluralists, differing only in the degree of our tolerance. [p. 61]

It is indeed difficult to envision the exaltation of technocratic or bureaucratic expertise in any civic culture where the formation of consensus is guided by agreement-oriented discussion and decision making manifesting generosity of spirit, concern for the welfare of one's neighbor, and caring in one's relationships with others.

Participatory democracy requires, although it is not confined to, a moral compact that captures our understanding of one another and obligates us to one another. By emphasizing our dependence upon each other *as we are*—as persons possessed of human dignity and worth—as being the basis for mutual respect, concern, caring, and tolerance, civic decency and association will go beyond ethnic, neighborhood, and even regional structures. Insofar as it is natural for us to want dignity, respect, and self-respect, it is in our best interests to pursue them. In joining the political debate, citizens will see the need for dialogue and consensus, especially if they see that it is in their self-interest to pursue them.

Notice well that there is no attempt here to connect an ethic of obligation with some metaphysical essence of persons. We must not succumb to that temptation. Rather, it will be recalled from the previous chapter that it is natural for us to want dignity and worth—"preciousness"—as well as respect, and if it is natural for us to want these things, as we just naturally find ourselves to be, then it is in our self-interest to pursue them.

Intuitively, at least, we understand that nothing accords better with self-interest than a civic culture promotive of an ethic of concern, caring, and tolerance. For example, when we cease to care for family and friends, what has been important in our social relationships vanishes, and so does an essential part of the self, namely, self-respect. Politically, we care for others by showing respect for them, and this engenders self-respect and promotes comity. We listen in an open way, are civil to others, take responsibility for what we say and do, and seek agreement-oriented debate to achieve consensus among citizens. In fact, each of us, provided we take our own interests seriously, will consent to be ethically obligated to others, which further obligates us to attempt the transformation of the civic culture.

This is an insight that is quite simple but powerful. Participatory democracy embodies ethical relationships among citizens that direct and orient them to act and feel in certain ways, about themselves and others. In this respect, democratic practice accords best with the ideals of service, cooperation, consensus, and comity. Being a participant in democratic practice is bound up with responding to others based on an interconnectedness expressed primarily in terms of dignity and respect. Hence, democratic citizenship is tied to a moral compact embodying the ideal of generosity of civic spirit, and to an ethic of obligation and commitment, or an ethic of service.

NOTIONS OF PUBLIC AND PRIVATE

If participatory democracy is conceived along the lines sketched herein, then it is essential that we come to grips with ideas about what is public and what is private. American society, from its inception up to our own day, has been characterized, on the one hand, by discourse and legislative activity based on public rights and, on the other hand, by a closely linked grid of private rights. Hence, these two notions, public and private, define the arena in which democracy is to function. But are these two so heterogeneous that they cannot possibly be brought to terms with one another?

Without a doubt, the term *public* is one of the most important and useful concepts employed in political and social theory. It continues to be surrounded by a sacred halo or, in practice, as is commonly the case, is imbued with mysterious overtones that have something to do with overreaching into the private sphere. Whatever the case, the impulse at work here is the association of *public* with such notions as *populace, population, citizens, voting public, common people, masses, rank and file,* and, of course, *silent majority.*

It is striking that the term *public* is best understood when marked off from its opposite, *private.* This distinction is something almost everyone recognizes and acknowledges, because it is visible in daily affairs. Both terms are what I call "trouser words," due to this quality of being understood through their juxtaposition as a pair.

Dewey (1927) conceptualized a *public* as those whose lives are significantly affected by a particular act of others; and he defined a *public act,* as opposed to a private one, as any act of human beings that has an extensive and indirect impact on a substantial number of people. Dewey held fast to the notion of a self-conscious public as opposed to an inchoate public. The former of these represents a group significantly affected by certain human acts, of which the affected group is aware, whereas the latter, an inchoate public, represents a group that also is significantly affected by the acts of others, but is unaware or ignorant of the consequences.

In this distinction between a self-conscious public and an inchoate public, Dewey (1927) offered a foundation for answering the question, What is a public act? Perhaps an example might help here. Consider somebody taking an afternoon swim in an abandoned quarry on a hot, muggy day. The quarry's water is very cold and extremely deep in spots. Though an exercise of human energy is generally good, and being cooled on a hot day by the quarry's waters is refreshing, there is a clear danger: Four young people previously drowned while swimming unsupervised in the same quarry. Hence, the activity has indirect consequences which go beyond the individual involved. Indirectly, others are affected, since the activity may result in the loss of life. Although not every quarry swimmer will necessarily drown, some have, and thus a concerned public, aware of the hazard unsupervised quarry swimming poses to citizens and wishing to prevent such an occurrence from happening, comes into being.

What the example brings out is the willingness of members of the community to act with genuine concern in behalf of others. It is no exaggeration to say that the self-conscious public just mentioned regards human life as "precious" and assumes that our identities are social in character and that is through a sense of community that we pursue a satisfying moral life. To see this is to appreciate, from the human point of view, the need for legal and practical prohibitions against unsupervised quarry swimming. The legal sanction against such activity is a collective decision taken to inform others that members of society are valued, human life is precious, and such risk taking is not justified as a private act in a society that is concerned about and cares for human life.

The reason importance is attached to Dewey's (1927) distinction between a public and private act is, as innocuous as it appears, it shakes up long-established ideas that have guided our thinking about what is public and what is private. For one thing, it does not suggest a civic culture in the sense of a set of dos and don'ts; rather, it offers a way of relating thoughts about government to our changing conditions of life, on the one hand, and the persisting need of human beings for "community."

Let us see what is involved here. For Dewey (1927), there are no fixed and immutable boundaries within which only government is to operate or only citizens are to operate. The limits of governmental action need to fluctuate from time to time, primarily in response to self-conscious publics created by extensive and enduring indirect consequences of conjoint human behavior. It is the quest for this kind of relationship between public and private that is generative of communities, in which consensus will decide what affairs are public and private. That is, precisely what is creating a public's needs, and where, when, and how government should intervene or withdraw, are matters to be determined by broad citizen involvement, characterized by agreement-oriented discussion aimed at producing consensus, as in the quarry example.

This analysis is useful because it makes an oxymoron of the phrase *private citizens*. Citizens, in Dewey's sense of the term, are first and foremost public, and the establishment of democratically organized citizens—the public—is an urgent need of American democracy. Too much cannot be made of this point. The crucial insight is that participatory democracy, the highest political manifestation of life, presupposes the existence of active, interested publics.

The democratic civic culture Dewey (1927) envisioned can be achieved only if there is complete freedom of inquiry into social problems, with a resulting dissemination of knowledge among the various interested publics. For too long, private enterprise has led to private greed or naked self-interest, a trait inimical to a full sense of community. Dewey tried to find democratic ways to achieve full publicity, the lawful dissemination of civic plans and policies about to be put into operation or currently in operation. He also discussed ways to promote the freedom of thought and expression so absolutely essential to informed discussion and debate, so that the direct effects of actions on citizens will be given wide publicity.

The task of establishing a democratic civic culture of informed, active, knowledgeable, and ethically obligated publics is a formidable one, for it must deal with the traditional notion of privacy carrying a sense of privilege. Dewey's (1927) demands on the public were huge, since he grasped an important dimension of that collective: its pervasive sense of puzzlement and confusion. He repeatedly stressed that what is involved in revitalizing the civic culture is not merely a critique of science and technology, but a recognition of a crucial moment of transition from privacy to our dependency upon one another, ultimately rooting democracy and citizenship in a "community" through which we pursue a satisfactory moral life. Practically speaking, Dewey directed attention away from democracy as formal governmental rules and procedures, rights and duties, and toward democratic processes reflecting actual social actions and their consequences.

Dewey's approach, admittedly optimistic, is not utopian but grounded in historical experience in that it shows us that it is natural for us to want human dignity and self-respect and that it is in our self-interest to pursue these together. Working together derives almost exclusively from a recognition and understanding of the value of each other, of what we are, which forms the basis for self-respect and self-esteem. Today, he would argue, we have seen the writing on the wall: Citizen participation in governance is not only a political necessity, it is a moral necessity as well. A moral citizenry, an informed public, must have the opportunity to make explicit the connection between political and moral necessity.

Thus, being a democratic citizen means defining and debating civic questions within the complex situations of human association, especially economic and political relations, with an understanding that admits to their moral implications as well as to the tangential, unfinished nature of the project. Indeed, one distinguishing feature of Dewey's (1927) position is its aim to connect moral reasoning with dependence on contingent viewpoints and prudential judgments, which are always seen merely as warranted but not true. The strengths of this view are the glory of reflective inquiry, the assumption of the epistemological equality of all involved, and a moral commitment to an ethic of obligation to others.

From the viewpoint of the philosophical liberal, such a civic culture seems a distinct overvaluing of the collective moral and psychological values. Indeed, the ethic of obligation, involving concern, caring, and tolerance, does sound more like private behavior than public, but only as the tradition of philosophical liberalism makes that division.

Much current confusion over the cultivation of a revitalized civic culture may lie in the historical character of the ethic of obligation. Historically, Arendt (1958) tells us, an ethic of nurture and concern, of caring for and tolerance of others, was associated with activities that took place outside the public sphere. This was evident not merely in the strong sense that they were not to be integrally related to political activities, but in the consensus that they were, by definition, by deliberate convention and not mere historical accident, set apart from the public realm. Nurturing activities were restricted to the private sphere, the family, for they were considered essentially private matters, to be contained within the household walls, well out of the public eye. The family, the ultimate private sphere, became for women their proper domain, within which an ethic of obligation including a healthy dependence on one another exhibited by concern and caring was to be fostered as a basically female and private virtue. This merely private realm and its agents were objects of contempt, declared impotent and cut off from the possibility of achieving real value in the exalted and respected public realm.

This historical account should enlighten and challenge us to become clear about the interdependency of citizens, of the need for an ethic of obligation for all citizens as a public good and not merely as a private good. I realize full well that to many these ideas will be counted impractical at best and, at worst, an attempt to legislate morality. But this is precisely the point. I have tried to show that we must work very hard to make the ethic of obligation authentically and recognizably represented in the new civic culture because it does accord with the fact of our dependence upon one another. It is our duty to engage in concerned, caring, and tolerant activities because it is in our self-interest to do so, even though the individuals who are virtuous in these ways may be unable to articulate the considerations that make these behaviors obligatory. In a word, not to be so obligated is not to take our own self-interest seriously. Moreover, citizens must be educated about the mythology of gender values in the public and private sphere, and I say more about this later.

It is perhaps not imperious to add that the suggested changes require much of us. What I have argued for is a more than modest attempt to bring about a measure of change. Undoubtedly, until we repudiate a citizenship of astringent self-interest and privatism, in favor of the pursuit of integrated commitment to self and others, we will continue to have distorted self-development. In addition, any claim to revitalize or transform the civic culture, to redefine citizenship, will seem impractical, unintelligent, and even absurd.

CIVISM, OR GOOD CITIZENSHIP

Thus far the discussion has emphasized that democratic citizenship requires the prior acknowledgment of what we are—persons possessed of human dignity and worth—and a recognition that our social nature requires us to have a moral community through which to pursue a satisfying civic life. Moreover, the principle of human dignity gives meaning to the phrase *mutual respect.* That is, in a democratic civic culture citizens are entitled to mutual respect because it is derived from their condition of human dignity or inherent worth. I have tried to show the sense in which that claim is justified. We saw, it will be recalled, that democratic citizenship is constituted by recognizing our human worth as the basis of our self-respect, self-esteem, and interconnectedness. Good citizenship, or civism, is the exercise of personal virtue in the public sphere.

We turn now to explaining the important considerations of civism and indicating its place and role in a democracy. Civism, at least in part, is the attempt to control or regulate the indirect consequences of self-interested human activity, by organizing publics around shared concerns that affect their well-being. People must engage in voicing their desires through and in the public sphere and at the same time be mindful of the ethical pull, or commitment, of civic obligation and service. The logic at work here is a conception of good citizenship based upon a relationship of mutual reciprocity between the individual and the community. This relationship of mutual reciprocity is vital; citizens must care about doing the "right thing," and it is the business of the school to engender and energize moral character.

It has been shown that philosophical liberalism conceives of the civic culture in terms of self-interested citizens having a relatively fixed endowment of rights and power that is actualized once external restraints are removed. Civism, in this view, is defined as activities that nurture and support rights, freedoms, and political involvement as a power struggle between competing interests. It is cloaked in the garb of astringent self-reliance and entrepreneurial opportunity, with a concomitant neglect of those less favored or fortunate. The good citizen may, if so moved, support those who are less fortunate, but doing so does not depend on one's obligation to do so or on humanity in general having the right to be helped or assisted.

Indeed, this view has encouraged the disadvantage of the many and one of the shabbier systems of communal provision in the Western world. Why? Because its sharply individualistic logic has resulted in an assemblage of citizens loosely organized and felt (except in political crises) to be unable to invest emotional commitment in other people that is sufficient to suffuse the civic culture and thus create the civic decency so basic to a moral community and the public good. Rather, it is content to promote an active voluntarism which encourages various ethnic and religious groups to run welfare programs of their own kind, largely for their own kind.

Philosophical civic republicanism, on the other hand, offers the Judeo-Christian and republican traditions of community, which nest civic activity within a moral compact. Good citizens, in this case, make a promise to share their concerns and to care for and tolerate one another. The business of politics at its best is to fulfill these compactual promises within the changing flow of events responded to by various publics. The central view is that we hold ourselves responsible, and we are held responsible by our fellow citizens, for practicing the civic virtues. From this mutual holding, the possibility of self-respect flows. The good person, in other words, exhibits concern, cares for and is tolerant of fellow citizens, and works for the public good. This suggests that what makes life worth living is the peculiarly human satisfaction of feeling oneself to be a person ("somebodyness"), a contributing member of a communal way of life ("belongingness") that appeals to one because of its moral and experiential validity.

Citizenship needs no justification, being inherent in the very existence of political communities; what does need justification is civism, or good citizenship. What justifies this view of civism is that political activity is taken as the natural fulfillment of human powers, not as an exercise of rights and freedoms, but as a common vocation, and the proper object of personal self-development.

It can be argued, I believe, that the citizens of America today

ought to view each other as equals—legally, epistemologically, and
morally. However they are treated in fact, they ought to be each
other's equals. Why? By virtue of what characteristics are we equals?
We are, all of us, human beings, persons, possessed thereby of inherent dignity and worth. There is no doubt that this thesis has
spiritual meaning, but it is not necessary to invoke an intrinsic de-
ity in this regard, although one may do so. It is not necessary because there is another path available. The concept of human dignity
is simply a way of representing certain restrictions or constraints on
our lives by others. It means that brutality, meanness, inequality,
gossip, murder, arson, lying, paternalism, and so on are suspect
prima facie and always in need of justification. Democracy, and hence
civism, is rooted in the principle of human dignity, and to override
it is always to act precipitously, in bad faith.

This notion of civism is compelling because it describes not only
a personal but a collective ideal as well. Good citizenship entails the
notion of *caritas*, not merely in the sense of love of your neighbor
but in the practical reality of being at home, of "belongingness," in
a community of shared concern, caring, and tolerance. Hence, what
is required of education for civism is activity that teaches us not to
take our own self-interest too seriously and to develop a healthy
sense of belongingness and interconnectedness, expressed primarily in an obligation of membership, of willing service to others.

Hence, both "somebodyness," being a person and having an
identity, and "belongingness," being part of a moral community,
suggest a self-developed, self-fulfilled person sufficiently integrated
to live up to consciously affirmed obligations of civic membership.
Such persons have a politically cultivated moral sense, resting on the
belief that they use their autonomy to achieve responsible interconnectedness in the public sphere. But does social disaster, the societal equivalent of a burst dam, await those who attempt to implement
this view of civism? Can this moral ideal of nurturance and generosity of spirit toward others, of obligations of membership, be
trusted to produce a vital, strong civic culture?

There is, of course, a fine line between responsible and constructive democracy, which commits its citizenry to obligations beyond its traditional capacities, and the reckless overextension of
obligations that flies in the face of empirical limitations, just as there
is a fine line between, say, responsible banking and wildcatting.

The fine line I have in mind is not conceived in a denial of empirical factors and moral impossibilities, nor is it based on unreality

and utopianism. Rather, it rests on the *fact* of interconnectedness or interdependence and on the *reasonableness* of our desire for dignity, mutual respect, and self-respect. My call for constructive and responsible democracy means that the basic institutions of society today, many of them economic structures, cannot remain unchallenged and unchanged. Nor can they be merely ignored or transcended. The danger of developing a new civic culture with new democratic institutions, Dewey (1927) tells us, comes from weak, ineffective civic associations. These must grow strong in order to mediate between the individual and the institutions and in order to produce a new, shared public spirit of obligation and generosity. How this challenge will take place in the school and how civic education is implicated are the issues that will be addressed in the following section.

THE PRACTICE OF COMMUNITY SERVICE IN CIVIC EDUCATION

In chapter 2 an account was given of civic virtue. It was argued that it is best acquired in the course of studying various subjects and through an ethic of practice whereby social habits of willing action beneficial to others are established. These habits, or reliable means of social action, are the desirable traits of an enlightened civic competence. Moreover, in chapter 3 an account was given of a civic ethic of service, a form of learning that embodies an ethical obligation to be a person who is concerned, caring, and tolerant.

The major challenge in this section is to fuse these accounts in order to situate an ethic of civic service within the school. This prescribes as the chief aim of civic education the schooling of citizens in willing service to others, that is, in community service. This endeavor will shape the good person and the good citizen, thereby creating the moral compact upon which the civic culture is based. We may risk a proposition: that community service can be the driving force, the unifying base, for a moral civic education.

This proposal, of course, will likely offend those who hold that the highest good of civic education is to instill a patriotic loyalty. In answer I would say that this proposal has two constitutive elements. First, all civic education must be *civic* education, and citizenship and its obligations are the focus of community service. Second, it should be civic *education*, which means that the school should attempt to form in students social habits of willing action beneficial to others, an obligation of membership, and a generosity of civic spirit. Through community service, they will learn the virtues of civic decency, the moral characteristics fundamental to democratic living.

Perhaps this proposition seems too much like a moral exhortation to raise niceness to others (altruism) to the level of a universal principle, resulting in the woolly-headed niceness of Mr. Chips. It may be more politically astute to say that in the tense, crucial struggle between philosophical liberalism and philosophical civic republicanism, the school represents a site open to the possibility of breaking down the strong separation between the bureaucratic and informal realms of life, which is more or less parallel to the distinction between public and private life. To do this is to mediate between the two, thinking of citizenship as conducted within a community in which flexible, warm, caring, sympathetic, decent persons feel obliged to practice social actions beneficial to others.

There is, admittedly, much room for dispute about what beneficial civic actions are, what a fully virtuous person is, what civic education may be taken to rule out, and so forth. Indeed, for rationnal, thoughtful citizens, the question of what counts as a democratic society will be a matter of considerable moral disagreement. It is not quite enough, however, simply to know this. The official tenet of philosophical liberalism, which is the individualistic logic, and its central principles of self-interest, personal freedom, and sacredness of individual effort, are inadequate and unsuccessful over the long haul. The old economic and moral problems are still there, only in some ways worse. These are problems that must be solved not only as a matter of social justice but as a question of moral decency. Civic education must be given its legitimate role in this process.

Since my most important proposition is that the ethic of obligation is central to the moral compact of democracy, and the moral compact of democracy entails the practice of community service, I conclude that the ethic of obligation entails the practice of community service. As a consequence, I shall now argue for the place of community service in the school, based on how service and civic competence are intimately correlated, conceptually and morally.

Student Volunteer Work in the Community or at School

It is generally recognized that it is easy to discuss democracy in the abstract, but it is much more difficult to offer concrete examples of democratic classroom practice. Dewey, according to Raywid (1976), held that a democratic society

(l) . . . is one marked by widely held common interests and much interaction and cooperation both within and outside the group; (2) . . .
is also a society in which all members share in service to others, while
each is simultaneously enabled to develop his individual or distinctive
capacities; (3) . . . [is one that] offers a guide to private as well as public life . . . which provides a moral standard for personal conduct.
[p. 38]

What this argument suggests is service to others as a means of
broaching the separation between public and private life as well as
providing a moral standard for personal conduct. This means that
an educational vehicle for learning to render service to others must
be found.

Traditionally, it has been the dominating premise that the
"democratic classroom" is the best means for preparing adults who
are inclined to participate in democratic living. Raywid (1976) challenges this idea, arguing a point that is widely felt but little grasped:

A different conceptualization . . . might have had a much better chance
for helping teachers, for both logical and empirical reasons. Logical,
because the notion of "democratic classrooms" leads to incompatible,
even self-contradictory notions; and empirical because a different and
clearer model, unassociated with conflicting signals, might recommend more consistent and successful procedures. [pp. 45–46]

Raywid contends that a new vehicle is needed to help students learn
and practice democracy as a way of life. I propose community service as a just, viable, coherent, and virtuous vehicle for negotiating
the terms of membership in a society by citizens exhibiting the virtues of mutuality, trust, kindness, concern, caring, tolerance, and
respect.

This notion also has been heartily endorsed by Boyer (1983),
who devotes an entire chapter to high school service, concentrating
on the following theme:

Beyond the formal academic program the high school helps all students meet their social and civic obligations. During high school young
people should be given opportunities to reach beyond themselves and
feel more responsibly engaged. They should be encouraged to participate in the communities of which they are a part. We recommend:

• All high school students should complete a service requirement—a
  new Carnegie unit—that would involve them in volunteer work in

the community or at school. Students could fulfill this requirement
evenings, weekends, and during the summer.
- Students themselves should be given the responsibility to help organize and monitor the new service program and to work with school
officials to assure that credit is appropriately assigned. [pp. 306–307]

What is revealing in Boyer's proposal is that high school students
should be given opportunities to "reach beyond themselves and feel
more responsibly engaged." In effect, what is being recommended
are social habits of willing action or practices of commitment which
set down patterns of obligation that will nurture the community,
perhaps even a national American community.

Encouraging students to participate in voluntary community
service for academic credit has as its goal the process of self-integration into community, a sense of solidarity with community. Students will grasp the ineluctable fact that they are members of a larger
community, the social unit that sustains individuals as they pursue
the good life. Civic education should be seen by students as the body
of principles, rules, and virtues which, as members of their community, they are required to act upon. Community service would
help them meet these requirements and accordingly acknowledge
them as obligations of membership. It would help snap the traditional isolation of schooling from social life by bringing students into
contact with the practice of commitment, obligation, duty, solidarity, public contribution, and public good, concretely showing that
personal fulfillment and public contribution are not inimical or antithetical. By close contact in service to others—including the sick,
poor, homeless, elderly, dependent young and aged, and handi-
capped—students will come to see firsthand that individualism, defined in terms of self-reliance and competition, leads to a harsh and
vacuous life, lacking, as it must, in social commitment.

Community service, in other words, provides the elusive essence of civic decency, formalizing our best impulses and qualities.
Boyer (1983) quotes Jerome Kagan, a Harvard University professor,
who wrote,

> Acts of honesty, cooperation, and nurturance are public events that the
> staff of a school can tally and use to assign individual evaluations that
> are understood to be essential complements to subject mastery. We do
> not keep such records as faithfully as course grades, because we do not
> believe the schools should judge motives and behavioral attitude to-
> ward others; that is a task for the home and police department. But

> judging youth on standards for action and talent would make it pos-
> sible for many more students to participate in, and identify with, the
> school community. [p. 210]

Any intelligent and honest assessment of American education informs that students, for the most part, are neither expected nor encouraged to practice acts of honesty, cooperation, and nurturance as *public events*, although many do as part of their own and their parents' design for self-development. In other words, there is a public-versus-private dichotomy to be overcome. Hence, to institutionalize community service is to require that what heretofore has been a private matter become a public matter. This action would, of course, be based on an acknowledgment of our interconnectedness and dependence upon one another, but would go beyond this insight to the willingness to admit that our identities are social in character and thus require a sense of public commitment or service to others, through which we achieve full self-development.

The notion of community service, as I have suggested, entails the forming of social habits of willing action beneficial to others. Becoming a good person involves not only acquiring the *capacity* to follow rules and act upon principle, but also the *disposition* to feel and respond in appropriate ways. The emotional dimension is vital; it energizes civic conduct. All of this presupposes a large undertaking, both for social life as such and for all forms of human association. To accommodate this, civic education should see the range of community service as broad, extending from tutoring children to helping distribute hot meals, cutting lawns, and grocery shopping for the infirm and elderly. The venues of community service will include convalescent and nursing homes, hospices, hospitals, museums, community care agencies, nutrition sites, day-care centers, and other social service institutions.

Community service can help students grasp that they are not independent, competitive, maximizing self-interested individuals; and it can disabuse them of the myth that the good of the community is the result either of an aggregrated pursuit of self-interest or of mere public opinion. Rather, they will come to see that the public good is the result of a moral consensus arrived at over time, in a nexus of practices and obligation. Community service, in other words, can help students learn that it is desirable to work for the good of the whole of which they are a part. They will grasp that social habits of willing action beneficial to others promote a positive relationship between the community and its members.

If teachers view community service in this way, then civic morality is implicated. Green (1985) put the issue as follows:

> Morality enters, in short, when we find the voice of conscience as sacrifice and when that voice gains its own motivational strength. Is it enough for the aims of moral education then, to find and to teach the reasons, even sound moral reasons, for such a sacrifice? No. We do not become moral by consulting the reasons that endorse our sacrifice. It is those reasons that philosophers . . . seek; and that is what a reflective person who is already moral would insist upon receiving. But what we require for moral education is the actual sacrifice of self-interest and not merely its rational defense. [p. 17]

Green (1985) understands moral education as entailing a sacrifice of self-interest, which in turn produces a moral person who is transformed into making moral decisions. But what does this mean in actual practice, in the affairs of everyday living? It would seem that students need to engage in service to others that goes beyond the limits of self-interest or the accepted norms of duty. That is, if students are required to perform community service that is not an act of sacrifice of self-interest and does not go beyond the demands of duty, then they are not being prepared for moral living, what Green calls the "formation of conscience."

We should note, however, that Green's (1985) proposal generates very strong criteria for developing moral character. It may be helpful to reflect on what is neglected in his account. First, the dicta of experience point us toward the notion that community service does not necessarily involve us in sacrifice of self-interest. It has been shown that individual self-development, based on human dignity, mutual respect, concern, caring, and tolerance, looks to a sense of solidarity with community to be fully articulated, a solidarity that can sustain the individual over time. Were we to disclaim a concern for human dignity and respect, we might seriously question whether a community spirit existed or even a sense of community existed. Green's condition of sacrifice of self-interest, however, is too strong, too demanding, since he fails to see that individual self-interests and public contribution are balanced in the pursuit of moral decency and civic virtue. Instead of sacrifice of self-interest, what is wanted is an authentic form of self-development through which we pursue a satisfying moral life, motivated by human dignity and mutual respect, and free from the limitations of altruism. We need to explore further the implications of this last point.

We all know of demands, in various traditions, to purify one's life through altruism or self-sacrifice. A life of self-sacrifice, including honorable service to the nation-state, although it has high value in most societies, cannot and should not be expected of anyone. Why? Perhaps an example will help. Consider, for a moment, the deferential wife. This is a woman who is utterly devoted to serving and caring for her husband and children. She wears the clothes her husband prefers, cooks and serves the dishes he likes most, makes love whenever he wishes to, and counts her own friendships and interests insignificant by comparison to her husband's and children's. Her morality tends to focus on self-sacrificing or self-indifferent acts which are viewed as laudatory, highly estimable, in the eyes of some people. But her behavior cannot be, and is not, moral, because it denies her a fully developed self-respect, since she is restricted in the pursuit of whatever personal goals and ambitions she might have for herself, apart from her family.

What this case points out is the absence of self-respect. The deferential wife does not sacrifice her self-interests due to humiliation or maltreatment, but has accepted society's view that the proper role of a wife and mother is to care for her family. Thus she is servile, not simply because she holds certain beliefs about herself, but because she has a socialized attitude concerning her rightful place in life. Why then, is servility a moral defect? A human being has, in addition to dignity and worth, the capacity for rationality, cognitive perspective, excellence, identity, privacy, community, and autonomy, and this capacity is worthy of respect. A person can have respect for herself only when the capacities are exercised and developed. The deferential wife, in sacrificing self-interest, neglects the development and nurturance of her full capacity, by virtue of which she is equal with every other person. In other words, self-sacrifice for her family takes caring too far and demands too much, as it requires abandonment of self-respect and prevents full self-development as a human being.

One reason for dwelling on this point is that the service we give to others should not become self-sacrifice or servility, that is, a willingness to disavow one's moral status, publicly and systematically, by displaying an absence of respect for one's own ends, thereby assuming a lower position than one is naturally entitled to. In essence, the objectionable feature of the self-sacrificing person is the tendency to disavow one's moral ends, hopes, and aspirations. Moreover, insofar as this occurs, then there is the strong possibility that one may not be in an adequate position to appreciate the ends and purposes of others. Thus, neither the individual nor the society is served by a too-willing disposition to sacrifice self-interest.

In addition, the service that one gives to others should not be seen as something that others have to earn, as a form of charity. Conversely, gratitude is misplaced, as is the accepting of the service —as a benefit which is one's by right—as if it were a gift.

Once it is recognized that service is not unconditional, that it has special constraints, then it is clear that community service rendered to others by students should not degenerate into mere self-indifference, servility, or charity. Teachers must help students see that a community is made up of many interests, that there are many people involved, and that the best approach to reaching self-interested goals is to cooperate with others in pursuit of the public good. A concern for self and a concern for others can be integrated in a community project or scheme from which all would benefit, compared with the alternative of some benefiting and others benefiting not at all. As suggested previously, individual self-development and public good are united in a sense of community service.

Unfortunately, the virtues of concern, caring, and tolerance are qualities whose manifestations are deplorably lacking in formal education today. But within the praxis of community service, students can learn and practice these virtues and accordingly acknowledge them as obligations of membership.

Community service, then, as an authentic form of civic education, can provide a vehicle by which students can cultivate a balanced sense of caring for others. This should have positive effects that could benefit the civic culture in the long term, by improving the persons involved.

Thus it appears that, in altering civic education by focusing on community service and creating an educational practice with expressive real-life content, everyone gains. No one remains boxed inside an overly defined or undefined civic education. Teachers, for instance, benefit from a more flexible view of the ends and purposes of civic education; students can practice harmonizing the civic virtues through community service; and parents can oversee their children's community service, which will make the parents more aware of their own obligation to benefit other members of the community. Finally, the issue of community *control* of civic education, along with the principle of vigilance, becomes superseded by the principle of indifference.

Student Experience as Part of the Socialization and Learning Process

It has been claimed that democratic citizenship entails willing participation in the public sphere by informed citizens conscious of their civic obligations. Consequently, civic education should help citizens develop civic virtues and social-action skills so that, even if they do not directly determine political policy, they can at least expand their influence on the making of policy.

It is understood that it is part of the nature of the socialization and learning process that schools are only one among many socializing agencies that work to shape the minds and character, habits, outlooks, and modes of thinking in today's societies, including our own. A civic education program cannot be a vehicle for linking the school with the community if it neglects this fact. For instance, research informs us that knowledge, skills, values, and attitudes are acquired from such primary associations as the family, various peer-led youthful coteries and conclaves, mass media, churches, recreation groups, and so on (Adelson & O'Neill, 1966; Jennings & Niemi, 1968; Torney, Oppenheim, & Farner, 1985).

Thus, learning occurs both consciously, as in formal settings, and inadvertently, through informal processes. In most cases, however, it is acquired inadvertently, in the course of daily activity, without the individual being aware of it. This is the manner in which individuals develop the bulk of their view of the community, government, the norms and rules of civic behavior, and the character of the political system, all of which operate to influence the direction, quality, and tempo of civic life.

Greenstein (1965), in a study of the circumstances of childhood learning, concluded that informal or inadvertent learning is a powerful tool of political socialization, creating, as it were, a consensus upon which society is based. As a form of legitimation, informal learning tends to sustain the traditions that create the consensus on which society is based. Therefore, informal learning is inextricably related to a particular conception of the civic culture. Greenstein is worth quoting on this issue:

> The most important source of children's conceptions of authority undoubtedly is the civic instruction which goes on incidental to normal activities in the family. Children overhear parental conversations; they sense, or are informally told of, their parent's stance toward political authority in general and partisan politics in particular. [p. 44]

Although these remarks apply to the learning of authority relationships in the family, they probably apply to one's ethnic group
and to the school as well, although to a lesser degree. None of this
means that schooling is unimportant or that it should not take special responsibility for civic education; rather, it means that we should
grasp that education must take into account informal learning. Thus,
on a similar tack, Sigel (1965) noted that inadvertent learning can be
a by-product of casual observation or the overhearing of a conver-
sation in a primarily nonpolitical setting, as well as in a political one.
As she observed, "much . . . learning is incidental to other experiences: . . . it is acquired in a subtle, nondeliberate way, often in a
context which seems totally void of political stimuli yet is often rife
with political consequences. . . . The child learns . . . without being
aware that he is learning" (pp. 4–7).

These observations cannot be ignored, because they shed important light on the ways students receive social and political ideas
that shape their civic conscience. Informal learning is, in fact, the
main consideration of student community service. It is essential to
offer a "favorable setting" that will give students the opportunity to
learn by practice the social habits of willing action beneficial to others. This means that students need to work collectively, practicing
in the community an ethic of obligation for those who exist outside
their immediate experience, pushing themselves to test their sense
of civic decency and commitment regarding human dignity, mutual
respect, concern, caring, and tolerance of others.

Providing students the opportunity to learn service to others in
a "favorable setting" is important not merely because this provides
them with a practical way to understand and broaden the familiar
terrain of everyday community life. It is also part of a pedagogical
strategy that attempts both to engage and to recover the experiences
that students have, so as to understand how such experiences are
part of community living, the stuff of the culture. It is through such
experiences that students will produce accounts of who they are and
constitute themselves as citizens, thus creating the consensus upon
which community is based.

There are a number of reasons for arguing this position. First,
it is clear that the very best ideas are of no use if they do not become part of the consciousness of the person who holds them. That
is to say, students cannot learn civic virtues only as ideas, no matter
how passionately we care about these ideas or the students we are
teaching. At stake here is the need for educators to understand how
experiences produced by community service give rise to the stu-

dents' understanding of their own civic world and, consequently, of their own experiences in the larger community. Unless educators address the question of how a generosity of civic spirit—citizens willingly committed to investing time and effort in benefiting other people—can best be constructed, it will be difficult for the school to tap students' healthy dependence on one another, which gives the basis for a new community consensus. Teachers and students must treat morality and community directly.

Second, it is foolish to argue for schools as sites for practicing civic virtue if some schools narrowly define and exclude the communities of which they are a part. Given the nature of the socialization and learning process, student experience is the stuff of civic learning, but its setting must be conducive to shaping civic character and behavior as an effortless act of moral development. Perhaps the key distinction in civic education is not between inadvertent and conscious learning, but between effortless acts of relevance and effortful acts to which there is no point. As Bastian, Fruchter, Gittell, Greer, & Haskings (1985) wrote,

> School isolation works to deny students a link between what they learn in the classroom and the environment they function in outside the school. . . . Isolation also denies communities the integrative and empowering capacities of the school as a community institution. Isolation denies schools the energy, resources, and ultimately, the sympathies of community members. [p. 47]

We must remember that civic education is a tool for making a society a moral community. We do not need such a tool to cultivate persons who have learned the civic values of dignity and mutual respect, as well as the ethic of obligation to help others to be democratic citizens. A good person is a good citizen. But we do need a tool to strengthen the tendency toward human dignity and mutual respect which is present in almost all of us, at least some of the time, but which also in almost all of us is not strong enough, most of the time.

Third, educators need to take seriously the notion of "favorable settings" so basic to community service. It is obvious that there are situations easily characterized as immoral, indecent, or unethical. Ordinarily, students are not placed in such situations in order to expose them to vices. Rather, social situations offering opportunity for expressions of an ethic of obligation must be found. If social situations call for participants recognizing their mutual dependence, a generosity of spirit can be taken up, and students can practice the civil virtues in these "favorable settings."

Thus educators must be willing and prepared to take civic education into the community, because it is there that good citizenship is made meaningful to students. By opening the schools to the diverse resources offered by the community, educators will create active, organic links with the community. Conversely, community involvement in the schools can help foster better school-community relations. Teachers can take a large step in organizing with parents and others in the community, so they may together secure a relative degree of control over education in general and civic education in particular, and may participate in its evaluation. The principle of vigilance will not be wholly negated, but it will be somewhat constrained. It is worth reaffirming that the great contribution of teachers and schools is to win for the community a strong sense of moral decency. Given this aim, especially if moral decency is thought of less as patriotic honorable action and more as social virtue, then parents have much to gain by abandoning the principle of vigilance.

Community Service Education Throughout the School Years

The fundamental phenomenon of community service is its *practice*. One could, I submit, not get far in trying to teach students the civic virtues as mere cognitive knowledge. The virtues are a type of knowledge that can be learned, yet there is also more than a hint here that they cannot simply be imparted by the teacher. This should, however, not daunt us. The practice of community service provides a kind of understanding or grasp that students need to have in order to make sense of and to judge the coherence and value of the civic culture. Service can help to create the consensus upon which a community is based. It is, therefore, in the school's community service function that the new civic culture can best be constructed.

Boyer (1983) makes the following specific suggestions for implementing community service:

> During each of their four high school years, students would do volunteer work in or out of school. They could tutor younger students; volunteer in the school cafeteria, office, audio-visual center; or maintain sports equipment and playing areas. They might also move beyond the school to libraries, parks, hospitals, museums, local government, nursing homes, day-care centers, synagogues, or churches. [p. 210]

As noted earlier, Boyer also recommends a new Carnegie unit, which would require that "a student invest not less than 30 hours a year, a total of 120 hours over four years, in order to qualify" (p. 210).

The service pattern sketched by Boyer (1983) is a shift from a school-bound notion of civic education to what has been suggested as a community-based civic education. He presents three examples of service programs already operative. For instance, in Detroit city schools students are required to complete 200 hours of out-of-school experience between the ninth and twelfth grades, in order to graduate. Each student receives a card that must be signed by her supervisor, recording the number of hours worked, either as an employee or a volunteer. The range of activities is broad, and Boyer reports that students accept the service requirement with little complaint.

A second example given by Boyer (1983) is South Brunswick High School in New Jersey, where the school service program offers two types of experience for students: service and career. Students are engaged in service activities at nursing homes, day-care centers, hospitals, nutrition sites, and so on. Career activities engage students at such work sites as computer centers and automobile repair shops. Once a week students meet in groups to review their individual experiences and to raise questions or problems they have encountered.

A third example, Metro High School, a public high school in St. Louis, requires that students work as volunteers in the community for 60 hours each year, at a nonprofit agency within the city limits. If students have not completed the required service hours by the end of their senior year, they will not graduate. They work on displays and research at the botanical gardens, as guides at the McDonnel Planetarium, as backstage hands on sets at the Theatre Project Company, as assistants in various jobs in local hospitals, and so on.

Boyer (1983) believes that a Carnegie community service unit during the four years of high school will do much to build a sense of community and common purpose within a school. I do not believe, however, that he stresses the obligation to serve others strongly enough. Aside from the question of how much and what the service requirement should be, I suggest that a community service program be divorced from the concepts of career training and opportunity, although some students will, as side benefits, gain job experience, explore careers and so on. A volunteer community service program is justified on the grounds of the fundamental interconnectedness of people, of the recognition of our dependency upon each other as possessed of inherent human dignity. To be fully human, in other words, one must serve others; and it is natural to do so. If students engage in tutoring other, younger students, develop big brother and big sister activities, and visit nursing homes and the residences of elderly citizens in order to entertain and care for them by writing letters, preparing meals, and offering simple companionship, they will come to see how nasty and unpleasant life would be if people rarely or never exhibited mutual respect, concern, caring, and tolerance for others.

It cannot be stressed too heavily that, one way or another, the core of democratic civic morality must be conveyed to students very early in their education. Many of the projects they work on are, of course, noncontroversial services. It does not follow, however, that there will be no issues raised by their work. For example, teachers should raise questions about freedom as the exercise of choice. Citizens have the freedom to choose, and a democracy is a formal arrangement allowing citizens to choose their freedoms. Thus students must discuss the idea that we exchange the freedom, say, of throwing a can or bottle out of a car on a highway for another freedom, say, safety or aesthetics, a freedom we want more, one for which our desire is greater. In short, students will be encouraged to discuss freedom in terms of exchanging one type of situation, one that we dislike, for another type that we think is better. From this chore teachers and students can never rest, for it is the business of citizens in a democracy. The risks that we take in not attending to this are frightful.

We also must not be so preoccupied with the advanced stages of formal education, the four years of high school, that we forget that this activity is best begun in the initial stages. Thus I propose that a community service program extend to the elementary grades, but two caveats are in order. If this is done outside of school, children may be exploited and harmed. It is important, in other words, that teachers and parents take responsibility for community service by closely monitoring the community experiences of students. Second, the knowledgeable teacher must make community service practice an integral part of the classroom. That is, educators must be aware that in their roles as teachers they are defining values, making duty and obligation commendable or objectionable, and establishing the guidelines for concern and tolerance of others. It is imperative, in other words, that educators realize that, no matter how far we agree on broad principles of social justice, civic decency, fairness, or respect, school and classroom practices will give concrete meaning to those principles. Awareness of this fact will encourage educators to keep in touch with those school and classroom practices productive of ways of seeing the world in terms of a generosity of spirit willing to invest emotional commitments in other people.

The last point suggests that community service education in the initial stages of school can only mean eschewing a generalized symbolic civic curriculum in favor of one closer to that of practice, of doing. There must be an ongoing concretizing of the values of human dignity and mutual respect. Teachers must be aware that, as abstractions, these principles are too nebulous, too far removed from the life experiences of young children and young adults. Concrete illustrations, such as role-playing the problem situation, are necessary to give these principles operational meaning within a context, which might be the ecology critique, the feminist movement, race relations, and so forth. Human dignity or worth is a topic or problem easily brought down to a young child's level in discussions concerning such specific contemporary concerns. So too can self-respect, rule by consent, due process, trust, and fairness, because even very young children can relate to and grasp instances of the denial of these, which helps them to appreciate their worth. This does not mean that each class must focus on drastic and harsh criticism of things horribly wrong in society. Rather, classes should be conducted as ideal free-speech situations, conversations whose politeness and fairness embody the best political language of the day.

In addition, a reasoned discussion of a problem in such a way that attention is given to the civic virtues offers promise of developing a sense of civic decency. Teachers might ask their students why they expect teachers to be fair, honest, and polite. Why do students expect teachers to expend their time and energy equitably, and why, in the most general terms, do students expect teachers to act out of good intentions?

Through an exchange of the teacher's and students' accounts of the situation, students may come to see why such expectations exist and, perhaps, why they are violated. It is possible, moreover, that in the process teachers and students may come to see that some teachers may violate these expectations because they hold conflicting ideas about what is fair student treatment. The discussion may lead students to see that, by looking closely at how people, including teachers and fellow students, respond in particular situations (the things they say and do to each other), we may detect the presence or lack of a generosity of spirit.

Finally, teachers must be willing and prepared to make the community service program responsive to the wider community. In doing so, they will have to redefine the role and nature of supervision and evaluation, as it is currently constituted around the notion of professionalism, a position that stands in opposition to wider school-community involvement. Since nearly every project will involve an adult in one way or another, significant community involvement is entailed in the supervision and evaluation of students. Community members may serve at one time or another as student supervisors, helping students in their projects and creating an understanding that there is a relationship of mutual reciprocity between the community and its members, and that community is the context within which we may pursue a morally satisfying life.

CONCLUSION

In this chapter, through several lines of analysis and argument, I have advanced the thesis that a democracy implies the idea of a moral society as an objective reality and not as a sloganized ideal. Central to developing democratic citizenship is the need for educators to reconstruct civic education, in order to bring about a revitalization of the civic culture.

This task, it has been argued, will have no real beginning until the question of how—the means—is looked straight in the eye. If one takes this point seriously, then the central issue is to make a community service program an integral element of civic education. This program must be aimed at developing an awareness of and sensitivity to the presence and values of others. This should not emerge as pseudo-tolerance or a mushy niceness, or, for that matter, as compartmentalized values-clarification; rather, what we are working toward is a genuine appreciation of human dignity and respect for others. Community service can serve as the occasion for reconstructing civic education by mobilizing the principles of human dignity and mutual respect, along with the ethic of obligation, which includes concern, caring, and tolerance for others.

School and classroom practices in this sense must be organized around the moral compact enunciated throughout this work, and they must be designed to mesh with knowledge acquired. This will prepare students to develop and perform, in and out of school, within the context of webs of solidarity, friendship, trust, decency, and honesty. In this way the civic culture can be revitalized.

CHAPTER 5

Social Heterogeneity and E Pluribus Unum

The purpose of this chapter is to address a phenomenon in American life, a stark social fact commonly called social heterogeneity. Its influence is manifested throughout our institutional arrangements, cuisine, language, architecture, dress, mass media, educational system, laws, and so forth. Because of this inheritance we have had an enriched tradition, but we have had to struggle to develop and nurture what slender common civic bonds we could, in order to maintain a civic union and vital civic undertakings. In other words, our political history is replete with a multiplicity of human collectivities, developed under a very wide range of institutions, acting in countless ways to forge a society beyond the anticipations of any one collectivity or institution.

Another purpose of this chapter is to address the issue of whether, in order to act as good citizens, it is advisable for persons to restrict their memberships in ethnic collectivities normally considered social or cultural groups. That is, do ethnic collectivities nurture and fortify those social institutions that mobilize the unpolitical in the public sphere, politicize the private sphere, and thus accord the private and informal with unwarranted stature in the public sphere? Are ethnic collectivities capable of not only cooperation and accord—providing a support system in which all members are cared for—but of vicious rivalry and exclusiveness used to justify a restricted sense of citizenship? Do ethnic groups "corner the market" on personal identity and threaten the loss of civic identity—estrangement and isolation—if their members should lapse?

This issue is, in another form, the question raised in chapter 3 in the discussion of the concept and ramifications of "caring for" others. We saw that caring for others is not a matter of all or nothing but of degree, and ordinarily we deeply care for those closest around us: immediate family, relatives, friends, and so on. Hence, we examined the question of why those closest to us are especially cared for.

In this chapter, this issue deals with the problem of whether we can exercise broad and objective democratic citizenship bonding that is promotive of civic collaboration if we make political decisions only in terms of particularistic ties to those for whom we passionately care—our inner group, ethnic group, or religious association. Is it simply asking too much to leave to ethnic identity the decision as to how much conscience will be mustered to carry out civic duties? Are there certain democratic conditions, constraints, necessities, requirements, or imperatives that can act to correct this? If so, do they apply regardless of the specific type of conscience one has?

A final question has to do with civic education. What can the public school do to help revitalize the civic culture and make it harmonious with a pluralist political and cultural system? The traditional solution to the situation has been to insist that virtually everyone should both recognize national loyalty as the highest priority of public schooling and explicitly renounce loyalties that might compete with the nation-state, including those of kith and kin. This approach has had an effect that has been neither uniform nor one way (Janowitz, 1983). In effect, according to Spring (1986), this resulted in the use of the school as a social agency to liquidate in students any other commitments, in favor of *Americanization*, meaning "cultural imperialism and the building of a national spirit that was suspicious of foreign countries and ways of living" (p. 168).

This demand, due to the nature of the case, could not be met without disastrous social and political consequences. For instance, it tended to impugn the essential bases of trust, friendship, and solidarity, which are the enduring objects of allegiance in ethnic collectivities. Consequently, Americanization was challenged and weakened in a nation-society that has always recognized that human communities are not like airtight compartments hermetically sealed from one another, that cultural diffusion regularly occurs, and that very little can be expected in a nation-society that is deeply and painfully divided along racial, religious, linguistic, and economic lines.

These issues, it seems to me, are the most crucial for a reconstructed civic education, and of course they are the points at which philosophical civic republicanism has its broadest significance. First, however, we will turn to a discussion of social heterogeneity.

SOCIAL HETEROGENEITY

We shall begin with the givenness of social heterogeneity, with the realization that the United States is a nation of immigrants. In this approach, we shall flesh out the meaning of the American cultural and institutional tradition of social heterogeneity. This tradition has come to be viewed, on the one hand, as out of date, unable to keep the tyranny of special interests at bay, and, on the other, as the only intelligent, humane course open to us. A dilemma of this sort can, very naturally, make us yearn for definitive answers, and I would certainly not contend that this is an unimportant matter. What often gets lost in the argument, however, is the important fact that American society was built on a system of countervailing human associations or factions and, like it or not, they now encompass, interpenetrate, and incorporate all of society. Our best hope for a revitalized civic culture may lie in assessing this tradition, for a failure to take into account the indisputable presence of social heterogeneity is to tax the human ability to make the ends and purposes of society intelligible and holds the potential for great tragedy in the civic culture. It is, ultimately, this very practical reason that gives urgency to the conceptual and historical task of explicating the relationship between social heterogeneity and American society.

An Evolving Nation

It is no exaggeration to paraphrase the historian Herodotus's remark that "Egypt is the gift of the Nile" by saying that "the United States is in large part the gift of immigrants." This point embraces the view that not only did the United States provide a haven or refuge for millions of newcomers, but in the process was enriched by them. The qualifier "in large part" is necessary because we must not neglect by error of omission the fact that significant intergroup contact occurred on the American frontier, between the immigrant settlers and this continent's indigenous peoples and the long-established Hispanics of the Southwest. In both instances, a dark page of American history was written, as hostility and prejudice developed out of conflict over land and its use.

There seems, however, to be little serious disagreement about the benefits of immigration. The Old World culture helped shape the New World experience and contributed to the phenomenon of social heterogeneity. Early in the nineteenth century came the first large wave of immigrants, over 2 million Irish between 1815 and 1860, as well as 1.5 million Germans, some driven westward by political persecution, but more by hunger and hardship (Bennett, 1963).

The inevitable result of unrestricted immigration was a second great wave of 10 million from 1860 to 1890, more than twice as large as the preceding period. These people were mostly Northern Europeans: English, Dutch, Swedish, and Norwegian. The third wave, from 1890 to 1914, was even bigger: 16 million, including a still-unmatched record of 1.3 million in 1907, when the population of the United States was only 87 million (Bennett, 1963). To the dismay of many of the newly established Northern Europeans, more than 80 percent of the newcomers were Southern and Eastern Europeans: Italians, Bulgarians, Poles, Greeks, Slavs, and Russians. This was the period immortalized by the words of Emma Lazarus, who wrote the Statue of Liberty's welcome to the "huddled masses yearning to be free."

Today, the picture of American society that begins to emerge from the consequences of immigration is awesome. Precisely for this reason, the fact of social heterogeneity is the single most important aspect of American society today. As far as racial makeup is concerned, while whites predominate, numerous other groups abound. In only one state, Hawaii, are whites a minority, making up one-third of Hawaii's population. Asians and Pacific Islanders are the majority there. At the other extreme, one state, Vermont, is more than 99 percent white, while New Hampshire is a close second at 98.9 percent ("July 1984 Estimates," 1985). Making up the largest American minority groups are 28.6 million blacks, up about 5 percent since 1980. Interestingly, the black growth rate has been steadily declining for more than three decades. The second largest minority are the 16.8 million Hispanics, having increased 14 percent in the four years between 1980 and 1984, with the increase from legal Mexican immigration alone making up 35 percent of this increase. The smallest racial or ethnic element of the United States is actually a cluster known as "other races." A current estimate shows that 6.7 million members of this category include about 4.8 million Asians and about 1.4 million Native Americans ("July 1984 Estimates," 1985).

At the same time, three states—California, Texas, and New York—have more than 1 million Hispanics, and nearly two-thirds of the nation's Hispanics live in those states. For example, Los Angeles County has experienced a new period of explosive growth of the Hispanic population that has surprised demographers and pushed whites into minority status for the first time in this century ("July 1984 Estimates," 1985). For years, Los Angeles had been heralded as a magnet for job-hungry immigrants from Latin America and Asia, but experts say the influx of newcomers is only indirectly responsible for the population spurt. Most of the growth has come from a baby boom among young Hispanics, explained by the unusually large percentage of Hispanic women of prime child-bearing age and by the fact that large families traditionally are preferred by Los Angeles Hispanic residents.

The high relative growth among Hispanics and Asians and their concentration in only a few states mean they will influence politics, economics, and education to an increasing degree. For instance, Asian-Americans will likely account for one out of every twenty-five Americans by the turn of the century, being the country's fastest-growing minority and heading for the 10 million mark a mere 15 years ahead ("July 1984 Estimates," 1985).

As immigrants continue to arrive, American society is an ever-changing mixture of many ethnic groups, and this is viewed with mixed feelings by citizens. The alarm bells have begun to ring, and there are dire warnings about the implications. Some speak in strident voices of an "immigration nightmare," proclaiming that our immigration policy is making us economically poorer, not richer, and arguing that immigration more narrowly divides the economic pie. Others argue that this is not so; immigrants, they contend, make the pie larger for everyone (Fallows, 1983).

The living realities of today's changing society and their political, economic, and cultural consequences are, in most cases, hotly disputed. Consequently, the important question about the new makeup of American society is, What is happening? What effects are the new immigrants having? Are they so numerous and powerful that they will alter political and social relations? What, if anything, will be their individual and cumulative impact on the civic culture? Above all, what sort of civic culture are they likely to respect? Will they, for example, accept the view that civic culture is defined by competition among special interests, or by the sharing of a common good, a public interest? At stake is nothing less than the shape of the good society, its purposes and goals.

In summary, we should note that social heterogeneity is a matter of both political choice and moral constraint. The former is seen in the fact that foreigners choose to become members of a historically established, ongoing political organization, called the United States of America. The latter aspect is seen in the fact that newcomers are granted membership, or here in the United States residence, and are thereby endowed with certain rights and obligations. Thus they are able, and expected, to regard themselves as potential legal participants in the politics of decision making. They may choose not to become citizens, but that is a matter of choice. Having and making the choice is to ponder concern for and reciprocity to one's fellow citizens and thus to consider moral matters.

Ethnicity

Our discussion so far has indicated some of the problems associated with the fact of social heterogeneity and has laid some of the groundwork for a new conception of the civic culture, one that begins with the reality of social heterogeneity and aspires to the eventual articulation of a revitalized American civic culture.

It is at this point that we must consider ethnicity and ethnic groups, so that we do not overlook the point that, on the whole, humankind has thought highly of such associations, and that, historically, ethnic group ties have been among the most important associational principles of Americans. American society, while it certainly must be conceived of as a collectivity, is also composed of an immense variety of subcollectivities, some of which are ethnic groups.

A collectivity, seen in these terms, is clearly not a concrete "group"; rather, the term refers to groups in the sense of systematically related pluralities of persons, seen in the perspective of their interests in and capacities for effective collective action. *Ethnic* groups, then, are self-conscious collectivities of humans who, on the basis of selected differences, such as a common origin or a separate subculture, maintain over generations a distinction between themselves and others. Thus an ethnic group may be cultural or racial, as long as these criteria are met.

Although there has been considerable disagreement in the social sciences over the usage of the term *ethnic*, the preceding definition seems basic to most conceptualizations. Maintenance of this sense of separateness is exhibited in the circumscribed social participation of the ethnic group's members, which is generally carried on in a restricted geographic territory and involves a distinct pattern of thought, values, or ideology or, also very important, a deeply felt consciousness of pride in a shared historical past.

The inclusion of racial groups as ethnic groups is maintained by this definition. In everyday usage, however, the word *race* is most often employed to mean people of color, indigenous and immigrant alike, while the term *ethnic* is reserved for minority whites. The implications that ethnic groups are only whites and racial groups are not also ethnic groups are both obviously false. Thus, for the purposes of this book, all groups in the United States, regardless of race, are taken to be ethnic groups, if they meet the criteria mentioned earlier with regard to being self-conscious collectivities with a sense of separateness and shared history.

Ethnic collectivities in the United States were originally founded upon some widely accepted purpose, not the least of which was to provide working associations in which a strong sense of solidarity and identity could be realized by members. It is a crucial feature of ethnic groups in the United States today that they serve as collectivities of great significance, understood in large part in terms of their possibilities for keeping the alien, the strange, the freakish, or the hellish of the dominant society under control. Ethnic communities, through both formal and informal agents and agencies, give members a feeling of "belongingness" and "somebodyness" as well as protecting their group privacy, even under conditions of near-constant physical proximity to others.

But to achieve this end, the end of being an ethnic group, requires its own means: the resources, freedom, and social power to continue its own work. It requires, among other things, standards, rules, and regulations that facilitate rather than limit the group's ability to provide for its members' self-development. The pursuit of such means frequently leads ethnic groups to take action far removed from the original purpose of group association, such as putting emphasis on the dominance of birth and blood over and above civic membership, or stressing the privilege of private over public functions of citizens. Here, then, is the rub: There is a limit beyond which no democratic state can tolerate for long the establishment of a fixed status between ethnic-group identity and civic identity, although there may be stages in the transition from ethnic identity to civic identity.

A slightly different way of looking at this problem is through a distinction made by Cooley (1909). He identified two types of human relations: primary and secondary. The former, he contended, are those relations in which we find ourselves in private, sometimes intimate, always informal, face-to-face contact with others. These associations are sometimes intrinsically valued and usually involve one's psychological being, the whole personality, rather than being restricted to, say, the cognitive functions that are used in the fulfillment of certain social functions. Secondary associations, on the other hand, are characterized by being formal, public, noncasual, and usually extrinsic, since they are employed as a means to an end.

Primary relations are truly primary in two senses. First, they are the original relationships in the life of the individual, since the nuclear and extended family commonly tend to be such an association. Second, they are primary in the sense that they have first call or weight in determining the group members' values, practices, and beliefs.

The distinction between primary and secondary associations is important because it helps us to see that ethnic membership can offer a powerful force in shaping individual self-development, since the force of ethnic socialization is reinforced by connections to the individual's most significant others, at least in the early stages of enculturation. The family provides the first site for self-development, and it is not uncommon to find a plurality of families formed as an ethnic group in which primary and secondary relations are confined almost exclusively to the group. In this case it would mean, for example, that at the primary level there is no intermarriage with other groups and that social activities are confined to one's own group. At the secondary level of association, the ethnic group would provide such services as schools, newspapers, hospitals, and cultural outlets exclusively for its members (Green, 1966).

If we were to extend this condition of exclusivity of ethnic-group primary and secondary relations to all groups in a society, then we would have social and political arrangements of a sort that could be described as "separatist." That is, we would have insular but coexisting groups arranged in a polity, functioning reasonably well in spite of deep separations based on privatistic boundaries called "ethnic differences."

Seen in this light the issue is this: Does the ethnic exclusivist element constitute a threat to the civic culture and to the unity of the nation-society? Is it a factor so strong, a sufficient barrier, that it will undermine the public exchange of citizen dialogue so necessary for civic collaboration and a revitalized civic culture?

These are difficult questions. Obviously, ethnic-group exclusivity in such areas of life as ritual, cuisine, language, humor, dress, and housing are significant because these are the practices that shape the community as a way of life. For Bellah, Madsen, Sullivan, Swidler, and Tipton (1985) these are the "practices of commitment" which lay down the patterns of obligation that define and legitimate the community. They constitute the social mechanisms through which the process of self-development in the community is articulated. They provide, in other words, an intelligible account of the world on a particular scale and, at the same time, allow group members to interpret and represent a larger world than one could experience if one were not a member of a group.

In understanding this phenomenon, due account again must be taken of the traditional problem of order. Any social system must possess a common normative system. "Solidarity," of course, is the principle by virtue of which the commitment to norms (which are based in turn on values) is articulated within collectivities. In the ongoing press of solidarity, the nation-society provides, among other things, schooling in civic values, in an attempt to override ethnic exclusivity and promote more extensive collective or common interest. Citizens commonly break through group exclusivity when they invest in the political system by seeking political office, public recognition, honors and awards, security and welfare, and, especially, freedom, equality, and social justice.

Everyone has had experience of this kind on one level or another. One problem with ethnic-group exclusivity is that it seeks to limit its members' secondary associations. Obviously, ethnic groups must limit their members' relations on the primary level, or else the groups would cease to exist; no subgroup or collectivity can resist controlling the primary associations of its members. However, the central problem of ethnic-group exclusivity occurs when an ethnic group creates a thorough structural separation between itself and the plurality of groups within the larger collectivity, at both the primary and secondary levels of association. In important respects, this severely limits the degree to which a group member has access to the institutional structures of other groups.

This type of pluralism, *insular pluralism*, can be a threat to the unity of a democratic society, since it establishes the monopoly of discrete groups committed to noncommon interests, over the larger civic collectivity and more extensive collective interest. In other words, ethnic-group interests take precedence over the public good.

Thus there is an urgency, due to the risk and danger embedded in this situation. In formal terms, the logic at work is that the civic culture is undercut by practices of ethnic-group exclusivity. Put plainly, ethnic-group membership, a high ideal in present-day American society, is potentially damaging to the process of instilling a vigorous civic collaboration, because, even with the exercise of excessive caution through public schooling and civic education, ethnic membership, bonding, and obligation could be elevated over civic membership, bonding, and obligation. An actual example of the suppression of civic citizenship is found in the political sphere when citizen X is chosen over citizen Y for political office primarily on the basis of X's membership in an ethnic collectivity and a professed identification with its particular goals and purposes.

One may argue that this action is not antidemocratic; it falls within the boundaries of accommodative democratic practice. But to go a step further, it also suggests in the strongest terms that a society of political and moral equals is not a lively possibility. Ethnic-group exclusivity in the social and political spheres may be disguised as a vision of social virtue by espousing great community service while pursuing ethnic-group advance. But the reality is that ethnic-group exercise of power is an important example of an atomized nation-society and a barrier to broad public interest and spirit, as well as to widespread citizen bonding.

It is important to see that the domination of the public sphere by informal, private, intimate, face-to-face relations—which legitimately operate in the institution of the family, extended family, clan, and ethnic collectivity—is a violation of human dignity and mutual respect. Primary relations are inappropriate objects of civic allegiance and collaboration and should be severely constrained, if not ruled out entirely, in the public sphere. It is not morally enhancing of dignity and respect to give a political office, or any position of power over others, to one's family, friends, or fellow ethnics, based on those narrow relationships. Political activity ought to be rooted in a moral conscience, and not just any moral conscience. Democratic political action must be rooted in a civic conscience, with a distinct undervaluing of private, informal, privileged considerations. So long as we must act in the public sphere as citizens, it is damaging to the interests and self-development of others to make decisions commanded by ethnic loyalty and partiality. Use of particularistic primary relations and ethnic-group criteria in the public sphere is an immoral, tyrannical, antidemocratic use of power (Walzer, 1983).

What kind of conditions are necessary to preclude this from happening? Ethnic groups must be encouraged to feel good about their heritage and not denigrated in terms in a narrow, biased judgment of what is truly "American." For instance, we must avoid any further attempts to apply social science to formal education by tailoring school curricula to the needs of "culturally deprived" children, or to translate all social issues, including ethnic relations, into technical problems. These efforts can be correctly viewed as part of a larger historic struggle to rid ethnic-group children of their culture, thus robbing them of their cultural identity.

Perhaps the important question is, Can any program of civic education succeed if ethnic identity is denigrated, if the political conditions for ethnic-group inclusion in participatory democracy do not exist, and if the relationship between ethnic minorities and the school is hopelessly estranged? Decades ago, millions of immigrants were willing to reject their cultural heritage because they firmly believed that formal education was the key to the American Dream of freedom and power, better jobs and pay. But is this true today, for a great many Hispanic, black, and Native American children? Is social mobility really available to any underclass citizen who can read, is "computer literate," and has critical thinking skills? Why should citizens whose cultures are denigrated invest in a civic culture that does not respect them?

Educators, perhaps more than anyone else, must realize that all individuals become the people and the citizens they are by growing up in a particular community, learning to speak its language, and participating in its life. There must be a community for one to grow up in to become a person and, importantly, a citizen. The particular qualities of the community make an important difference; no one can be socially and culturally neutral. We must take social heterogeneity seriously by recognizing our duty to maintain a genuine community, never being indifferent to the lot of any member, irrespective of nationality, ethnic origin, religion, or any other differentiating characteristic.

Assimilation

The foregoing discussion of ethnicity points us toward a fact that has been part of a basic social problem of American society for the past 200 years. Although seldom stated explicitly, we now have seen enough to put it into words: Social heterogeneity is immigration's vexing child. Historically, assimilationists have attempted to deal with the problem by stressing the value of dominant social processes, including public schooling, in bringing diverse cultural groups together in a social unity with a shared common culture (Gordon, 1964).

Assimilation, obviously, has been more than an ideal in the United States. To trace the range of its effects is a staggering chore and is not necessary here. Suffice it to say that the achieving of civic bonding among different ethnic, religious, and racial groups has been, in this view, the main means of overcoming the limitations and fragility of social heterogeneity. This difficult and important task rests on the belief that people from widely diverse backgrounds, if given the chance to know one another in meaningful ways, will become cordial neighbors, members of the same business associations and social clubs, and perhaps even close friends; and, of course, their children would eventually intermarry. If there is a central hypothesis characteristic of the assimilationist view, it is the "contact hypothesis." In the words of Green (1966):

> The value of diversity, however, entails two further assumptions: in the first place, it means that there must be contact between the divergent groups in society, a household may be richer for including persons of different aspirations, values, dispositions, and points of view. But these differences will not be enriching to any particular individual unless he talks with, eats with, or in some way has an exchange of view with those who are different. The value of diversity implies contact between persons and not simply incidental, temporary and casual contacts. Secondly, this fundamental value implies that the diversity which is enriching is not itself endangered by the contact which is valued. The diversity must be sustained through contact. [p. 11]

But, of course, diversity *is* endangered by the contact, primarily by interracial or interfaith marriage. What happens in the latter situation? How are the children of these unions to be raised, and in whose faith? These are difficult questions, and they are not easily resolved. Most commonly, the result is a weakening of ethnic objects of allegiance, and this explains why assimilation is based on the logic of rejecting social heterogeneity. The worlds of cultural unity and cultural diversity exclude one another. Assimilated individuals are endowed with an ethic and set of values that clearly and massively make them citizens of the nation-society, but the process exacts the price of obligating them to renounce their heritage. This logic, without a doubt, continues to be, for many Americans, a desired, effective way of dealing with the vexing problem of social heterogeneity and social order.

PLURALISM

The search for a better resolution of this problem—which raised the specter of national disunity and cultural instability, from the traditional assimilation perspective—led enterprising thinkers into the complex developments of social heterogeneity. A popular answer to the traditional problem of *E Pluribus Unum* was pluralism, but especially cultural pluralism. This conception of the social order judged assimilation as ignoring the degree to which its processes are relations of domination and subordination. That is, while it may be true that decisions made in the context of an assimilationist polity carry an aura of indelible pragmatic necessity, they also involve substantial commitments to the dominant group's values over those of all others, which pluralism sees as unjustifiable, even in the name of unity.

In the American model of political pluralism, originated by James Madison and extolled in our time by Dahl (1956) and others, social groups are seen to have a distinctly political role. The civic culture rests on the many interest groups that serve as guardians of the welfare of their constituencies. The essential point is that individuals perceive their own best interests, organize around that interest, and voice their desires through voluntary associations, ready to do battle with other individuals similarly organized, in order to gain the goods and services of society (Connolly, 1971). The pluralist, in other words, observes the web of social diversity, the balancing of interest-group pressure at work, and concludes that this is democracy at its finest. In the multiplicity of associations and the diffusion of power, democracy is judged to be alive, safe, and well.

This is the preamble of democratic pluralism, but it is woefully incomplete. The history of American society strongly suggests the fact of social heterogeneity, that great multiplicity of human associations sometimes referred to as "cultural diversity," developed and was nurtured under a wide range of changing empirical conditions, acting in countless ways to forge a nation-society, a political unit, a politically organized society over a territorial area. Formal and informal rules, moral agreements, and a legal system coalesced in regulating this vast and complex social process.

I have argued that an inescapable aspect of any political system is the problem of order or control. In democratic pluralism, the nation-society's compact among citizens—which includes the formal and informal rules, the moral agreements, and the legal system—is formed by conceptions of justice and morality that spring from citizens' perceived self-interest and is expressed in partisan group interest. To be accepted as rightful and legitimate, the nation-society must allow partisan group interests to dominate human action in every sphere. Order and control are exercised through a netlike system of organization, and not only do individuals circulate among its threads, but so do groups.

The point is, then, if we are interested in gaining a deeper understanding of the relationship of social heterogeneity to social order and of what this means for civic education, we must answer the question raised by pluralism: What kind of organization of collectivities will best fulfill the functions of a democratic state?

Cultural pluralists, like political pluralists, reject assimilation by encouraging diverse ethnic groups to display their differences proudly. The logic is not that social heterogeneity will disappear or become invisible, but rather that diversity will evolve into new cultural forms expressly enriching the society. This logic further assumes that a civic accommodation among diverse cultural groups is basic to society's well-being, since a multitude of such interdependent groups, working together, is the very basis of human survival. The test and measure of this is the realization of fellowship in the groups themselves, in the struggle for a more exclusive community.

The political and cultural pluralist tradition contains disagreement and ambiguity, but the direction of its social goal is clear: human dignity, community, and social justice in a socially heterogeneous society. If we have chosen to invite vast hordes of immigrants to our shores, then we absolutely must have the means and the will necessary for articulating their well-being, as individuals and as groups. The common foundation is that concern, caring, and tolerance for others entail honoring and respecting a plurality of values and traditions in American society. The great democratic challenge is to build as many safeguards, both formal and informal, as are necessary to take care of the need. Hence, in this tradition, prejudice, discrimination, and bigotry are not to be tolerated, for if they are ignored or go unchecked, hostility and antagonisms in ever-widening circles will divide and weaken the civic culture beyond repair.

It is this last point that weds cultural pluralism to philosophical civic republicanism, on the one hand, and, on the other, divorces them. Both traditions value human dignity and mutual respect, and they are linked by their sense of moral urgency, holding that citizens not only owe each other dignity and respect but concern, caring, and, above all, tolerance. Moreover, both traditions agree that "somebodyness," "belongingness," face-to-face social relations, and warm and powerful family and group ties must not give way to domination by bureaucratic management and specialist expertise. In these contexts, each citizen must be allowed, even encouraged, to maintain and nurture a lifestyle that gives significance and worth to living. Each citizen, in other words, must work hard to protect and nurture diverse human associations and life as a shared tradition.

Perhaps Green (1966) captured this best when he said that

> a pluralist society is one in which a plurality of associations expressing different values and interests must be allowed to flourish; but, on the other hand, it means that individuals must have freedom to associate with such groups as they may find acceptable. . . .
>
> Pluralism as a social ideal contains, however, the further value or belief that diversity is a good thing. The view is that any society is richer if it will allow a thousand flowers to blossom. The assumption is that no man's culture or way of life is so rich that it may not be further enriched by contact with other points of view. The conviction is that diversity is enriching because no man has a monopoly on the truth about the good life. There are many ways. Diversity is further valued because it provides any society with a richer pool of leadership from which to draw in times of crisis. [p. 10]

It is clear that pluralism is an echo of philosophical civic republicanism insofar as the notion of a rough epistemological equality, so basic to philosophical civic republicanism, is no less so in pluralism. Moreover, there is a linking of the values of concern and tolerance for others, so that "different values and interests [may] be allowed to flourish." More to the point, Green's (1966) depiction of pluralism celebrates the principle of human dignity and mutual respect, qualities intrinsic to philosophical civic republicanism, since pluralism requires a certain kind of ethical relationship toward others reflective of a consensual, shared, mutually reciprocal realm. Above all, both traditions articulate an understanding that the fact of interdependency among citizens is not only a political but a moral relationship.

On the other hand, pluralism diverges from philosophical civic republicanism in that the former relentlessly struggles to restrict human dignity and mutual respect as well as the ethic of obligation primarily *to one's own group*. It is pluralism's vision of group interest and caring for one's own that is in tension with the common interest or public good espoused by philosophical civic republicanism. In the pluralist tradition, it is first and foremost the nuclear family and extended family—kith and kin—who constitute the objects of one's obligation, not a broad civic membership.

The tension between the two traditions reflects most clearly in the duties of democratic citizenship. In the pluralist view, being a good group member either takes precedence over being a good citizen or the two, group member and citizen, are conflated into one, so that the good group member is the good citizen. The chief posi-

tion of philosophical civic republicanism is that the good person is
the good citizen. Consequently, the latter view shuns a particularistic view of concern, caring, and tolerance, in favor of an ethic of
obligation extending across a wide range of people and associations. It eschews the politics of "ethnic interests," viewing them as
narrow and unjust since the public good, the display of the full ca-
pabilities of human society, is too frequently discriminated against
within the particularistic circumstances of pluralism. Decisions about
the public good must be arrived at in terms of impartial, objective,
or nonbiased decision making, with due regard to amicable agreement.

RECONCILING PLURALISM AND
PHILOSOPHICAL CIVIC REPUBLICANISM

Producing a fit between pluralism and philosophical civic republicanism in order to revitalize the civic culture is not an easy task.
Indeed, it seems to be impossible. Pluralism, fueled by the efforts
of ethnic groups, has moved the private and public sectors closer
together, brought about a new order of complexity to the governance of public affairs, and challenged our democratic infrastructure. Its threat to democracy is its admittedly powerful, private,
somehow privileged, face-to-face, informal ways of acting and their
use to establish supremacy over the more public, formal, impartial
ways of acting in the public sphere.

On the other hand, in citing this condition of a real conflict between pluralism and philosophical civic republicanism, we should
not be blinded to the fact that social heterogeneity is valued by
American men and women whom we cherish, love, and respect. But
while this is true, it is only part of the truth, because the democratic
ideal exists, and it too is valued by those we cherish, love, and respect. Thus these indelible facts of American society challenge a rational revitalization of the civic culture to take into account the two
views and seize upon the conditions that must prevail in order for
this project to be accomplished.

The common ground of philosophical civic republicanism and
pluralism, as we have seen, is their high valuing of human dignity
and mutual respect. As conceived here, a combinatorial strategy involves stressing two important implications. First, pluralists are held
together by common values or principles of human dignity and mutual respect. Thus, the two traditions are not completely inconsis-

tent insofar as both are rooted in a deep sense of mutuality and a habitual readiness to acknowledge a commitment to a community of active solidarity in which human dignity and mutual respect are fundamental expressions of trust and a part of self-worth. Awareness of the pluralist disposition to treat certain others with dignity and mutual respect can be the foundation for attacking its ideal of ethnic-group privilege and the resulting conflicts among group interests. Pluralism values the idea of a moral society as an objective reality, in essence advancing the view that members of a community are bound together by values and that these enable the community to cohere.

Second, it is both a peculiarity and a defining characteristic of pluralism that it historically has been very closely linked to both democratic ideals and the values of social heterogeneity. Although the mobilizing of pluralism in the direction of particularistic ties has helped to disassociate these, it is important to recognize that there is an inherent aspect of pluralism that values the democratic ideals of social justice, community, and fairness. This aspect clearly involves some subordination of ethnic-group association to the larger collectivity, the nation-state, in cases where the two are in actual or potential conflict. Hence the justification of ethnic-group interest as compatible with the more extensive collective interests or public good is seen. This is evidenced when city officials invite the ethnic enclaves to come out from their peripheral position in public life and to harness their neighborly solidarity to join in the larger effort of transforming the city, physically and culturally, into an expression of citizenry and fellowship. Thus ethnic-group interest and public contribution are not necessarily antithetical.

The combinatorial process addresses the problem of the relation of ethnic-group interest to collective responsibility, which is one of the basic tensions in American society. It would be a huge mistake to ignore the tension, but it also would be foolish not to capitalize on the common elements of the two traditions and seek a resolution. The culprit, in other words, is not social heterogeneity or pluralism. On the contrary, it is the lack of a vital moral compact based on dignity and mutual respect. The combinatorial process seeks to redress this problem, and therein lies the motif that inspires what is basic to both traditions. What unites these traditions is a consensus about what is constitutive of the good life. Both admit that our identities are social in character and thus require a sense of community and a minimum moral measure through which to pursue a satisfying moral life.

E PLURIBUS UNUM

The task of revitalizing the civic culture appears overwhelming. An account of *E Pluribus Unum* may shed some light on the matter. The *unum* of the new culture requires that citizens believe in the principle of human dignity and mutual respect and accept the ethic of obligation regarding others. Yet, at the same time, the fact of social heterogeneity cannot be wished away. The *pluribus* requires that citizens be allowed, even encouraged, to preserve their cultural, linguistic, and religious collectivities.

One may wish to pause a moment to consider what is being advocated here. It is obvious that many of the disputes over the nature of the civic culture today issue, at the deepest levels, from the continuing fact of social heterogeneity. There are, we are aware, numerous reasons for this: long-standing ethnic jealousies, racial prejudice, religious bigotry, discrimination, and nation-society atavisms. In any case, it is clear that, even with the best intentions on all sides, there are no instant solutions to this state of affairs.

But, going a step further, the many strengths of diversity and pluralism are matched by equally serious deficiencies, yet social heterogeneity and its problems cannot be wished away or ignored. Thus the question we must deal with is this: How can we fit all varieties of ethnic groups into a relatively coherent democratic community that serves the ends and purposes of public interest? Moreover, what sort of communal provision is appropriate in this project?

Surely there must be a fruitful way of answering these questions. Building on the combinatorial process, it may be to the point to argue, quite plausibly I believe, that citizens of a socially heterogeneous nation-society owe one another a great deal. What I mean by this can be clarified and tested by the employment of the common conditions of self-development: community, identity, privacy, and autonomy. In other words, it has been argued that these conditions are common to all human self-development, although self-development is not limited to these. Particular conditions, really moral virtues, united with the common conditions, form the self-developed, self-fulfilled person. The common conditions of self-development, *writ large*, are made applicable to a society, to any community in fact, by the particular conditions. Why is this so? A society, like the persons who comprise it, must endeavor to provide a moral basis for the relationship of mutual reciprocity between the society and its members. What is significant about this is that the

moral basis or compact legitimates all relationships, creates solidarity, and perpetuates the society. The virtue of a necessary web of
mutual reciprocity between the society and its members, including
civic obligation, is that social cohesion is accomplished through the
coordinated work of a variety of interconnected persons and groups.
This is the reality of interconnectedness or mutual dependence, the
basis of community. In other words, the necessity of mutual reciprocity between the society and its members, for coordination of
diverse persons and groups within a large-scale human network,
requires a sense of community, a sense of "belongingness," for its
members. Thus the idea of community entails the fostering of var-
ied points of view, of shared concerns, a strong reliance upon the
recognition of mutual interests, and a commitment to caring for and
tolerating others. Community, employed in this fashion, has a distinctly moral core, because it is composed of obligated members who
owe a great deal to each other.

Care must also be taken that society provide its members with
a sense of identity, of "somebodyness," which is the major status of
the human in society. Identity is not simply the result of "banding
together"; it involves a decision about what kind of person one takes
oneself to be in relation to others. The social outcome of mutual
reciprocity is social connectedness, and it involves deciding to whom
one will be obligated and why. When the principle of human dignity and mutual respect serves as the enduring object of our allegiance, then, socially, the corporate identity of the civically
concerned, caring, and tolerant citizen is formed.

What needs expression, however, is the idea that corporate
identity is connected to ends that seek to restore human dignity and
mutual respect by creating a sense of being valued by, and competent in, a social enclave. The project of forming meaningful identity must be separated, at least in part, from its strictly individual
connotations and must acknowledge the role of community as that
of breathing life into the enterprise of self-development. This may
be seen in the value attached to shared civic festivals, perform-
ances, activities, and holidays. In this sense, neighborhood block
parties, local coordination of hot meals for senior citizens and the
homeless, and a decentralization of schools sustain a corporate
identity absolutely fundamental to a revitalized civic culture.

In addition, society must provide for the protection of its citizens in terms of privacy. Human dignity and mutual respect figure
prominently here. The present century has given a peculiar turn to
contexts in which violations of privacy take place. One finds that it

is sometimes very difficult to locate blame for invasions of privacy. Upon inspection, the loss of privacy is brought about by the spread of sophisticated information technology which finds no person able or willing to say, "I did this (horrible) thing to you. I knew what I was doing, and I will accept the consequences of invading your privacy."

Patently, most of us have had experience of this kind, and not always on a trivial level. Because of a mistake in bureaucratic paperwork, a document we regard as private, very personal, becomes public; in another instance, our home address is sold for profit to direct-mail companies. An error in a computerized bank statement or credit card account is widely circulated to credit investigators. The protection of privacy is essential because its loss makes citizens vulnerable, creates a loss of respect and esteem, threatens their identities, and gives rise to distortions within the community that make citizens feel mistreated, like victims. Clearly a primary value of any society is that it provides an element of restraint on the invasion of privacy. Otherwise, the very notions of dignity and worth, mutual respect, and community begin to dissolve.

Finally, a sense of autonomy is a value and clearly worthy of respect. But this notion should be treated cautiously because it does have its limits, in that autonomy does seem to require restrictions when weighed against other considerations. For instance, community, for the unrestrictedly autonomous, is a bargain struck on the grounds of collaborative noninterference rather than of mutual reciprocity. Autonomy, as conceived within the framework of a moral compact, is achieved in the recognition of a healthy dependence on one another, is tempered by a strong sense of interconnectedness, and is expressed primarily in terms of autonomous decisions made for the public good.

Returning to *E Pluribus Unum,* and more specifically to the problem of "the one and the many," we can now say a revitalized civic culture must bind self-interest, group interest, and the public good. This is to be done through a new ordering of the ecology of social relationships, one that creates a moral civic community based on dignity, mutual respect, trust, and friendship and embraces an ethic of obligation to others. Hence, the civic community's political activity will be rooted in a moral compact whereby a citizen's conception of self-interest and an ethnic enclave's conception of itself as a social entity are shaped into forms that are respectful, nurturing, caring, and tolerant of all others.

IMPLICATIONS FOR CIVIC EDUCATION

In an attempt to state the role of the school, and particularly of civic education, in bringing about a new ecology of social relationships, we commence with the fact that the individuals who at any given time constitute the larger collectivity, the nation-society, are held together (1) by formal rules and informal values governing social and political association and (2) because of the fact of mutual interdependence, by a relationship of mutual reciprocity between the society and its members, a reciprocity that is the mechanism of the society's perpetuation.

What unites the community is the practice of social obligation, which gives precedence to the interest of the larger whole over one's personal self-interest. This sets down the patterns of responsibility, which in turn perpetuate the community. The practice of social obligation, in other words, creates the informal patterns of responsibility that allow t.\e process of self-integration into the community to be achieved. Sel\-integration fulfills the need of the human self for a life of inclusion in a community that celebrates human dignity and mutual respect. Once achieved, self-integration promotes a sense of solidarity with the society, a solidarity that sustains the individual in the nation-society.

Arendt (1958) looked for the foundation of this process, and she found it in the capability of responsible citizens to make and to keep promises: "We mentioned before the power generated when people gather together and 'act in concert,' which disappears the moment they depart. The force that keeps them together . . . is the force of mutual promise or contract" (p. 244). She regards as the basis of community and political legitimization the moral contract between free and equal parties, by which they place themselves under mutual obligation.

In less formal terms, we know that a nation-society may be held together, in the words of Dewey (1927), as "a community of interest" (p. 39). This happy circumstance occurs when "those indirectly and seriously affected for good or evil by the actions of others form a group distinctive enough to require recognition and a name" (p. 35). The name he selected, it will be recalled, is the public.

This brief reentry into the thoughts of Dewey is aimed at offering a foundation for a civic education that will integrate pluralism with philosophical civic republicanism, in order to achieve a revitalized civic culture. The basis for this project is Dewey's "community of interest." The strength of the proposal is found in the premises of philosophic civic republicanism and pluralism: the value of human association based on the principle of human dignity and mutual respect as well as an ethic of obligation to serve others.

Dewey used the term *community* to fuse the notions of individual self-development and public contribution. He saw that participatory democracy requires a citizen's identification with community. This means a balanced concern for self and others in the pursuit of common interests, as in the case of local communities working to achieve a more healthy environment, to protect their citizens, and to care for the homeless and disadvantaged. "The Great Community," Dewey (1927) said, "in the sense of free and full intercommunication is conceivable. But it can never possess all the qualities which make a local community. It will do its final work in ordering the relations and enriching the experience of local association" (p. 184).

This is a powerful idea. Taken seriously, it suggests that a community of interest is necessarily a local community or, at least, is characterized by the face-to-face relations of primary associations. Dewey realized, of course, that it is impossible to maintain the viability of local values as enduring objects of allegiance in the face of an expanded corporate-bureaucratic society dominated by formal social relationships. He did, however, see people coming together over perceived mutual interests, and he saw how they might be organized for effective pursuit and control of these.

A reconstructed civic education should take note of Dewey's conclusion that human collectivities share more than their "humanness." Educators must understand that identities are social in character and thus require a sense of community in which to pursue a meaningful, satisfying life. Students should participate in practices and rituals—moral, aesthetic, and pragmatic—that define them and their associations.

Equally important, Dewey realized that many citizens deny these requirements; thus he described the United States as only a "Great Society," rather than a "Great Community," because the various human collectivities had consistently been unable or unwilling to develop the conditions of practice, particularly the moral decency and compassion, required to perceive and meaningfully deal with common concerns and interests (Dewey, 1927).

What this view suggests for civic education is that citizens may associate and interact for many reasons, not the least of which is ethnic membership. It also is the case that ethnic collectivities may tightly regulate and censor the pursuit of a larger sense of community—the public good—by wittingly or unwittingly sponsoring narrow, selfish, privatized action in public affairs. Moreover, ethnic collectivities may abet antidemocratic prejudices and atavistic hatreds. Where they usually fail, in a Deweyan sense, is in bridging the gap between narrow group interest and broad public interest. This results from the tendency of ethnic collectivities to deny what has been called "consociational democracy"—the ability to function reasonably and harmoniously in a civic culture in spite of deep communal divisions, especially those of language, race, and religion (Canovan, 1981). This condition lends an extra urgency to civic education.

In a reconstructed civic education, group interests are only the starting points for dealing with a perceived public issue. What is desirable or what should be desirable may in fact not be admitted as a mutual concern by ethnic collectivities out to protect their special interests regardless of the broad social consequences of their acts, that is, without regard for the public good. Dewey asks us, in effect, to be prepared to work and reason together, to participate in the practices of obligation we owe each other and create a "Great Community." In a word, we must grasp the truth that individual and group interest, moral decency, and public contribution are inextricably bound up together in a democracy.

Care must be exercised, however, not to draw absurd conclusions from this account. There is, for instance, a tendency to think that it is a highly romanticized view, not realistic or tough-minded enough for a reconstructed civic education. But this is not the case. There are deep historical roots for this account, mirrored in large part in the example of Switzerland. Without a doubt, Switzerland is the prime case of "consociational democracy." The 6 million Swiss are culturally diverse, divided between two historically opposed religions (Catholic and Protestant) and four different language groups (Swiss-German, French, Italian, and Romansch). Yet it combines democracy and social heterogeneity by a system of governance that leaves the local political communities (cantons and communes), very considerable autonomy. More significantly, the political culture embraces amicable agreement rather than a legally unrestricted majority rule. It is presumed that all interests should be taken into account and compromises reached that are acceptable to all concerned.

By far and away the most interesting illustration of the possibility for a kind of cooperation that requires neither the philosophical liberal's formula for making and enforcing contracts nor Green's

(1966) self-sacrificing altruism is in the work of Axelrod (1984). What he examines is a hypothetical game situation called *The Prisoners' Dilemma*. In this situation, two criminals are arrested for a crime that they have in fact jointly committed. They are kept in separate rooms and brought before the prosecuting attorney individually. They are urged to confess, but if neither talks nor implicates the other, then neither will be convicted or incarcerated. This is winning through *cooperation*, and in Axelrod's game a score of three is given to each player who cooperates. If, on the other hand, each confesses and implicates the other, each is punished by a score of one. If one criminal confesses, implicating the other, whereas the other criminal does neither, then the latter scores zero whereas the former scores five. The aim of the game is to develop a strategy that enables a player to score high over a series of several games, when the score for each game is revealed to both players only at the end, and neither is ever able to communicate with the other.

Within the usual boundaries of game theory, desertion is the rational, dominant, and maximum strategy for each individual. Self-interest, in other words, is best served by deserting rather than co-operating with others. However, if a cooperative strategy could be shown to be rational, then this would point to a way out of the self-interest box and toward the development of a moral compact as suggested by philosophical civic republicanism. The stipulation of playing the game over a long series is important, because in every-day life we cannot successfully continue to lie about our intentions; that is, double-crossing is not a viable social strategy because we must play again. Our failure to cooperate may bring retaliation and injure our long-run interests.

Now, game-theory constructions are abstractions from the real decisions that face citizens, but as this game shows, they can model certain social relations. In this regard, Axelrod (1984) asked various theoreticians how they would, over a long series, play *The Prisoners' Dilemma*. Anatol Rapoport, a Canadian psychologist, won out against all other theoreticians with his submission, called "Tit for Tat." Rapoport's scheme begins on the first round by both players coop-erating, that is, by neither player confessing nor implicating the other. After that, player A always does what player B did in the pre-vious round. If player B cooperated on the previous round, player A cooperates. If player B defected, player A punishes the other by de-fecting on the next round, but only the next round, and so on.

What is illuminating about the "Tit for Tat" strategy is, as Ax-elrod (1984) put it, it is always "nice" or "optimistic." It never defects first, preferring to assume good intentions until proved wrong. Second, it is retaliatory; it does not ignore betrayals, but retaliates or brings injury immediately. Third, although retaliatory, it is not spiteful. It extracts only an equal amount of vengeance for each betrayal.

This cooperative and optimistic strategy, neither spiteful nor exploitative, might be called mutual trust or moral decency. In analyzing lengthy computer tournaments, Axelrod (1984) quickly established two strategies or categories. The first he called "nice"—the moves that assumed good will on the part of the other player and did not defect first. The second was called "not nice" and was generally built around the moves of not cooperating, trying to defect or betray the other player. On Axelrod's analysis, the first strategy always did better. The "nice" strategies, with only one exception, were all located at the top, while the "not-nice" ones were bunched at the bottom. Moreover, when played over a long time sequence, the "not-nice" strategies eventually faded into disuse or extinction, while the "nice" strategies all survived.

This analysis also revealed something else. Axelrod (1984) and his students reported that they were strongly tempted to behave as if *The Prisoners' Dilemma* were a zero-sum competitive game, which it was in fact deliberately designed not to be. That is to say, the players were strongly tempted to assume that, in order to do better for themselves, they had to do better than the other person, so any gain by one player had to be at the other player's expense. But, of course, if they succumbed to a defection strategy, then their defection provoked counter-defections, and so both players, until and unless this defecting strategy was reversed, proceeded to do progressively worse. Axelrod draws the moral that in *The Prisoners' Dilemma* the first rule is to eschew a zero-sum position; competition is destructive. Even in game series in which the players started noncooperatively, it was possible on repeated trials for mutual trust to develop and for players to break out of the prisoner's trap.

The important moral for our purposes is that human association does not necessarily entail a zero-sum game of ruthlessly exploiting every advantage one has, to the detriment of others. Nor is it a totally self-sacrificing or other-regarding situation where one would rather spend a year behind bars with another than be free while the other is in jail. Rather, each individual makes herself better off through the willingness to cooperate in an exchange (for example, price collusion among would-be competitors). Thus individual self-fulfillment and relations of trust, friendship, and solidarity are not antithetical. But note the major point of significance: It is not necessary or fruitful to abandon the notion of self-interest. Rather, this game clearly shows that individuals see the advantages of cooperation in repeated playings and adopt an other-regarding view. If we are all incorrigible philosophical liberals, then we are doomed to use defecting strategies. If we are philosophical civic republicans, a cooperative outcome is dictated. And if we assume a moral compact among citizens, then we will choose to cooperate in the safe expectation that others will, too, since it will be in everyone's interest to do so. Compulsory cooperation is not necessary. What is challenged is not the assumption of social cooperation, but the assumption of a self-interested, competitive, individualistic person and society.

The strengths of the Swiss and *The Prisoners' Dilemma* cases have the combined result of suggesting for civic education that its indispensable first effort is that of promoting citizen self-integration into the community, based on a moral compact of cooperation, mutual trust, and being morally decent. Recent developments such as movements for police review boards, consumer protection, Mothers Against Drunk Driving (MADD), and Students Against Drunk Driving (SADD), along with an increased desire on the part of citizens to support the imperative of a public good, suggest a cooperative basis for a revitalized civic education.

This lesson should not be lost on those who teach civic education. Civic educators, and by this I mean all teachers, must take the naturally rewarding relationship between self-fulfillment and cooperation into consideration as they teach students and future teachers and as they carefully examine their own civic consciences. This issue, as I have argued throughout, becomes critical because of the intended and unintended stress on competition, self-interest, and self-reliance so commonly found in school. Teachers must, in countless classroom moments, present and nurture the view that a concern for self and a concern for others can be delicately balanced in the pursuit of the good life, in the pursuit of moral decency.

The first effort of civic education further demands the creation of public sphere opportunities for the many different publics, including ethnic collectivities, to come together for a free circulation of ideas, evidence, and argument. Through such activities, these publics can come to see that ethnic insularity exemplifies the inherent contradictoriness of pluralism; that is, they will discover that, despite their often daily efforts to deal successfully with the broad range of social structures and interdependent relationships of everyday life, they will be frustrated as long as they insist on finding their true selves independent of any consideration of a wise, interconnected common or public good. It is this stubborn insularity that is so at odds with today's interdependent reality.

The lesson for civic education, I believe, is evident. The public good of the nation-society must be shaped and nurtured, for it is the means through which citizens can be brought to participate in civic affairs and national ceremony. In theory and in practice the dictates of government are enforced by the sanctions of individuals and groups. It is a hallmark of democracy that individuals and groups effectuate the policies they determine. Where individuals and groups understand and accept this role, their civic performance will be all the stronger. Citizens, in short, act for the nation-society in response to the community with which they identify themselves. Hence, the community can serve as the fulcrum of national endeavor. While repudiating the notion that individuals should, out of loyalty, support a public good that has little or no meaning to them, mutuality, solidarity, friendship, decency, trust, and so on supply the guts of national purpose or the public good. The merger of individual or self-interest with group or civic interest is a means of both combatting chauvinistic patriotism and assuring that loyalty to the nation-state is never a mere symbol, but is quite real and heartfelt.

Yet there is no real beginning until the question of how, the means, is looked straight in the eye. If one takes this point seriously, then we must deal in the concrete. To illustrate what is needed, Table 5.1 provides five areas of community concern, along with specific topics that relate to each area. I do not wish to suggest that the problem areas be taught as units; they are provided as illustrations of categories that all teachers, regardless of subject-matter specialty, could deal with. Generally speaking, discussion of these topics should be designed to help teachers and students, kindergarten through the twelfth grade, to develop a civic disposition, a readiness for practices of commitment and a generosity of spirit, which perpetuate a "community of interest" in the pursuit of the public good.

A careful consideration of the Table 5.1 topics in all classrooms should impact on the practice of civic education, not as an additional competing subject in schools, but as appropriate to the education of all students in all classrooms, whatever the subject. The discussions and projects should be undertaken in a way that focuses on what might be called the foundation for democracy, in-

Table 5.1 Topics for Civic Education

AREAS OF CONCERN/Topics	Goals
CULTURAL DIVERSITY	
Religion and education	Respect for cultural diversity
Immigration policies	Freedom from racism, sexism, and
Aliens and citizenship	other forms of discrimination
Religious property and taxation	Civic tolerance for others
Equality of educational opportunity	Acceptance, caring, and concern
Minority beliefs and values	for others
Cultural relativism	
Ethnicity and subcollectivities	
Membership needs	
Need and merit	
Family and kinship	
Honors and awards	
COMMUNITY	
The poor	Generosity of spirit
The disadvantaged	Doing what is needed as defined by a
The handicapped	civic conscience in accord with self-
Community spirit and welfare	chosen democratic moral principles
Peace and order	Amicable agreement
Privacy and association	
Personal and public identity	
Crime and delinquency	
Law and order	
Cooperation and competition	
Fraternity and trust	
Friendship and solidarity	
Neutrality	
Recognition and honors	
RIGHTS	
Rights of the majority	Knowledge about rights, duties, and
Rights of minorities	obligations
Rights of minority political parties	Knowledge and skills to identify where
Private vs. public interests	and when to go for citizen and consumer
Due process	protection
National security	
Contract rights and obligations	
Censorship	
Education as a right	
Citizenship	
Public honor and desert	
ECONOMICS	
Organized labor	Ability to protect one's interests,
Corporate-bureaucratic society	self-esteem, and career
Monopoly and cartels	Knowledge as a consumer in estab-
Conservation of natural resources	lishing the value of a product or
Social Security and old age	service
Job and income benefits	
Technology and mass media	
Income and status	
Distributive justice	
Commodities and use	
Work and leisure	
Property and power	
Occupations and professions	

Table 5.1, *continued*

AREAS OF CONCERN/Topics	Goals

FREEDOM

Equal protection before the law	Mastery of intellectual tools for
Standards of freedom in other countries	resolving conflicts involving freedom
U.S. Constitution and other	Intellectual eagerness to defend
"American Creed" documents	freedom
Authority, power, and consent	Willingness to protect the freedom
Academic freedom	of others
Bill of Rights as freedoms	Skills of communication and consider-
Hierarchies and caste systems	ation of mutual interest
Sovereignty	
Paternalism and its limits	
Military conscription and protest	

cluding democracy in learning, namely, the principle of human dignity and mutual respect, and the ethic of obligation. The program should include teaching a historical perspective and the basic social-action skills of debate, negotiation, and compromise. In addition, it should teach the questioning and negating of stereotypes of human characteristics, lifestyles, occupations, status, gender, or one's particular culture. (Recall the goals of civic education given in chapter 1.) Of course, the main purpose here is not merely to denounce such stereotypes, but to help students see stereotyping is never justified because it denies a "generosity of spirit" among citizens and weakens self-integration into the community.

Teachers must take the responsibility of selecting content not only from the suggestions in Table 5.1 but also from a rich and wide variety of resources available in the classroom and in the community. The civic education curriculum should start with the problems and needs of students. Teachers must recognize that the world of students' feelings and ideas, of what is happening to them in life outside the school, moves much more quickly than the slowly developing pace of classrooms.

A revitalized civic education may seem so long overdue that the time needed for its proper development and implementation can barely be afforded, but a well-thought-out overall strategy is nevertheless required. Civic education curricula based on a high regard for democracy reconstruct classroom life as an arena for a new form of community infused with generosity of spirit. It eschews individualistic and competitive approaches to learning, in favor of cooperative projects involving teachers and students working collectively, both in terms of their production and in terms of their evaluation. This means that students learn within an ethical framework of concern for self and a concern for others, balanced in the pursuit of moral/civic decency.

Giving students the opportunity to practice generosity of spirit in civic matters means that classroom emphasis must be of the order that discussion of the subject includes a free consideration of reasonable alternatives, rather than an attempt to structure the one "best" solution. Thus a discussion of military conscription and draft protest would necessarily consider the conflicting values of human dignity, freedom, and national security as students reflect upon the role of the individual and of law and security in a nation-society. They would need to explore the requirements and limits of national defense, the need to accommodate conscientious objection, and the role of political dissent as basic in dealing with often conflicting courses of action that might be deemed appropriate to a particular situation.

These prescriptions are neither rare nor of small consequence. As Torney-Purta (1983) reports,

> a close connection [exists] between the content of civic values (freedom, toleration, fairness, respect for truth, and respect for reasoning) and the process by which the teacher helps students to see things from the point of view of others, to be critical about sources of political information, and to recognize political dimensions in school and on the job. . . . In schools where [such a] program has been successful, it can largely be attributed to the training of teachers to create a classroom climate in which the content and process of civic values are congruent. [p. 32]

The significance of these points is that teachers must not disconfirm the civic virtues by permitting a classroom climate and practice that deny the grounds on which these virtues stand. These points can be clearly illuminated by a single example. Durkheim (1904/1961) said that the first step in moral education is discipline, the setting of boundaries, the bringing of order to the child's behavior. Teachers can, if they think about it, make a living connection between classroom discipline and the principle of human dignity and mutual respect. The problem of classroom discipline should not be approached as strictly a managerial problem, namely, how to control a class so as to teach history , mathematics, or English effectively to all students present. Rather, it could be approached through the notion of respect for persons. This value, albeit a rather abstract principle for most children and youth, can be grasped by students in terms of the intimate relationship of rules and discipline. If rules must be established in the classroom, they can be discussed and students helped to understand their need and justification. Most important, however, the rules must be enforced with the highest regard for human dignity and respect for persons. A disciplining action must be conducted with an appropriate sense of the student's moral significance, that is, with due regard for the student's best interests and rights, subsumed within the obligations due to the community of students. Without much difficulty, students will come to understand the connection between establishing rules they can respect and administering the rules with a proper consideration of human dignity and respect for persons.

What this example shows is that a teacher can justifiably discipline a student for an infraction of a rule, but it is morally necessary and prior to other concerns that the teacher and students engage in a general discussion of why rules are needed, how they are justified, and how they are applied. Teacher and students, then, might regard the rules as legitimate moral obligations, and compliance with them as "practices of commitment." In this way they set down the patterns of responsibility that create the "classroom community," which allows the process of self-integration into the classroom community to be articulated.

Thus civic education is, among other things, an education in moral formation. It means a great deal to the purposes of civic education whether students comply with rules for moral reasons, from a sense of moral obligation, or for nonmoral reasons, out of mere compliance with rules as rules, with no consideration of their moral legitimacy. Creating a moral classroom community requires that teacher and students achieve a sense of their mutality and interdependence, publicizing morality in their participation in the practices and rituals that define their group.

CONCLUSION

In this chapter I have advanced the thesis that a revitalizing of the civic culture must take into consideration the fact of social heterogeneity, but not be limited by it. We began with the question of whether, in order to act as good citizens, it is necessary for individuals to avoid isolation as members of human collectivities generally considered private and informal. It was argued that the common result of such isolation, the domination of the public sphere by ethnic collectivities, misses what seems to be most needed today, namely, a revitalized civic culture based on a vision of the public good.

Pluralism, social heterogeneity's vexing offspring, is a form of social thought that takes the pursuit of the good life to be a matter of maximizing group interest, particularly ethnic-group interest, in the public sphere. It is in the context of ethnic collectivities that meaningfulness in life is discovered. Individuals discover who they are in terms of informal, face-to-face, relations with kith and kin; and they achieve a sense of self-esteem ("somebodyness") in so doing.

The long-standing ideal of *E Pluribus Unum* was examined, and it was shown that American society has suffered from the lack of a morally developed and coherent civic culture adequate to celebrating social heterogeneity as well as cherishing fundamental democratic values. Historically, the impulse at work has been to view the culprit as social heterogeneity, but this is not the case. The real culprit is a lack of a vision of the public good, a lack of understanding of and commitment to the philosophical civic republican principle of human dignity and mutual respect, and the virtues of concern, caring, and tolerance for others. When ethnic collectivities systematically refuse to apply these to all citizens in the public sphere, then social heterogeneity is seen as the villain in the piece, but this is merely an illusion. The central tension is not between social heterogeneity and democracy, but between group interests and a responsibility to a larger moral/civic collectivity, embodied in the notion of a public good.

What must bind Americans together, regardless of the fact of social heterogeneity, is a civic community that is nurturing of democratic institutions. The civic community unites citizens in the realization that our identities are not merely ethnic but social in character. Understanding that fact provides the grounds for promoting the common elements of pluralism and democracy, as mirrored in the philosophical civic republican tradition. From this may emerge a truly radical separation between the informal, face-to-face ethnic collectivities, with their privatization of morality, and the moral/civic commitment of each to all that marks the public good. A failure to make this separation can have enormous and quite frightening consequences for the future.

A reconstructed civic education can give students a more explicit understanding of what human beings have in common and that the goals we seek to attain together—dignity, mutual respect, cooperation, tolerance, trust, friendship, and moral decency—are only possible through a civic culture that values these. Thus, it is in our best interest—and even our obligation—to pursue such ends, provided we take our own interest seriously.

CHAPTER 6

Civic Competence

Any contemporary attempt to revitalize the civic culture encounters two obstacles, one philosophical and one social. The philosophical obstacle derives from the way in which the traditional democratic social theory, philosophical liberalism, has become the order of the day for most of us. Moreover, philosophical liberalism's offspring, self-interest and self-reliance, appear insufficient in resolving the moral quandaries of modernity and sustaining moral commitment, a sense of community or comity. Today the private is separated from the public, self-identity from collective identity, and the concept of the good person from the good citizen.

The social obstacle derives from the network of political and economic life—the democratic civic culture—and the social structures, including intermediate associations, that nurture it. Herein work is separated from leisure, the personal from the collective, and the emotional from the intellectual. So there is a splintered notion of selfhood, a fragmenting of social life, and a lack of consensus about what is constitutive of the just society.

Although many Americans sense and acknowledge the bankruptcy of philosophical liberalism and its institutional structures, we have yet to articulate fully the idea of a revitalized civic culture constituted by a moral compact, a relationship of mutual reciprocity between the community and its members rather than of collaborative noninterference. For instance, it is recognized that much of what is thought and done within the civic culture is prompted by less than high citizenship motives, most notably an unwillingness to take ourselves seriously as principled moral agents engaged in promoting the public good. The intimate relationship of good citizenship and a moral compact between citizens has remained murky. The problem, as we have seen, has been compounded by the fact of social heterogeneity and by the fact that too few publics have ready access to the means for sustained and effective participation in the public sphere. The result is either a lack of community collaboration or, at best, a truncated sense of community.

Sullivan (1982), a theorist who would very much like to transform the civic culture, described the current situation as follows:

> As the questioning of the liberal assumptions of contemporary public policies for managing interests becomes progressively more fundamental, the self-confidence of the governing groups in America continues to weaken. The much-decried turning away from politics by many is surely related to these developments. However, the tremendous rise of interest in psychological and religious movements, the apparent national obsession with healing wounds, real or imagined, in the self are first of all social events. They undoubtedly reveal something of what the current American crisis of values is about. Instrumentalist, liberal politics is being abandoned not only because it is seen as ineffective; it is also being deserted because it is seen as corrupting and empty of a genuine sense of orientation. . . . Part of the meaning of the current American retreat to privatism is a continuing search for what counts in life, a hunger for orientation that neither the dynamics of capitalist growth nor the liberal vision of politics provides. [p. 159]

This is an important matter for a society that purports to be democratic and just. But what could be an answer to the "hunger for orientation?" Throughout this work it has been argued that the resources of philosophical civic republicanism are especially well suited to this task. Clearly, the kind of civic culture we have depends on the kind of people we are, that is, on our civic virtues or character. Good citizenship is a function of being a good person. For this reason, a reconstructed civic education is of particular import in shaping the moral character of a good person so necessary for good citizenship and for a reconstructed civic culture.

The issue of a modern democracy's need for a reconstructed civic culture has been the impetus and the challenge in this work. What is wanted, it has been argued, is to develop the conceptual means, the schooling mechanisms, for generating the viable civic education so badly needed in the American present. This project is, of necessity, a contingent process, yet it must be intelligently assessed and dealt with because the traditional definition of American citizenship has been called into question.

It is particularly important for a nation-society that purports to be democratic not to ignore this situation. As democratic citizens, we need to be concerned about the state of the civic culture, especially the question, Can we construct a morally collaborative civic culture? Unfortunately, this question is often relegated to the realm of private anxiety, as if it would be awkward or embarrassing to make it public.

ABSOLUTE AND RELATIVE CIVIC COMPETENCE

We shall begin by exploring the possibility of using the notion of competence in the activities of civic life as the basis for deciding the proper content and processes of civic education. First, however, we must come to grips with the notion of civic provision. Citizenship, we have learned, is required for a democratic society: All future citizens must be able to exercise their skills and talents in order to promote a larger good, a just society. Civic provision, then, assumes that the citizen's right to play a meaningful role in shaping society is guaranteed. Minimally, each citizen must have a civic literacy, an informed understanding of what contributes to the genuine growth of responsible community life.

We have seen that civic education should strive to provide students with an appreciation of an obligation of community membership itself as a first step in acquiring a genuinely self-chosen commitment to being a citizen. In short, civic education has the task of helping students find a path that assures their civic literacy while advancing an ethical, "other-regarding" concern, a sense of moral obligation. This attitude gives other-regarding citizens the dimensions of a life plan and disposes them for lives that are characterized by planned activity. There is, of course, no guarantee of a path to civic competence, but a democracy does demand it, at least in a majority of its citizens.

There remains the fact, not to be diminished by its obviousness, that a specialist/expert view of decision making makes a universal civic competence extremely difficult to achieve. When experts stress the "principle of complexity" in public matters, seeking to employ surveys, computer analyses of data, public opinion research, and so on, they erect a barrier against the exercise of universal civic competence. Again, this is not meant to deny the value of expert knowledge, but the office of the expert is an insolence in that it seeks to make a particular body of knowledge the exclusive condition of those who will make the political decisions. It is a clear case of domination when experts seek to isolate political decision making within the principle of complexity, where their expertise or competence is already certified and, to some degree at least, monopolized.

One remedy for conditions brought about by an artificial maintenance of the monopoly of the public sphere by "expertise" is to learn what experts know. But that course of action, although possible in principle, is inefficient and costly. For instance, if we were to try to raise the competence of all citizens in, say, science and technology, how civically invigorating would this be? First, what of the cost? It would be financially prohibitive to prepare thousands of qualified teachers whose training in science and technology would also make them very attractive to the private sector. Practically speaking, the cost of educating and keeping such a large cadre of high-caliber teachers would be staggering. Second, even if we were to achieve this advance, the literacy students achieved would inevitably become obsolete by the time they attained full voting status in society. Thus, an education in science and technology, along with a consideration of their uses and abuses, must, it would seem, be continuously supplemented by the ongoing education of adults, and this too would be no small or inexpensive undertaking. One can only insist, however, that it be done, if citizens are expected to have a civic competence in scientific and technological matters.

On another tack, although there are very good reasons for constraining the expansion and denying the monopoly of expertise in the public sphere, we do want competent people to serve us. The question is, How do we assure competent, qualified, professional service to citizens, without having the experts rule? Clearly this is a vexing question, but one that cannot be sidestepped in a democracy.

In order to answer the question, it may be useful to draw a distinction between two conceptions of competence, one *relative* and the other *absolute*. In the former case, in some civic tasks, such as paying taxes, obeying laws, and serving in the military, there appears to be a continuum of competence and little justification for drawing a line between the competent and the incompetent at any particular level or threshold of performance. In other civic tasks, there does appear to be something approaching such a division, as in being literate (in English or another language), in being able to perform jury duty, in running for public office, in applying knowledge of U.S. history and the Constitution, and so forth. While these tasks clearly involve a situation where the performance can be indefinitely improved, there is a threshold above which these differences are relatively unimportant in the functioning of civic responsibility. Additional expertise is required only by specialists of an appropriate type. Those below a certain threshold, however, are regarded as severely restricted in their civic competence.

Ideally speaking, the activities essential for civic competence would be of both types, with social convenience and the demands of democracy tending to insure that these functions are not too difficult for most adult citizens. Any society in which this was not so

would have a large number of citizens who could not make the political decisions that affected their lives; they could not, in effect,
manage the society.

The two conceptions of competence can be linked to the two
varieties of democracy—protective and participatory—discussed in
chapter 4. If we take an absolutist view of competence, where there
is a fairly clear line between competence and incompetence, then
democratic activities or functions are restricted to those who have
competence, or expertise, of the appropriate sort. By this standard
of competence, the true rulers of society ought to be the citizens most
skillful and knowledgeable about managing the economic and political systems, in order to insure against a crisis or the bringing of
the whole to a fatal collapse. Regardless of what changes occur in the
actual membership of those considered competent in the absolutist
view, there is always one group excluded from the list—the great
mass of citizens in society. Most persons, it is assumed, simply lack
the absolute competence to participate in the governance of the society. The experts rule, not because of the exigencies of political
matters, but because no one else is capable.

If, on the other hand, we take a relativist view of competence,
assuming that citizens can acquire sufficient knowledge and skill to
be competent in essential civic functions, then the gap between the
proficient experts and the supposedly benighted masses is bridged.
Moreover, the domination of the mass of relatively competent citizens by the experts in the activities of the public sphere is not warranted. From this follows the central hypothesis that a democratic
nation-state can exercise legitimate power only so long as it requires relative civic competence. A mortal danger to a democracy lies
in a form of civic education that does not prepare citizens to exercise relative civic competence. In other words, the danger is in giving all power to those who have absolute competence, with no
consideration given to the ways the masses of citizens are to exercise their relative competence.

The relativist view of competence must be placed in context,
however. It assumes that, though we may hope to bring students
eventually to a relative level of civic competence, we do not normally hope to make them competent in an absolute sense. We need,
however, to be aware of the direction in which absolute competence lies, and we need to give students an awareness of this standard, though we cannot, and need not, educate them to that point.
Further, this view assumes that, where the populace as a whole may
not be absolutely competent to deal with the sociopolitical complex-

ities of the nation-society, their relative competence, if nurtured, can hold political representatives accountable, in the sense of deferring to the ultimate decision of the electorate.

In the effort to mitigate the power of experts, the first guideline is that experts, along with office holders, are to serve citizens. Second, experts have no exclusive right in the process of public policy determination. Third, experts are not entitled to operate at citizens' expense, that is, for their own benefit. Finally, as agents of citizens, experts are to serve communal purposes; therefore, their work is subject to the review and control of the citizens of the community. In effect, experts are accountable to citizens. This suggests that changing the conception of public policy making from professional or expert management to that of relative civic competence is part of the task of civic education.

In thinking about what has gone wrong, we need to see that civic education's task is not to make all citizens competent in an absolute sense, but to make them relatively competent, so that they will be able to mark off and negotiate the boundaries of expertise in the public sphere. It must be one purpose of civic education, then, to help citizens understand that, although they must enlist the aid of experts and qualified professionals in making public policy decisions, they must resist the rule of experts as despots. How? The rule of experts must be examined, in part, as the rule of the enemy. Students should come to see the limiting consequences of expertise, to recognize and be offended by the insolence of benevolent expertise, and discuss the positive purposes of government, persistently pursuing the kind of government appropriate for a democracy.

One problem with this is that teachers and schooling are not themselves immune to seizing the monopoly of expertise, exercising it to assure themselves a privileged position, either professionally or socially. As Giroux (1986) argued, "As it stands, teachers tend to legitimate their roles as professionals through appeals to knowledge and expertise that is highly exclusionary and undemocratic. Professionalism as it is presently defined has little to do with democracy as a social movement" (p. 37).

This view might be a bit strong, but it is an easy matter to achieve the mystification of expertise. The usual procedure, whether in school, home, or community, is the settlement of issues, intellectual and moral, by appeal to the authority and expertise of the teacher, parent, or official. Obviously, dispositions formed under such conditions, where the essentials of citizenship are formed, are so inconsistent with a relative civic competence that in day-to-day political activities they may be aroused to act in antidemocratic ways for antidemocratic ends. Coercion and the suppression of civil liberties are readily undertaken in professed democratic societies when the cry is raised that "law and order" are threatened.

While it is no easy task to achieve it, we can find adequate grounds or justification for the demystification of expertise in the demand, which is characteristic of philosophical civic republicanism, that citizens, not experts, rule. In order to insure the rule of citizens, it is essential that they be prepared to share control of communal institutions, associations, and agencies vital to the well-being of the society, including the control of schools. Again, Giroux (1986) is helpful in this regard, reminding us that, "by creating active, organic links with the community, teachers can open their schools to the diverse resources offered by the community" (p. 37). In other words, making a commitment to participatory democracy the focal point of the performance of relative civic competence is only a start. It also is necessary that teachers take seriously the democratic ideal that a democracy is government of, by, and for the people. The office holders are elected to head local, state, and federal offices, but they are not the government, nor are the specialist/experts; they are only the executors of the people's government. The point of relative civic competence is to make citizens aware of this ideal's embodiment in practice and to subject office holders to the rule of citizens.

So we are led to this challenge: How shall students be prepared for relative civic competence? Knowing what one should do and acting upon one's knowledge are sometimes difficult when there are dangers to be faced or temptations to be resisted. It is important to be clear about how the standpoint of relative civic competence, which is presupposed by participatory democracy, differs from that of absolute civic competence, which is presupposed by protective democracy. Experience informs that relative civic competence cannot be promoted by merely talking about the value of human dignity and mutual respect, the ethic of obligation, and moral decency in the abstract. Nor can it be reduced to mere civic literacy, with the stress on the practice of patriotic ritual, the nuts and bolts of civic rights and duties.

In addition, the concept of relative civic competence, although notoriously difficult to pin down, must be coordinated with two conceptually distinct but related entities: civic conscience and practical reasoning skills. (These two will be discussed in more depth later.) Students must be involved in actions that promote concern and tolerance for other people. The concern I have in mind is like the attitude of parents and friends toward one another. Students will experience the feelings that accompany these actions as satisfying and very congenial to other people. Students will be presented with opportunities to act in ways that demonstrate but they also must confront the problems and conflicts that are obstacles to these goals. If students are helped to chart their paths through these obstacles and resolve conflicts intelligently, their lives will represent the work of practical reason.

The goal of civic education is the development of citizens who choose to act reasonably, intelligently, and creatively while manifesting a sense of fairness, obligation, or duty to others. There is no incompatibility between being reasonable and humane, or between possessing benevolent virtues and good judgment, but the coordination of these is absolutely necessary for good citizenship. Relative civic competence, which involves the coordination of civic conscience and practical reasoning, is a channel into which the elements of moral decency and practical reasoning skills flow.

CIVIC CONSCIENCE AND PRIVATE CONSCIENCE

Most efforts, I believe, to instill relative civic competence are successful when they embody feelings and attributes, which are at once both local and general, personally experienced and yet characteristically social. The emotional dimension is vital, for without it there would be nothing to energize moral conduct. This type of learning is usually informal and takes its character, focus, themes, or particular conditions from its societal setting, that is, from the whole lived experience of the society, including its material life, social organization, ideas, and beliefs.

On this account, if society does not admit that our identities are social in character and thus require a sense of community through which to pursue a satisfying moral life, then a mere formal knowledge of civics, no matter how well done, will probably be offset by the informal, lived experience of students. Giroux (1986) said, "To ignore such experiences is to deny the grounds on which students learn, speak, and imagine" (p. 36). He quotes Williamson as "putting this issue as well as anyone." She argues, "Walter Benjamin has said that the best ideas are no use if they do not make something useful of the person who holds them; on an even simpler level, I would add that the best ideas don't even exist if there isn't anyone to hold them" (p. 36).

Seen from this view, relative civic competence can no longer be thought of as a mere addendum, such as moral education or values clarification, to the process of learning subject matter. If the ideas of civic education are to motivate students to behave in mutually beneficial ways, then they must be accepted with justification, such justification serving to make students *want* to be good citizens, to be obliged to act in other-regarding ways.

Consequently, the fostering of relative civic competence has to be understood, at least in part, as the formation of a civic conscience. The term *conscience* has traditionally meant an inner "small voice" providing us with a sense of right and wrong, of moral obligation—an inner monitor of our actions and thoughts. It prevents the hardest and least attractive walks of life from being deserted entirely; it keeps the teacher at his desk long after students have left school; it holds the accountant to her books; the law official to the sea of paperwork; and the parent to the erring child.

A general argument that bears on the question of the place and role of civic conscience in the public sphere or commons has recently been put forth by Green (1985), in an analysis that is rich and provocative. He talks about the formation of various types of conscience. A critical feature of his account is the defense of conscience of membership as it relates to moral education:

> *A conscience formed for conduct in the skills of public life is more likely to be a conscience suited to private life than a conscience formed merely for private life is likely to be suited for public life. . . .*
> A radical reversal of practice is contained in such a thesis. It is one way of framing, in modern terms, the ancient claim that the community is prior to the individual. By stating the thesis in this way, however, I seek a modern version of that ancient claim. . . . To say that the community is prior to the individual may imply simply that although our conscience is, indeed, uniquely our own and therefore, in a sense, private, nevertheless, conscience is never formed at all except within that public. In other words, the proper unit of consideration in the conduct of moral education is not the individual, not even the individual conscience. Rather, *it is the member.* Conscience as membership is the fundamental reality that moral education must take as its object. [p. 8]

Green (1985) seems to assert, with respect to moral education, what I have argued about civic education, namely, that a civic conscience, so vital to civic competence, must involve a self-development that occurs within a membership, a community. What unites these two views is that both moral education and civic education look to a sense of solidarity within community and to an individu-

al's active identification with the community, and these help define
the good person and good citizen. As I have stated before, human
self-development and community are deeply connected. We must
remember that it is not in groups but in isolation that citizens are
most apt to be morally underdeveloped.

Green's (1985) notion of a public versus a private conscience also
suggests that, although a conscience is uniquely private and informs a particular individual, a conscience also may be formed for
participation in the public sphere. Thus a public conscience refers
to an inner voice formed for informing us as to what to do in situations having wide-ranging consequences, or what are called public
acts. Such a public conscience is general, common, communal, joint,
collective, civic, popular, open, and for all the world to know. Private conscience, on the other hand, is a voice that is confidential,
particular, intimate, privileged, not to be made public, nonpolitical,
and nonofficial.

A public conscience, according to Green (1985), involves moral
formation within community membership and is calculated to inform citizens in the public sphere. The individual's moral development and community membership are mutually reciprocal, for the
actions we take as citizens in the public sphere or commons have
enormous ramifications for ourselves and others. This suggests that
it is in the nature of civic conscience, so essential for civic competence in a democracy, that it be regulated by publicity and open-
ness. This is because civic conscience formation takes as its subject
matter questions of choice and decision having to do with some collective, common, or public interest. Politically speaking, this means
that it operates in making decisions as to what is best for the public
citizen to do, not what is good for the individual to do. The public
good cannot be served best by the inherent privileged confidentiality of private conscience. Political action most commonly involves a
considerable collectivity, and our moral principles must be applied
out in the open and, if possible, in the actual presence of other citizens.

This places the citizen inescapably in a public network of political decision making, which serves as a safeguard against secrecy,
which may be used to oppress and exclude, a confidentiality, which
may enhance various forms of social abuse. In this vein, Bok (1984)
proposes that

> secrecy . . . protects the liberty of some while impairing that of others.
> [Secrets] . . . guard intimacy and creativity, yet tend to spread and to
> invite abuse. Secrecy can enhance a sense of brotherhood, loyalty, and

> equality among insiders while kindling discrimination against out-
> siders. And in situations of moral conflict, secrecy often collides with
> a crucial requirement for justifying a choice: that the moral principles
> supporting it be capable of open statement and defense. [p. xvi]

Bok's note of caution regarding secrecy applies equally to confidentiality. There are, of course, acceptable uses of secrecy and confidentiality, especially in the matter of national security. But, as we
are well aware, in an atmosphere of international tension, the quick
assumption that more secrecy necessarily brings about more security is severely strained. The question is, in actual practice, how
much secrecy is justified? The advantages of secrecy have to be
weighed against its risks.

All societies prizing citizen participation in political matters
must nurture the exercise of civic conscience. It is indispensable in
the long run for a democratic society because, when it is exercised
in the public sphere, it establishes the public's view of what it has
a right to expect and reduces the hesitation that citizens otherwise
feel about whether or not to disclose their reasons for acting. In addition, the open exercise of civic conscience works against the inevitable tendency of governmental secrecy and confidentiality, legal
privilege, to spread and to invite abuses. It does so by providing the
justification for a widespread publicity that is more than mere public relations disclosure. As John Stuart Mill (see Bok, 1984) asked,
how, without disclosure, could citizens either check or encourage
what they were not permitted to see?

These points can be clearly illustrated in a single example. Consider the situation where a certain sect of evangelicals (Bellah et al.,
1985), composed of a dedicated and active body of religious believ-
ers with a loosely formulated set of dogmas and doctrines, feels duty-
bound, by religious conscience, to see that, through diverse methods and righteous indignation, "corrupt" public policy, including
educational policy, is changed. Moreover, they attract support from
a growing number of nonsectarian evangelicals who also do not
generally favor the same lines of action taken by policy makers of
recent years. To seek justice in a corrupt society, to remain faithful
to one's religious conscience, is not easy. Dedicated sectarian evangelicals recognize a need to plan, organize, motivate, and control.
What this recognition implies is that success can only be achieved
through a tightly knit grid of group cooperation. Thus, group action
is encouraged, along with a sense of belonging to a vital and relevant membership; and a sense of self-actuated worth derives from
both the context and the exercise of group action. To raise Green's

(1985) point once more, are these politically active people exercising a conscience that is more suited to the conduct of private life than public life? Put differently, is it necessary to mark off a separation between civic conscience and religious conscience?

At the most general level, civic conscience is properly identified with Green's (1985) public conscience, and religious conscience with Green's private conscience. Civic conscience is public insofar as it is constituted in terms of adopting moral principles embracing an obligation to something higher than one's own preferences or one's own spiritual self-fulfillment. The "something higher," it seems, is secular, in the sense of citizens seeking social arrangements that cultivate a kind of moral decency, a generosity of spirit, or concern for the public good. Civic conscience informs citizen conduct that is always general, common, communal, and secular. In short, civic conscience is an amalgamation of moral principles formed for active participation in political affairs. It is the mainspring of political action, formed for the most part under the influence of the customs of a nation-state. Its shape and nature vary from state to state, but in most cases it is designed to insure the mutual reciprocal relation of the citizen and the nation-state.

Religious conscience, on the other hand, involves a sectarian, sacerdotal, nonsecular, or worshipful set of moral principles informing conduct that is private, privileged, particular, intimate, personal, confidential, and devotional. Because religious devotion is a wholly personal matter, the "something higher" is an intimate recognition of a healthy dependence on a higher being, offering not only guidance but hope and faith in this respect. It is precisely because religious conscience connects the self to God that it sustains itself by informing the personal, the private, by specifying what is best for one to do in one's understanding and covenant with God, that is, with the meaning of one's own life, not all others' lives.

The relevant element in civic life, in political matters, is not one's relationship to God, but political justice. Citizens do not necessarily need religion, but people of religious faith need full exercise of citizenship. All citizens need the protection of those basic civil liberties, including freedom of religion, whose exercise is so fundamental for democratic living. Civic conscience, then, is fundamental for democratic citizens because it is what keeps us within the bounds of ordinance, encourages the use of pragmatics or political compromise, and promotes a civic decency.

This last point highlights the importance of Green's (1985) thesis that a civic or public conscience is more likely to serve the needs of private life than a private conscience is to serve public life. What this means is that a civic conscience has a certain *quality* and an *instrumental value* in private life that is superior to the action of private conscience in public life. Clearly, this quality of public conscience involves behaving morally toward others as a response to their basic dignity and worth. We acknowledge, in other words, our dependence on each other for the very things that we value most: human dignity and self-respect. The instrumental value of public conscience involves the recognition that behaving morally toward others enhances greater social cohesion, solidarity, and hence greater social protection than acting immorally. Both aspects seek to unite the diverse members of society into a just, equitable social order, a nation-society. The welfare of the citizen and the society are seen as symmetrical because these aspects of civic conscience will result in improved individual and group well-being. Here, precisely because citizens are encouraged to see social life as mutual and reciprocal, a just society is born. In this view, the public good cannot be far behind.

CIVIC CONSCIENCE AND NORMS

So far we have examined civic competence from the point of view of a public or civic conscience, and we have looked at how this is articulated in the public sphere. We now need to extend our inquiry by probing the connection between civic conscience and norm-governed behavior.

First, consider that values are in themselves without causal power; individuals must choose to give them effect in their lives. Ordinarily, we are helped in this by others who link action to good works, thus serving as exemplars of action and value; and by still others, if only in a secondary way, who impose the connection between action and values upon us, say, via punishment. In any case, we can isolate two aspects of the linking of civic action with norms. First, there is the willing act, the open avowal to do something because we believe it is right or correct. Second, one can act because of a fear of punishment.

In the distinction between a willing and a coerced act is found the difference between rule-following and rule-obeying behavior. The former suggests a *state of mind*, an internal condition, wherein there is a decision to accept as proper, justified, fitting, appropriate, correct, even good or right, a rule or set of rules. In other words, in this case the rule is internalized. For example, it may be argued that conformity in a community to certain modes of behavior is enormously beneficial, and these benefits are widely distributed. The self-sacrifice individuals must make in conforming to these modes of behavior is generally insignificant in comparison with these benefits. It is therefore justified or correct for us to require of one another conformity to these modes of behavior.

Rule obeying, on the other hand, is a *state of affairs*, an external imposition of rules through a use or threat of punishment by somebody in authority (Chambers, 1983; Straughan, 1982). In such a case, citizens do not see themselves as reasonably required to conform to certain modes of behavior, but obey them because they either admire the rule maker or are compelled or coerced to do so. A power/authority relationship of superordination and subordination exists with regard to the modes of behavior.

Rule obeying and rule following play different roles in developing civic conscience. Adherence to the former produces a very restricted, pre-moral type of conscience. Obeying a rule because it issues from an admired source or from fear of punishment is importantly different from following a rule because it is judged to be a good rule, a sensible rule, or a rule required for efficient and fair management (Wilson, 1977). Rule following, in other words, is suggested by the notion of justificatory reasons. Giving students the opportunity to learn rules is important, but they need to understand that rules must be justified, not merely obeyed. Civic conscience as moral formation, then, is part of a pedagogical strategy that attempts to go beyond the teacher as a respected or even admired rule giver and the student as a trusted rule obeyer. If a student obeys the teacher by refraining from talking because of wanting to please the teacher or to avoid disapproval or punishment, the student is merely obeying rules. But if the student judges that there are good and sensible reasons of a nonpersonal kind for refraining from talking—because it disturbs other students and creates a noise problem—the student is following rules for justificatory reasons.

This is, of course, not to say that all students who are honest, fair, truthful, and observant of the "no-talking" rule are so because they see the reasonableness of these requirements. Someone may be silent when asked to be because he or she believes that unsolicited talking is against God's law. All that is being suggested here is that students should be taught to seek good grounds or reasons for conforming to rules.

With this view, teachers must be willing and able to make their classrooms more responsive to the educationally moral task of helping students gradually come to feel the need for and force of justificatory reasons in shaping civic conscience, as distinct from other motivational factors, such as wanting to please the teacher. Experiencing rule formation in this may well be the chief means by which students can develop a responsible moral decency in public matters.

The connection between civic conscience and norms is also grasped in the recognition that part of what distinguishes a social group from a mere aggregation of individuals is that the behavior of a social group's members is governed by authoritative social norms. But we must carefully consider what this means. When a sociologist says that a particular community has or follows a norm—say, no children on the streets after 10:00 P.M.—what is meant is a description of the behavior of the community in that particular respect. It is a mere description of a behavior; no judgment is made by the sociologist about whether it is a good or bad norm. The sociologist, we say, is asserting an empirical claim about observed and verified social functioning in the community.

To put this a bit differently, the sociologist verifies the existence in a society of normation in terms of observing the actual practice of norm-controlled behavior. If parents are expected to keep their children off the street after 10:00 P.M., it is observed that, when a child is found on the street after 10:00 P.M., adults tell the child to go home and, commonly, the erring parent is admonished by other community members for this transgression.

Verification of norms by those who live under their sway, however, may entail an entirely different dimension. Townspeople, if asked about the norm, most likely would not talk merely about the existence of the norm, but also of its acceptance or rejection by members of the community. In other words, the townspeople believe they have a certain duty, an obligation, that places them under certain constraints about what actions must be done and classifies as morally impermissible other acts that might be done.

This, in general outline, suggests a distinction between a social norm *describing* how members of a group actually behave and a social norm *prescribing* how a group ought to or should behave. The latter sense of normation is, of course, a moral norm, really a moral rule, since it is a "should" or an "ought."

Now it may be useful to notice that in the distinction between a statement describing the existence of a social norm and a statement prescribing a moral norm is found a difference in the attitude one has toward the social norm: The former sense merely informs us about what is social practice; the latter sense informs us about the social practice as a reason for conforming to it.

Shoulds and oughts are moral rules of social, personal, or institutional practices. There is no doubt that the existence of a rule such as a curfew for children is a reason for action. One ought to keep one's child off the streets after 10:00 P.M. because *everyone else does so*. Similarly, the validity of rules of etiquette is based on the fact that they are practiced. But not all rules are of this nature. Many moral rules are claimed to be of universal validity, regardless of whether or not they are practiced. In other words, one can always say such rules ought to be practiced, whether or not they are practiced. (We have encountered this type of statement in the discussion of the principle of human dignity and mutual respect, along with the ethic of obligation.)

I believe that an important implication for civic education can be deduced from these ideas. It seems that, whenever proponents of civic education enunciate a particular conception of it, we need to notice (1) whether this is essentially a move calculated to inform us about certain social norms—practiced rules—to which we, as members of a public, ought to subscribe; or (2) whether the move reflects mandatory social norms, which are mandatory because they are morally compelling and hence valuable for all citizens. The latter is the voice of civic conscience in the philosophical civic republican view. An individual subscribes to a mandatory moral rule if and only if he believes that there is a justified reason for adhering to the norm when the conditions for application obtain and that there is a justified reason for disregarding conflicting impulses. In other words, to develop a civic conscience appropriate for a moral civic competence is to find moral rules to which individuals will give their willing assent, thus engaging in rule following, as distinct from rule obeying. Individuals who can choose where their obligations lie will gladly fulfill them in active civic service.

The task of developing a civic conscience appropriate for relative competence in a democracy is in essence to find rules of practice that students accept for justificatory reasons. These are required for social life as such. Truth telling and refraining from theft are necessary for any system of cooperation, without which there could be no social life. Even young children recognize that truth telling and refraining from theft are good; that our dependency upon each other is the basis of our self-respect, self-worth, and self-esteem. These may not at first be appreciated by the very young in terms of a justificatory form of reasoning, but it can be educationally valuable to discuss such matters with them and to administer rules of practice fairly and consistently in the classroom.

By recognizing that we are dependent upon one another and that it is natural for us to want a sense of worth or dignity, self-respect, and self-esteem, we come to understand that it is reasonable,—that is, in our self-interest—to pursue these goals. Students will thus learn that caring for and being tolerant of others is not merely a matter of giving our assent to mandatory moral norms, but of consenting to a moral compact, a generosity of spirit directed toward other people.

Furthermore, students can learn that the moral norms against murder, coercion, manipulation, intolerance, and lying are valid summaries of what is commonly demanded of us by virtue of being in contact with mutually dependent others; and that they also suggest an obligation on our part to be morally decent and civil, if we take ourselves seriously as moral agents.

Mention of moral norm acquisition involving taking ourselves seriously as moral agents is not accidental. Not only does this requirement give rise to the practices of obligation and emotional commitment that create the community, it nurtures a sense of solidarity with community, which sustains individuals as they pursue the good life. Community, in other words, involves a mutuality of dependence, communication and sharing, and facilitates a social identity based on individuals adopting an obligation to and a concern for the welfare of their neighbors, thus conferring on them all a special and desirable worth.

Giving students the opportunity to recognize and understand that the good life requires moral decency suggests that to develop relative civic competence requires the continual exercise of strategic judgment. Students must be provided genuine opportunities for the exercise of such judgment within the immediate context of their lives, as well as for critical reflection on the outcomes of such judgment. In this regard, teachers can draw from the common, day-to-day experiences of their students' lives, such as the rules made by parents regarding the times to be home for dinner and to go to bed, rules prohibiting yelling from room to room, and so forth.

As Hook (1946) argued, "This means that ultimately a democracy is committed to facing the truth about itself. Preaching and edification have their holiday uses but they do not inspire initial loyalty—only practice does—nor do they sustain loyalty against critical doubts, for they present no rational grounds" (pp. 118–119). Hook's point may be generalized to mean that the shaping of civic conscience should not focus merely on the themes of democracy and that we seek fulfillment in relationships with others. Students need a relative civic competence, which requires *practice* that unites intelligent and virtuous behavior.

CIVIC COMPETENCE AND REFLECTIVE THINKING

As has been noted throughout, students need repeated performance in order to develop a relative civic competence. If they are to achieve this, they must learn how to ask and answer questions, to inquire seriously whether proposals as to what is to be done and how to proceed are correct. What is needed is a constant companion to the moral development of citizens: an intellectual dimension that is performance oriented. The importance of the intellectual component of civic education cannot be overstated. The exercise of relative civic competence requires that citizens be earnest thinkers able to take a "hard look" at those who wield political power, and this means understanding a political action as something for which someone is accountable. In other words, citizens must know and appreciate that it is always appropriate to ask elected officials for an intelligible account of their actions. To achieve this on a wide scale is to teach students practical reasoning by inducting them into a set of intellectual tools or cognitive strategies.

Hence, it is not only the ethical virtues of moral decency which the good citizen exhibits, but a requisite amount of applied intelligence and critical judgment. In the absence of critical reflection or good judgment, civic virtues could result in citizens who are either dangerous fanatics or self-indulgent prigs. Surely a democratic nation-society that believes in the principle of human dignity and mutual respect, and that all citizens should be equally entitled to relevant concern, care, and tolerance, must have able and earnest thinkers who can examine the implications of these ideals as well as the proper methods or means for achieving them.

According to the position I have developed in this chapter, relative civic competence requires a civic conscience, a set of rationally chosen moral principles, which civic education helps students acquire and practice. Nonetheless, the best efforts of teachers and students must go beyond this stage of development, because something additional is needed to connect our actions with our morals. In other words our actions must be rationally justified. This is reflected, for example, in teaching students an appreciation of rule following rather than rule obeying, involving the exercise of moral judgment. The pay-off should be the moral enhancement of individual and collective action in the public sphere as well as emphasizing concern for the public good.

It follows, then, that a failure to consider reflective thinking indicates a substantial stumbling block to developing a civic education for relative civic competence. Indeed, the intimate relationship between civic competence and reflective thinking is so obvious that it is hard to imagine citizens exercising their civic duties in its absence. Reflective thinking, as a central element of civic competence, is socially necessary work; it needs to be taught, and that means someone must be found to do it. Traditionally, the conventional solution to this problem has been to assign the responsibility to schools.

To take for granted, as an empirical fact, that the school does indeed teach reflective thinking may be ingenuous. Teaching students to be reflective thinkers is to cultivate conceptual abilities, skills, habits, and dispositions that embody the ideal of rationality. Rationality, in turn, is to be understood as being coextensive with the relevance of reasons. In short, a reflective thinker is one who recognizes the importance and convincing force of reasons. Thus, when assessing statements, making judgments, considering explanations, and evaluating procedures and practices, the reflective thinker seeks reasons on which to base her assessment, evaluation, or judgment.

The general obligation to seek reasons compels us to recognize that we can set down some conditions for reflective thinking that will hold for the most part. Reflective thinking is, *inter alia*, principled thinking. Judging according to principle entails judging nonarbitrarily, impartially, and objectively. Logical criteria governing proper inference, as well as criteria governing the assessment of empirical evidence, are thereby relevant in this regard. Hence, the reflective thinker seeks not merely reasons to guide and control judgment, but reasons that must accord with the principles insuring proper control. Reflective thinking, therefore, must be objective, impartial, nonarbitrary, and based on evidence of an appropriate kind when properly assessed.

It is widely held that a critical thinker can assess claims and make judgments on the basis of reasons, and understands and conforms to principles governing the evaluation and force of those reasons. It goes without saying, then, that a reflective thinker knows a good deal about the nature of statements, types of statements, how they may be disputed, how reasons are assessed, what principles govern such assessment, and the justification of the principles themselves.

On first consideration, reflective thinking seems to be a great deal to expect of both teacher and student. But suppose a student masters all of this. Can we then truly say that she is a reflective thinker? The answer is an unqualified no, although such a student would be well on her way to becoming a reflective thinker. What is missing? What else must a student have besides critical thinking skills and a grasp of principles governing reasoning?

In order to be a reflective thinker, a student must have a certain disposition, what we might call a critical attitude. It is not enough for a student to be able to evaluate statements on the basis of evidence; she must be disposed to do so. There must be, in other words, an *obligation* to conform judgment to principle, not simply an ability to do so. A student who possesses a critical attitude has moral character traits as well as the skills already mentioned. Thus we can say that a critical attitude is the positive capacity for acting rationally when certain motives are apt to incline one to do otherwise. A critical attitude is not simply an ability to judge impartially, but an obligation to so judge, even when impartial judgment is not in one's self-interest. Hence, a reflective thinker is predisposed by duty to seek reasons and evidence; to demand justificatory reasons; to ponder and investigate statements.

But, it will be said, some students may not find it in their self-interest to think reflectively. Rather than cultivating the critical attitude that reflective thinking demands, some students cultivate a kind of nonreflective disposition that means leading narrow, restricted, and privatized lives ruled over by an arbitrary particularity of the moment. It is the task of the teacher to help them understand that, in making such a decision, they are, in their existential ways, creating themselves and community, for there is a crucial relationship of mutual reciprocity between the community and its members. The social and political outcomes of nonreflective citizenship are inappropriate, even disastrous, for a democratic civic culture. It is an unfortunate truism that when reflective thinking is ignored in civic action, citizens find themselves situated in a civic culture that places at risk the minimum moral measure applicable to all human beings, notably human dignity and worth, mutual respect, and social justice.

There is a clear, intuitive idea here that I seek to capture. If civic education is to have any significant effect on revitalizing the civic culture, schools have no choice but to engage students actively in reflective thinking and the forming of a critical disposition. These are essential for a democratic civic culture. For instance, with the use of reflective thinking, new civic possibilities are opened. Citizens can notice how they are behaving; they can decide to have their behavior conform to social norms or not; they can produce reasons for and against their political beliefs and critically discuss them, weighing the reasons; and so on. In short, reflective thinking and a critical disposition define the social and political roles of citizens within the civic culture, redefining and broadening the political nature of their civic tasks, which are to listen, think, and mobilize in the interest of a more just and equitable civic culture. By linking reflective thinking practice to wide social views and movements, teachers can begin to influence the nature of the civic culture. In doing so, they can provide the basis for students' engaging themselves in certain causes in the struggle for the establishment of equality, freedom, and justice.

In short, if relative civic competence is democratically reconceptualized, then reflective thinking and a critical disposition are necessary conditions, along with moral norms and their performance—moral practices of obligation—in rendering political decisions that are communitarian in the best sense of the word.

PRACTICING PERSISTENT QUESTIONING

The foregoing discussion raises the question, How well can we succeed in stimulating students to become active moral agents and reflective thinkers, exercising, in other words, a relative civic competence in the pursuit of a revitalized civic culture? The approach sketched here seems promising, but it is reasonably clear that more specifics are required. What we must do is consider a civic education that will provide the necessary skills for practicing reflective thinking and help cue or shape a critical disposition.

The first step is to introduce in the curriculum the *practice* of sincere, persistent questioning. How we understand this is extraordinarily important, because it will influence our view of relative civic competence, the place of civic education in the curriculum; the importance of civic education as opposed to teaching traditional subject matter; the flexibility we allow teachers and students in accommodating local, regional, national, and international differences; and so on. Other instances of importance might also be mentioned, but I shall merely say that, if relative civic competence is to have its due influence in determining the direction of the civic culture, then we must understand the practice of persistent questioning and its relationship to civic competence.

A second step is to recognize fully that a democracy, especially participatory democracy, is never a given; it can never be taken for granted. Hook (1946) has claimed that "a democracy is the only society which in principle believes that men [and women] can accept the truth in every realm of thought and live with it" (p. 119). What is the cost of neglecting this point? The results are cognitive and behavioral inertia and a blasé attitude, which assume that democratic institutions and practices are part of the natural order of things. But this is false, of course. Democracy is something we have to achieve. Teachers, as agents of civic education, need to mobilize student interest and participation in defining and redefining the nature and importance of democracy.

As Dewey (1966) argued, "A democracy is more than a form of government; it is primarily a mode of associated living, of conjoint communicated experience" (p. 87). Following Dewey's line of thought, Rich (1976) contended that "undemocratic societies establish barriers to the free exchange and interplay of ideas, whereas a democratic society makes provision for all members to participate and develop thinking abilities which will enable them to participate intelligently and secure changes in social life" (p. 57).

If we take these warnings seriously, it appears as if something valuable is lost whenever democracy is taken for granted, whenever we embrace the institutions of democracy without understanding how they came into being and for what reasons. Carnoy (1983) warned that democracy was not created without a struggle: "Democracy has been developed by social movements, and those intellectuals and educators who were able to implement democratic reforms in education did so in part through appeals to such movements" (pp. 401–402).

On a similar tack, something valuable is jeopardized when we come to regard the basic doctrines and institutions of democracy as unassailable, as impervious to our questioning. The point is that civic education should be defined, at least in part, by the practice of persistent questioning of the meaningfulness of democracy itself. Teachers and students must address the issues of authority, knowledge, power, equality, opportunity, freedom, and justice, among others. If they cede their responsibility in this regard, then they will fail to cultivate a relative standard of civic competence and risk instead either a subminimal standard, since informed and rational judgment would be denied students, or an absolute standard of civic competence. I believe, in other words, that there is a high cost to denying the practice of persistent questioning: The unexamined life is a less valuable life than the examined one. The sanction against denying the practice of persistent questioning is thus a value sanction. This is no trivial point.

My argument that a persistent questioning of the meaningfulness of American democracy is justified leads to another question: Under what conditions can civic education include such questioning? This query is of immense importance and deserves serious attention.

If a persistent questioning of the meaningfulness of democratic politics, of democracy itself, is to help students rethink the purposes of democracy, we must take note of certain problems or obstacles. The immediate problems are those of mystification and symbolic obfuscation, which in subtle fashion dominate our thoughts, legitimate our values, govern our decisions, and dictate our behaviors. In other words, teachers and students need to identify the subtle values and mechanisms of democratic politics so that relative civic competence may come to include the understanding of politics as a pattern-maintenance type of organization. This needs to be overcome if civic education is to be reconstructed in the interests of a revitalized civic culture.

The potential for achieving this is restricted by a devastating observation: Traditional civic education obscures rather than reveals the foundations of democratic politics. Finkelstein's (1985) writing is instructive on this issue:

> Radical critics have rejected, as incorrect and mischievous, the central intellectual assumptions on which the concept and conduct of civic education have rested. First rejected is a concept of the civic individual conceived independently of social relationships, or in light of what some might call a socially ungrounded civic vision. Second, is the traditional view that civic bonds arise not out of primary or primordial attachments and loyalties in home, church, and neighborhood, but exclusively from rationally calculated associations among aggregates of individuals, who in pursuit of self-interest, enter into exchange relationships, the better to secure social, economic, and intellectual advantage. Third, there is the view based upon an assumption that social solidarity, reciprocity, mutual aid, cooperation, and respect for human

dignity can or should emerge out of contractual relationships, or even individual moral decisions. Finally, there is an implicit definition of civic education as preparation in the art of calculating self-interest, securing exchange relationships, and understanding the processes of government, the better to contain and direct the regulatory structures through which the "Public Will" can be expressed and realized. [pp. 15–16]

Finkelstein claims, in other words, that we have based traditional civic education, unwisely and with negative effects, on the democratic theory of philosophical liberalism. The pursuit of self-interest is, in her view, a misconceived project for a democratic society and a poor basis for the framing and justification of civic education.

If Finkelstein is right, and I believe she is, then our present situation is an unhappy one. How do we demystify the above beliefs? How do we overcome the symbolic obfuscation of citizenship that has been developed along the lines of national loyalty or patriotism? How can teachers engage students in a persistent questioning of the meaningfulness of democracy itself without being accused of being "radical" teachers or, worse still, indoctrinators?

For one thing, a realistic appraisal of the problem suggests that a reconstructed civic education requires more of teachers than the skills they commonly possess. The curriculum of relative civic competence, minimally, requires practical reasoning and the skills of clarification and justification. What is problematic about the account presented herein is that teachers are woefully prepared in these areas. Teacher education programs generally do not prepare teachers to engage in reflective thinking, let alone teach the skills of reflective thinking. Also, experience informs us that teachers do not have the requisite training required to entertain normative issues seriously in a collective setting, acknowledging the legitimacy of others' views and interests, as others see them, without lapsing into either naive ethical relativism or dogmatic authoritarianism.

Furthermore, another major barrier to transforming civic education may well be that there is little agreement among educators that a curriculum of relative civic competence is necessary. In other words, no meaningful role for the bulk of teachers has been defined and implemented that includes developing a special qualification in teaching civic competence, beyond the narrow, traditional view. Teachers clearly cannot fulfill a role for which they have not been prepared.

A related area in need of demystification also exists. The merit of the view of relative civic competence presented here is found in fusing ethical norms of obligation with a reflective thinking ability and a critical disposition. By emphasizing our dependency upon each other, as we are, as the basis of our mutual respect and duty to serve others, it is argued that we are ordinary citizens, not moral saints. A nurturing, caring, and tolerant view of others, it is recognized, traditionally has been reserved for women in our society (our "moral saints"), while reflective thinking and a critical disposition traditionally have been reserved for men. In this artificial separation between the affective and cognitive domains, we catch a fleeting glimpse of the ideology of male supremacy. It prescriptively forms a restrictive culture limiting women to the expressive and nurturing roles of mother and beautifier of the home—the domain of all that is informal, flexible, warm, sympathetic, creative, and nurturing. Thus, women's "place" is a private retreat from the everyday world and the public sphere (Gilligan, 1982; Noddings, 1984; Ruddick, 1982).

Something must be made of this doctrinal bifurcation, for it is part of the politics of knowledge. Educators must, as reflective thinkers, anticipate and recognize this "illiberating" view. Martin (1981) argued that "what is needed is a *gender-sensitive* ideal, one which takes sex or gender into account when it makes a difference and ignores it when it does not. Such an ideal would be gender-just" (p. 17). We would do well to grasp that the idea of a relatively competent citizen is a worthy one for all, not to be genderized or appraised differently for males and females. Educators must reflect upon the processes and content of their teaching, in order to purge sexist ideas about the various traits and dispositions that a citizen requires, particularly the belief that reflective thinking and a critical disposition are unfeminine.

I wish to extend this point, for its implications for relative civic competence and, hence, the civic culture are profound. There was, clearly, no time in recorded history when gender discrimination in society and schools was defensible. But the demystification of this unspeakable state of affairs is further demanded by the need for a revitalized civic culture. Teachers and students should not exclude sexist beliefs, policies, and practices from the purview of persistent questioning. They furnish an almost infinite array of possibilities for pondering the meaning of collective life; for understanding theoretical power issues; for analyzing civic rights and obligations, privileges and immunities; and for giving dramatic illustrations of the denial of human worth and dignity, a lessening of self-respect and self-esteem. To ignore or refuse this challenge is to fail to tap into the habits of the heart that give relative civic competence its unique voice and the momentum for moral decency.

A reconstructed civic education requires that educators be alert to the internal stresses this doctrinal dichotomy creates. Teachers can, without a great fear of community outrage, provide *all* students with social-action skills, including those of reflective thinking, along with strong moral virtues reflecting the view that the search for the public good is a quest for moral decency. The classroom can provide a civic safeguard from the effects of gender mystification and ideological obfuscation, if well-informed teachers with strong moral convictions who have been trained in ways to take effective action—to practice commitment or obligation to others—set about to discover a sense of community.

The practice of persistent questioning, then, can give students access to an understanding of the democratic political and moral traditions that nourish and, thereby, reinforce the public good. By focusing civic education through the lens of this practice, a generalized sense of community, a thoughtful, collaborative, social, and moral endeavor can be undertaken. Let me say it as plainly as possible: Learning to question persistently the values and structures of society, both in the United States and elsewhere, can and commonly does serve as an instrument of counterpolitics. This practice will foster a critical view of, say, the media, by offering a new set of ideas and information at variance with those supplied by the dominant media. Moreover, it would aim to teach a clear understanding of business corporations as massive structures of great bureaucratic power, largely unresponsive to citizen needs and certainly not the best forums for shaping the future direction of the civic culture, civic education, and relative civic competence.

In this practice teachers and students may discover an inescapable fact in thinking about civic life; namely, that there is a relationship of mutual reciprocity between the society and its members. A confrontation with questions about our collective life engages us unalterably, both cognitively and emotionally, in a process that fuels this reciprocity—the engine of the society's perpetuation. Engaging in the practice of persistent questioning, then, involves more than gaining a great deal of knowledge, skill, and information. It promotes the development of a historical perspective which allows us to see the connections among national and international societal successes and failures, or the reasons why there are the fortunate and not-so-fortunate. Also, it necessitates the learning of social-action skills, especially reflective thinking. Finally, students will learn to pose critical questions about their own cultural conditioning (see chapter 1 in this respect).

Thus it is through the practice of persistent questioning, as the focus of civic education classroom activity, that a student may actually be transformed, exhibiting both a cognitive, reflective disposition and the emotional form of civic conscience. Why is this so? To engage in persistent questioning with someone is a moral act, because in doing so a moral dialogue is set up and is itself a moral response to the other's basic concern. It is also a means toward a satisfactory accommodation with the other, so often an effective means toward resolution of conflict. It involves an acceptance of the norm of mutual respect, the force of shared concern, a first-order caring for another, as well as an epistemological equality between the participants. In short, all the necessary ingredients are in place to help students acknowledge each other as the basis for our human dignity and self-respect.

CONCLUSION

Disputes about civic competence are, at the deepest level, interpretations of good citizenship. To argue that the public schools should be training grounds for civic participation on a relative competence standard is to argue that civic participation must transcend the mere plebiscitary function of civism. Teachers and students must be free to examine and persistently question the meaningfulness of democracy itself, and in the process resist the demand to reduce civic education to mere civic literacy or drill in patriotic values.

There is no reason why we cannot ask those who work in schools to operate in this way, under the tension of the principle of vigilance and the fostering of a relative civic competence. Whether this approach will be successful is not predetermined, but civic competence will be strengthened and, inevitably, so too will the civic culture. This is no small task, but it is one of the things members of a democratic society, especially those entrusted with the education of the young, owe to one another.

Epilogue

Moral habits, induced by public practices, are far quicker in making their way into men's private lives, than the failings and faults of individuals are in infecting the city at large.

Plutarch's Lives
"Lysander," Section 17

In this work I have pointed out that the present condition of modern society makes it clear that, if we are to do more than merely survive, if we hope to prosper, the civic culture must be revitalized. There is, in other words, a civic imperative today which can no longer be ignored. I have argued the thesis that the democratic social theory called philosophical liberalism is outdated and its present deficiencies are attributable to inherent moral defects in its tenets and principles, its moral base. Without sentimentality, it is a social philosophy currently "running on empty." As a first step in revitalizing the civic culture, philosophical civic republicanism must be considered. We have now to adopt a moral compact composed of the principle of human dignity and mutual respect, the ethic of obligation, and civic moral virtues. These are needed to set a minimum moral measure or framework for uniting the interests of individuals *qua* individuals and individuals *qua* members of society. The moral compact serves to help us discover a way of living well and on behalf of others and also serves as the criterion for understanding both the significance and the limitations of the public good.

One thesis of this work is that the requirement of the minimum moral measure must be adopted in formal education, uniting subject matter and an ethic of civic service. Educators should understand that the possession of civic virtues is not enough by itself. In the absence of good judgment characterized by impartiality, nonarbitrariness, and objectivity, the civic virtues or character traits may constitute a person who would be, at best, an irritating prig and, at worst, a dangerous fanatic.

It is in the school that students can develop a disposition toward community service, of social habits of willing action beneficial to others ("habits of the heart"). This disposition is the mark of the good person, and the relation between being a good person and a good citizen is a pattern established in the weave of our life, in the ample space of community and school. It is the thesis of inseparability: The good person is a person of good civic character, a good citizen. Any sort of concern for a revitalized civic culture or for the public good is *prima facie* a candidate for reflection on this thesis. If the thesis is correct, then the behavior of a good person is apt to be neither different from nor preferable to the behavior of a good citizen.

An ethic of civic service has been proposed as a necessary practice of civic education, in order to bring out the role of morality in the life of a human community. One becomes a moral agent in the course of growing up and becoming a member of a community. Whatever one does, one learns that there are in human relations obligations to others; there are some things we must do, irrespective of inclination or self-interest, having to do with living together and bettering the lives of all. An ethic of civic service, most notably community service, calls for students to take actions in the service of others which exemplify the virtues of friendship, trust, mutual respect, concern, caring, and tolerance for others. Community service is life in earnest, engaging students in the formation of social habits of willing action beneficial to all. To be a good citizen is to pursue self-interest in ways compatible with enriching and edifying community life. Personal self-interest is adapted to, and not pursued at the expense of, the community's purpose.

Recommendations for action presented in this work entail practicing their commitment to the principle of human dignity and the civic virtues. There must be morality wherever there is social life. Moreover, we know that social life is necessarily carried on in communities, and certain moral principles are necessary if there is to be any social life at all, any community existence. Becoming a moral agent, a good person, involves the capacity to be a follower of rules and to act upon principles, as well as the disposition to feel and think in appropriate ways. What these are depends upon the character of the community's way of life. It has been shown that in a democracy there are certain obligations people are under by virtue of being democratic citizens. This is a general institutional fact of massive inescapability.

There is, in other words, no valid reason for being puzzled about what a democracy requires of its citizens. If we wish to revitalize the civic culture, then the strategy needed is a sweeping revision of democratic social theory, a shift from philosophical liberalism to philosophical civic republicanism. This shift is absolutely essential in order to have supportive, morally justified communities, and thus necessary for the sort of life we regard as characteristically democratic.

To illuminate both the significance of the idea of the good person as good citizen and the obstacles to cultivating this sort of citizen has been the aim of this book. We must be aware that to try to make civic education carry more weight than it can bear is a mistake. There is no doubt, however, that to deny that it can carry any weight at all, to dismiss it, is also a mistake. If educators and parents are sufficiently conscientious about this point, then everyone should benefit from an unmistakably better world. In writing this book, I hope to have given meaning and believability to a much-needed project of human enlightenment and emancipation.

References

Adelson, J., & O'Neill, R. (1966). The growth of political ideas in adolescence. *Journal of Personality and Social Psychology, 4,* 295–306.

Arendt, H. (1958). *The human condition.* Chicago: University of Chicago Press.

Arendt, H. (1963). *On revolution.* New York: Viking Press.

Arendt, H. (1986). Communicative power. In S. Lukes (Ed.), *Power* (pp. 75–93). New York: New York University Press.

Axelrod, R. (1984). *The evolution of cooperation.* New York: Basic Books.

Bachrach, P. (1967). *The theory of democratic elitism: A critique.* Boston: Little, Brown.

Bastian, A., Fruchter, N., Gittell, M., Greer, C., & Haskings, K. (1985). *Choosing equality: The case for democratic schooling.* Philadelphia: Temple University Press.

Bellah, R., Madsen, R., Sullivan, W. M., Swidler, A., & Tipton, S. M. (1985). *Habits of the heart: Individualism and commitment in American life.* Berkeley: University of California Press.

Benne, K. D. (1987). The meanings of democracy in a collective world. In K. D. Benne & S. Tozer (Eds.), *Society as educator in an age of transition* (pp. 1–23). Chicago: University of Chicago Press.

Bennett, M. (1963). *American immigration policies.* Washington, DC: Public Affairs Press.

Bok, S. (1984). *Secrets: On the ethics of concealment.* New York: Vintage Press.

The bold quest for quality. (1983, October 10). *Time,* pp. 63–68.

Boyer, E. L. (1983). *High school: A report on secondary education.* New York: Harper & Row.

Brown, L., & Wolf, E. (Eds.). (1985). *State of the world: A Worldwatch Institute report on progress toward a sustainable society.* New York: W. W. Norton.

Butts, R. F. (1980). *The revival of civic learning: A rationale for citizenship education in American schools.* Bloomington, IN: Phi Delta Kappan Educational Foundation.

Butts, R. F. (1982). The revival of civic learning requires a prescribed curriculum. *Liberal Education, 68,* 377–401.

Canovan, M. (1981). *Populism.* New York: Harcourt Brace Jovanovich.

Carnoy, M. (1974). *Education as cultural imperialism.* New York: David McKay.

Carnoy, M. (1983). Education, democracy, and social conflict. *Harvard Educational Review, 53,* 398–402.

Chambers, J. (1983). *The achievement of education.* New York: Harper & Row.

Cleary, R. (1971). *Political education in the American democracy.* Scranton, PA: Intext Educational Publishers.

Commoner, B. (1979). *The politics of energy.* New York: Alfred Knopf.

Connolly, W. E. (Ed.). (1971). *The bias of pluralism.* New York: Athernon Press.

Cooley, C. (1909). *Social organization.* New York: Charles Scribner.

Cranston, M. (1964). *What are human rights?* New York: Basic Books.

Dahl, R. (1956). *A preface to democratic theory.* Chicago: University of Chicago Press.

Dahl, R. (1961). *Who governs?* New Haven, CT: Yale University Press.

Dewey, J. (1927). *The public and its problems.* Chicago: Swallow Press.

Dewey, J. (1966). *The child in the curriculum/The school and society.* Chicago: University of Chicago Press. (Original work published 1900)

Dewey, J. (1966). *Democracy and education.* New York: Free Press. (Original work published 1916)

Dewey, J. (1975). Moral theory in practice. In *The early works of John Dewey* (Vol. 3, pp. 93–103). Carbondale, IL: Southern Illinois University Press. (Original work published 1891)

Dewey, J. (1975). *Moral principles in education.* Carbondale, IL: Southern Illinois University Press. (Original work published 1909)

Domhoff, G. W. (1983). *Who rules America now? A view for the '80s.* Englewood Cliffs, NJ: Prentice-Hall.

Durkheim, E. (1961). *Moral education.* New York: Free Press. (Original work published 1904)

Dworkin, R. (1977). *Taking rights seriously.* Cambridge, MA: Harvard University Press.

Fallows, J. (1983). The new immigrants: How they're affecting us. *The Atlantic, 252,* pp. 45–106.

Finkelstein, B. (1985). Thinking publicly about civic learning: An agenda for education reform in the '80s. In A. Jones (Ed.), *Civic learning for teachers: Capstone for educational reform* (pp. 13–24) Ann Arbor, MI: Prakken Publications.

Foshay, A., & Burton, W. (1976). Citizenship as the aim of the social studies. *Theory and Research in Social Education, 4* (2), 1–22.

Friedman, I. (1980, 10 November). We can end inflation. *Industry Week, 207* pp. 60–65.

Gauthier, D. (1969). *The logic of Leviathan.* Oxford, England: Clarendon Press.

Gilligan, C. (1982). *In a different voice: Psychological theory and women's development.* Cambridge, MA: Harvard University Press.

Giroux, H. (1986). Authority, intellectuals, and the politics of practical learning. *Teachers College Record, 88,* 22–40.

Gordon, M. (1964). *Assimilation in American life.* New York: Oxford University Press.

Gouinlock, J. (1986). *Excellence in public discourse: John Stuart Mill, John Dewey, and social intelligence.* New York: Teachers College Press.

Goulet, D. (1977). *The uncertain promise.* New York: IDOC/North America.

Green, T. (1966). *Education and pluralism: Ideal and reality.* Syracuse, NY: School of Education, Syracuse University.

Green, T. (1971). *Predicting the behavior of the educational system.* Syracuse, NY: Syracuse University Press.

Green, T. (1985). The formation of conscience in an age of technology. *American Journal of Education, 94,* 1–32.

Greene, M. (1984). Excellence: Meanings and multiplicity. *Teachers College Record, 86,* 283–297.

Greenstein, F. (1965). *Children and politics.* New Haven: Yale University Press.

Habermas, J. (1969). On systematically distorted communication. In H. P. Dreitzel (Ed.), *Recent sociology* (pp. 115–148). New York: Macmillan.

Habermas, J. (1971). *Knowledge and human interest* (J. S. Shapiro, Trans.). Boston: Beacon Press.

Habermas, J. (1973). *Theory and practice* (J. Viertel, Trans.). Boston: Beacon Press.

Harrington, M. (1980). *Decade of decision.* New York: Simon & Schuster.

Harris, K. (1982). *Teachers and classes.* London: Routledge & Kegan Paul.

Harrison, G. (1982). Relativism and tolerance. In M. Krausz & J. W. Neiland (Eds.), *Relativism: Cognitive and moral* (pp. 226–243). Notre Dame, IN: University of Notre Dame Press.

Hirsch, F. (1976). *The social limits to growth.* Cambridge, MA: Harvard University Press.

Hobbes. T. (1958). *Leviathan* (Parts I and II). Indianapolis, IN: Bobbs-Merrill. (Original work published 1651)

Hofstadter, R. (1955). *The age of reform.* New York: Vintage Books.

Hook, S. (1946). *Education for modern man.* New York: Dial Press.

Janowitz, M. (1983). *The reconstruction of patriotism: Education for civic consciousness.* Chicago: University of Chicago Press.

Jennings, M. K., & Niemi, R. G. (1968). The transmission of political values from parent to child. *American Political Science Review, 68,* 169–184.

July 1984 estimates: American demographics (1985, September 18). *Columbus Dispatch,* p. 14.

Kant, I. (1981). *Grounding for the metaphysics of morals* (J. W. Ellington, Trans.). Indianapolis, IN: Hackett. (Original work published 1797)

Kemp, J. (1968). *The philosophy of Kant.* London: Oxford University Press.

Kirst, M. (1984). *Who controls our schools?* New York: W. S. Freeman.

Korner, S. (1955). *Kant.* New Haven, CT: Yale University Press.

Locke, J. (1946). *A letter concerning toleration* (J. W. Gough, Ed.). Oxford, England: Basil Blackwood. (Original work published 1689)

Locke, J. (1946). *The second treatise on government* (J. W. Gough, Ed.). Oxford, England: Basil Blackwood. (Original work published 1690)

Lukes, S. (1973). *Individualism*. Oxford, England: Basil Blackwood.

MacIntyre, A. (1984). *After virtue: A study in moral theory*. Notre Dame, IN: University of Notre Dame Press.

Macpherson, C. B. (1962). *The political theory of possessive individualism: Hobbes to Locke*. London: Oxford University Press.

Macpherson, C. B. (1977). *The life and times of liberal democracy*. Oxford, England: Oxford University Press.

Martin, J. R. (1981). The ideal of the educated person. In D. R. DeNicola (Ed.), *Proceedings of the thirty-seventh annual meeting of the Philosophy of Education Society* (pp. 3–20). Normal, IL: Philosophy of Education Society.

Matthews, D. (1984). The public in practice and theory. *Public Administration Review, 44*, 120–125.

Merriam, C. E. (1931). *The making of a citizen*. Chicago: University of Chicago Press.

Mills, C. W. (1956). *The power elite*. New York: Oxford University Press.

Milne, A. J. M. (1986). *Human rights and human diversity*. New York: State University of New York Press.

Noddings, N. (1984). *Caring: A feminine approach to ethics and moral education*. Berkeley: University of California Press.

Nozick, R. (1974). *Anarchy, state and utopia*. New York: Basic Books.

Nozick, R. (1981). *Philosophical explanations*. Cambridge, MA: Harvard University Press.

Pico della Mirandola, G. (1965). *On the dignity of man* (C. G. Wallis, Trans.). Indianapolis, IN: Bobbs-Merrill.

Pocock, J. G. A. (1975). *The Machiavellian moment: Florentine thought and the Atlantic republican tradition*. Princeton, NJ: Princeton University Press.

Raywid, M. A. (1976). The democratic classroom: Mistake or misnomer. *Theory into Practice, 15*, 37–46.

Rich, J. M. (1976). Problems and prospects for democratic education. *Theory into Practice, 15*, 54–60.

Ruddick, S. (1982). Maternal thinking. In B. Thorne (Ed.), *Rethinking the family: Some feminist questions* (pp. 76–94). New York: Longman.

Shaw, G. B. (1956). *The apple cart*. Baltimore, MD: Penguin Books. (Original work published 1929)

Sigel, R. (1965). Assumptions about the learning of political values. In R. Sigel (Ed.), *Political Socialization: Its role in the political process* (*Annals of the American Academy of Political and Social Science, 361*, pp. 4–7). Beverly Hills, CA: Sage.

Spring, J. (1986). *The American school: 1642–1985*. New York: Longman.

Stanley, M. (1978). *The technological conscience: Survival and dignity in an age of expertise*. New York: Free Press.

Straughan, R. (1982). What's the point of rules? *Journal of Philosophy of Education, 16*, 63–68.

Sullivan, W. M. (1982). *Reconstructing public philosophy*. Berkeley: University of California Press.

Three nations beat U.S. for quality of life. (1986, December 21). *Columbus Dispatch,* p. 4.

Tocqueville, A. de. (1969). *Democracy in America* (G. Lawrence, Trans.). Garden City, NY: Doubleday Anchor Books. (Original work published 1840)

Torney, J., Oppenheim, A. N., & Farnen, R. (1985). *Civic education in ten countries: An empirical study.* New York: John Wiley.

Torney-Purta, J. (1983). Psychological perspectives on enhancing civic education through the education of teachers. *Journal of Teacher Education, 34,* 31–38.

United Nations. (1948). *Universal declaration of human rights.* New York: Author.

Walzer, M. (1983). *Spheres of justice.* New York: Basic Books.

Willis, P. (1981). *Learning to labor.* New York: Columbia University Press.

Wilson, J. (1977). *Philosopy and practical education.* London: Routledge & Kegan Paul.

Winner, L. (1978). *Autonomous technology.* Cambridge, MA: MIT Press.

Wirth, A. G. (1987). Contemporary work and the quality of life. In K. D. Benne & S. Tozer (Eds.), *Society as educator in an age of transition,* (pp. 54–87). Chicago: University of Chicago Press.

Wynne, E. A., & Walbert, H. J. (1985). *Developing character: Transmitting knowledge.* Posen, IL: ARL.

Yankelovich, D. (1981). *New rules.* New York: Random House.

Index

About the Author

RICHARD PRATTE is Professor of education at The Ohio State University. He is past President of the Philosophy of Education Society and of the Council of Learned Societies in Education. Among his books are *The Public School Movement* and *Pluralism in Education.* His major research interest in the past decade has been the study of social heterogeneity and pluralism.